The Elusive "I" in the Novel

American University Studies

Series I
Germanic Languages and Literature

Vol. 46

PETER LANG
New York · Bern · Frankfurt am Main · Paris

Hamilton H. H. Beck

The Elusive "I" in the Novel

Hippel, Sterne, Diderot, Kant

PETER LANG
New York · Bern · Frankfurt am Main · Paris

Library of Congress Cataloging-in-Publication Data

Beck, Hamilton.
The elusive "I" in the novel.

(American university studies. Series I, Germanic languages and literature; vol. 46)
Bibliography: p.
1. Hippel, Theodor Gottlieb von, 1741–1796. Lebensläufe nach aufsteigender Linie nebst Beilagen A, B, C. 2. Hippel, Theodor Gottlieb von, 1741–1796—Technique. 3. Narration (Rhetoric) 4. European fiction—18th century—History and criticism. 5. Sterne, Laurence, 1713–1768. Life and opinions of Tristram Shandy. 6. Diderot, Denis, 1713–1784. Jacques le fataliste et son maître. 7. Kant, Immanuel, 1724–1804—Influence. I. Title. II. Series.
PT2358.H5L433   1987   833'.6   87-2596
ISBN 0-8204-0279-6
ISSN 0721-1392

CIP-Kurztitelaufnahme der Deutschen Bibliothek

Beck, Hamilton H.H.:
The elusive "I" in the novel: Hippel, Sterne, Diderot, Kant / Hamilton H.H. Beck. – New York; Bern; Frankfurt am Main; Paris: Lang, 1987.
(American University Studies: Ser. 1, Germanic Languages and Literature; Vol. 46)
ISBN 0-8204-0279-6

NE: American University Studies / 01

© Peter Lang Publishing, Inc., New York 1987

All rights reserved.
Reprint or reproduction, even partially, in all forms such as microfilm, xerography, microfiche, microcard, offset strictly prohibited.

For my mother and father

Contents

Acknowledgments ix

Chapter 1. Hippel and his Critics 1
   1. Hippel's *Lebenslauf* and the *Lebensläufe* 1
   2. Traditional Views of the *Lebensläufe* 7

Chapter 2. The Eighteenth-Century Novel and the Role of the Narrator 23
   1. The Novel and Historiography in the Early Eighteenth Century 23
   2. The New Evaluation of the Relationship between Novel and History 30
   3. The Emancipation of the Novel 36
   4. Parodies of the Novel 40
      A. Sterne 41
      B. Diderot 46

Chapter 3. Sterne and Hippel: the Relationship Reconsidered 67

Chapter 4. Kant and the Use of Documents in the *Lebensläufe* 99
   1. Documents in Hippel's Works 99
   2. Kant and the *Lebensläufe* 101
   3. Documents and the Problem of Self-Knowledge in *Tristram Shandy* 117

Conclusion 127

Appendix 131

Bibliography 167

Acknowledgments

I would like to thank Professors Hans Joachim Kreutzer and Albrecht Schöne, who encouraged me to write on Hippel when I studied at the University of Göttingen. The members of my thesis committee at Cornell, Professors Sander Gilman, Inta Ezergailis, and W. W. Holdheim, were always helpful, as was Professor Eric Blackall. This book is a revised and expanded version of my doctoral dissertation.

For permission to reprint passages from articles that appeared in their journals, I would also like to thank the editors of the *Journal of the History of Ideas*, where part of Chapter II appeared; *Studies in Eighteenth-Century Culture*, where part of Chapter III appeared; and *Kant-Studien*, where part of Chapter IV appeared.

I would also like to thank Dr. Joseph Kohnen of Luxembourg for his encouragement.

1
Hippel and his Critics

1. Hippel's *Lebenslauf* and the *Lebensläufe*
"Was ich für Wahrheit halte ist drin, allein es ist und bleibt die Frage die wichtigste in der Welt: Was ist Wahrheit?" With these words, Theodor Gottlieb Hippel (the "von" was added later) sent to his friend Johann Georg Scheffner some pages from the first part of his novel, *Die Lebensläufe nach aufsteigender Linie, nebst Beilagen A, B, C*.[1] Its appearance coincided with some major steps in Hippel's career as a civil servant in Königsberg. Volume I appeared in 1778, the same year Hippel became a *Stadtrat* and judge of the Burgfreiheit and Roßgärtchen districts. Volume II appeared in 1779. One year later, Hippel suddenly and unexpectedly became the mayor and chief of police of Königsberg. 1781 saw the publication of the *Kritik der reinen Vernunft* by his friend Kant and also volume III, parts one and two, of the *Lebensläufe*. All the volumes of the *Lebensläufe* were published by Voß, Hippel's favorite publisher, in Berlin. (Except where noted, all Hippel's publications appeared with Voß.) All appeared anonymously.

Evidently Hippel's civic duties took up most of his time in the ensuing years, for he published virtually nothing during the rest of the decade. He was one of the *Moneten* at work on the reform of the Prussian legal code, and won prizes for his contributions. Hippel always had had the habit of writing down entire conversations that he thought interesting. In 1785 he wrote down such a "Gespräch über die *Lebensläufe*", in which an unnamed acquaintance of Hippel's advanced an unusual, not to say eccentric, interpretation of the work, little suspecting that he was talking with the work's author.[2] In 1786 he became a *Geheimer Kriegsrath*. After the death of Frederick the Great, the new King, Frederick William II, named Hippel *Stadtpräsi-*

dent of Königsberg. This same year he wrote a treatise *Ueber Gesetzgebung und Staatenwohl*, which, however, was first published posthumously in 1804 (Berlin: Voß, 1804; rpt. Königstein/Ts.: Scriptor, 1978). 1787 saw the publication of a minor historical work with a long title, of which I give only the beginning: *Bedenken über die Historisch-kritische Beleuchtung der Frage: "Hat die Preußische Ritterschaft das Recht, ein beständiges Corps zu formiren* [. . . .]" Hippel answered this question in the affirmative, which seems to agree with his generally pro-aristocratic views. It was at about this same time that he had restored to his family name the "von", which had been dropped years earlier. Elise von der Recke visited Königsberg in 1788, and Hippel recorded a long conversation with her and Kant in a letter to Scheffner dated December 17.[3] In 1789 Hippel began to keep a diary, which he continued until 1792, and wrote his testament.

In the last period of his life Hippel began a series of evening play readings with his relatives, with special emphasis on the works of Lessing. Hippel's nephew called the years 1790–1794 "die Sonnenwende seines Lebens" (XII, 213). In 1790 there appeared a satire, *Zimmermann der I. und Friedrich der II*, (published, according to the satiric note on the title page, in "London: In der Einsamkeit", but actually published by Lagarde in Berlin) and a bit of idyllic nature-prose, *Handzeichnungen nach der Natur*. The following year appeared a short legal work on the Königsberg *Stapelrecht* (Berlin: Lagarde; not included in the *Sämmtliche Werke*).

It was not until 1790–91, almost a decade after completion of the *Lebensläufe*, that Hippel again undertook a major work, his autobiography. This, too, first appeared posthumously, and in two versions.[4] Towards the end of this year he also wrote a short essay to the Prussian Minister von Schrötter *Ueber die bürgerliche Verbesserung der Juden*, in which he took an extremely hostile attitude towards the question of rights for Jews. This work, too, first appeared posthumously.[5]

Hippel took a much more enlightened approach towards the emancipation of women, and is rightly considered the first champion of their cause in Germany. In 1774 and 1775 had appeared the first two editions of his *Ueber die Ehe*, in which, however, his views on the role of women were more traditional than progressive. By 1792 this had changed, and the arguments he advanced in the third edition of *Ueber die Ehe* (with illustrations by Chodowiecki) and in *Ueber die bürgerliche Verbesserung der Weiber* were decidedly progressive, almost revolutionary.[6] In this same year also appeared two unjustly neglected works, *Ueber die Mittel gegen die Verletzung öffentlichter Anlagen und Zierrathen*, and the *Nachricht, die von K . . . sche Untersuchung betreffend* (Königsberg: Nicolovius), in which Hippel, the presiding judge, reports on a case of infanticide.

In 1793 appeared the fourth and final edition of *Ueber die Ehe*, in which Hippel took a position even more radical than in the previous edition. On 29 May of that year, Hippel departed for Danzig to organize the administration of the city after the partition of Poland. There he lost an eye due to the strain of overwork, and returned to Königsberg in March 1794. Hippel's second novel, *Die Kreuz- und Querzüge des Ritters A-Z*, a two volume satire on the nobility and the freemasons (Hippel was a member of both), appeared anonymously in 1793–94.

It was to be the last of his works to appear in his lifetime. The completed first twelve chapters of another novel, *Der Pächter Moritz*, were found among Hippel's papers but were never published, and now must be presumed lost. Weakened and exhausted, Hippel, after a short illness, died on 23 April 1796, of "Brustwassersucht". He was buried in the Neuroßgarten cemetery. Aside from his papers he left behind a collection of books (numbering either 700, according to the Schlichtegroll biography, or 2,500, according to his nephew), and a valuable collection of art works, including engravings of works of Dürer and oil paintings by Rubens and Cranach. His estate amounted to 140,000 *Thaler*, a huge sum, especially when one considers his modest origins. He had inherited virtually nothing, and acquired most of his wealth in the course of his career as a lawyer and politician.

* * *

Hippel was born in the East Prussian town of Gerdauen on 31 January 1741, the son of the rector of the school there. For most of our information about Hippel's youth, we can turn to only two sources, each of them of dubious reliability: the fictionalized account of the hero's upbringing in the *Lebensläufe*, and the autobiography's idealized version written late in life. Here, for example, Hippel describes his father not as an educator but as a church official (XII, 36).[7] The fact is that we have virtually no independent corroboration for any of the events in Hippel's youth; almost all our information is supplied by Hippel himself. It is certain, though, that in 1756 he enrolled at the university in Königsberg. At first, his field of study was theology, though he did hear Kant and others lecture on philosophy as well as other subjects. For a time he lived with the Dutch *Justizrath* Woyt, and tutored his step-grandson (XII, 104 ff). Hippel also delivered five sermons in Königsberg and Gerdauen during his early years at the university (the sermons have not survived). In 1760, during the Russian occupation of East Prussia during the Seven Years' War, he interrupted his studies for a trip with a friend to Kronstadt and St. Petersburg, an experience that opened his eyes to what was for him an entirely new world. (In his autobiography, begun thirty years later, Hippel traces his life only up to this high point and concludes with his return to Königsberg.) It was probably this experience that moved Hippel, upon his return, to change his field of study to law.

At the same time, Hippel lost his position as tutor with Woyt. He became a *Hofmeister* at the estate of Freiherr von Schrötter in Wesselshöfen, and evidently fell in love with his eight-year-old daughter. She was, however, "in Ansehung des Standes und Vermögens weit über ihm", a circumstance which made any hope of marriage impossible.[8] In the 1760s Hippel first began to have his poetry published, usually by Kanter in Königsberg. He also wrote theater reviews for Kanter later in the decade. (None of the reviews and only a few of the poems are included in the *Sämmtliche Werke*.)[9]

Hippel's comedy *Der Mann nach der Uhr* premiered in the

spring of 1765. It met with moderate success, and was mentioned by Lessing (who identified the author as "Herr Hippel in Danzig") in the twenty-second number of the *Hamburgische Dramaturgie*.[10] That summer Hippel was admitted to the bar at the city court in Königsberg. The first letter to Scheffner included in the *Sämmtliche Werke* also was written this summer. Another comedy, entitled *Die ungewöhnlichen Nebenbuhler*, appeared in 1768, the same year as the *Freimäurerreden* (Hippel had joined the lodge *Zu den drei Kronen* in 1762) and the essay (published by Kanter, but not in the *Sämmtliche Werke*), *Ist es rathsam, Missethäter durch Geistliche zum Tode vorbereiten zu lassen*?

Hippel's public career began to move forward in the 1770s. In 1771 he became a notary and lawyer at the royal court, the following year municipal court adminstrator and assessor of the *Stipendiencollegium*. 1772 also saw the publication of Hippel's *Geistliche Lieder* by Haude and Spener in Berlin. Though dedicated to Klopstock, Hippel had first sent them to Gellert for his evaluation, and, in one of his last letters, Gellert had written a favorable reply (see Schlichtegroll, p. 396 f.) The first division of Poland, whose second partition was to play such an important role in Hippel's life more than twenty years later, also fell in this year. In 1773 Hippel became a *Kriminalrath* and *Beisitzer des Armencollegiums*, the following year Director of the Criminal Court and *Hofhalsrichter*.[11] The first edition of *Ueber die Ehe* appeared in 1774, calling forth Hamann's response in his *Versuch einer Sibylle über die Ehe* in 1775, the same year as the second edition of *Ueber die Ehe*. Without knowing that Hippel was the author of the anonymous work, Hamann called him "ein gelehrter witziger Kautz". Hippel quotes this in a letter to Scheffner (XIV, 6 f.). Another of Hippel's masonic works, the *Pflichten eines Maurers bei dem Grabe eines Bruders*, was published in Danzig by Flörke in 1777. It was the last work of his to appear before the *Lebensläufe*.

* * *

"Was ich für Wahrheit halte ist drin [. . . .]" What exactly is it that is in this novel? The plot is soon told. The hero of the novel is Alexander, a name given in ironic reference to Alexander the Great. In a retrospective, first-person account, he proposes to tell the life of first his parents, then his grandparents, and so on further back in time and up the genealogical tree (hence "nach aufsteigender Linie"). Like Tristram Shandy, however, who promised to tell his readers not just his opinions but also his life, only to fail brilliantly in his self-appointed task, Alexander disappoints the expectations he has set up in the title and concentrates for the most part on his own life. The first volume tells of Alexander's youth in a small town set in Courland, and contains loving descriptions of Alexander's parents and their foibles. It is clear that the hero and his parents are thinly veiled and somewhat idealized portraits of Hippel himself and his parents.

The second volume deals largely with Alexander's departure from home and experiences at the university in Königsberg, as well as his love for a virtuous young woman named Mine (short for Wilhelmine), who is, however, the object of the nefarious intrigues of the profligate nobleman v. E. With the aid of the local sheriff this villain pursues Mine, who dies of grief and a broken heart before v. E. can catch her.

In volume three, part one, Alexander suffers through a deep depression, and spends most of his time with the so-called *Sterbegraf*, a man obsessed with the thought and rituals of death and who tries to remove his fear of death (indeed, tries to become friends with death) through such means as sleeping in a coffin and inviting the terminally ill into his castle so that he may observe their final days. In volume three, part two, Alexander joins the Russian army fighting against the Turks and is made a member of the nobility by Catherine the Great (for whom Hippel always held great admiration). Alexander returns to Königsberg, discovers that he has really been a member of a noble family all along (and is thus doubly ennobled, both by blood and by deeds), and marries Tine, whom he renames Mine in honor of his first love (Tine goes along with this enthusiastically). In the novel's final pages Tine/Mine bears Alexander a son, Leopold, and there is a happy ending. Until, that is, one turns what had appeared to be the final page only to discover that the work continues, now in the form of a diary dealing with the tragic events of the narrator's present: the death of young Leopold ("Mit ihm ist mein Stamm hin" [IV, 247]) and the grief of his parents.

Let me say at this point that the plot is one of the less interesting parts of the novel, and to summarize the work in this bald fashion and leave it at that would be to give a serious misimpression of the whole. For comparison, think of the different impressions that would be left by reading Sterne's *Tristram Shandy* and reading a plot summary of the work that restored everything to its original chronological order. Though Hippel does not take the same freedoms with chronology that Sterne does, Hippel has from the beginning been considered perhaps the most accomplished Sternean author in Germany in the eighteenth century. Hippel's extensive digressions, asides, obscure references, and, perhaps, self-indulgence lend some support to this traditional view of Hippel as a follower in the footsteps of Sterne.

2. Traditional Views of the *Lebensläufe*

It would lead too far afield to trace the reception of the *Lebensläufe* in its entirety. I propose, therefore, to concentrate upon the emphasis reviewers from the past two centuries have placed on the Sternean elements in Hippel's novel.[12] Later, I propose to examine the *Lebensläufe* from another angle and argue that what Hippel is up to is the very opposite of Sterne.

The anonymous reviewer in the *Teutsche Merkur* of December 1779 did not need to mention Sterne by name in order to make the thrust of his criticism clear, since he emphasized the conversational style of writing which Sterne had made fashionable. "Writing," Tristram had written, "when managed properly (as you may be sure I think mine is) is but a different name for conversation."[13] The critic for the *Teutsche Merkur* apparently did not think that Hippel had properly managed his writing, for he says, "Kurz, mündlich, in einem Zirkel von Freunden, die an einander gewohnt sind, mag die schnakische, halb abgerupfte, auf Stellen der Bibel und anderer Bücher anspielende Sprache und Ton den man eben sowohl für Ernst als Scherz annehmen kann, nicht nur allgemein verständlich seyn, sondern so gar gefallen; nicht aber in einem Buche, das für ein ganzes Publikum geschrieben wird."[14] Hippel understood the implied reference to Sterne, for he wrote to Scheffner, "Mit der Merkuranzeige hätt ich Ursache zufrieden zu seyn, wenn der liebe Mann mir nicht alles durch die Shandische Brille sehen möchte." (XIV, 124)[15]

The organ of the Berlin Enlightenment, the *Allgemeine deutsche Bibliothek*, was more explicit than the *Merkur* in its review of the first two volumes of the *Lebensläufe*. The Berlin critic at first puts the relationship between Sterne and Hippel in a positive light, saying, "Unter unsern Humoristen nach Sterne's Manier wüßten wir keinen, dem es in dieser Art der Composition, ohne *Yoriks* Nachtreter zu seyn, so gelungen wäre. Er überläßt sich, eben so wie dieser, den Ergießungen seiner Laune, aber über andere Gegenstände als solche, die nur unter die Rubrik der Empfindsamkeit gehören; speculative Philosophie und Lebenspraktik begegnen einander hier wechselsweise unter den zufälligsten, doch ohne Zwang herbeyeilenden Veranlassungen; jedoch nicht in der Amtskleidung des langschleppenden theoretischen Talars, sondern in dem Farbenkleide des Witzes, unter dem Aufputz kecker Metaphern und eines allegorischen Schwunges [. . . .]"[16] But soon the reviewer is criticizing both Sterne and Hippel. "Es gehet dem V. wie es sogar dem guten Sterne zuweilen ergangen ist: nicht alle Einfälle eines launigen Schriftstellers sind Kinder einer glücklichen Laune, oder dem Leser auf eben die Art empfindbar, wie dem Autor im Augenblick des Niederschreibens" (Ibid., p. 470). Hippel's reaction this time was one of resignation. "In der Recension ist nichts mehr und nichtsweniger, als was andere gesagt haben." (XIV, 196. The letter is dated 24 November 1780.)

Borowski, writing years later (1797) but with the old reviews in hand, remarks that the *Lebensläufe* was "mit Kaltblütigkeit gewürdigt" by the *Allgemeine deutsche Bibliothek*.[17] Thus when Hegel wrote in 1828 that Hippel was "der Einzige" of all the prominent members of the non-Berlin Enlightenment "der den Schmähungen jenes Mittelpunktes nicht ausgesetzt war," he had evidently forgotten that all Hippel's works appeared anonymously.[18] Otherwise the Berliners would have mentioned Hippel as well in their attacks on Hamann, Herder, Kant and all the rest.

Though Jean Paul himself did not look upon Hippel as merely the *Kometenschweif eines Sternes*, he was aware that there were many authors in Germany who could be considered so. "Als man Sterne in Deutschland zuerst ausschiffte, bildete und zog er hinter sich einen langen wäßrigen Kometenschweif damals sogenannter (jetzo ungenannter) Humoristen, welche nichts waren als Ausplauderer lustiger Selbstbehaglichkeit."[19]

Hegel was unstinting in his praise of Hippel, though he too saw Hippel as a Sternean. In his discussion of subjective *Humor* Hegel criticizes Jean Paul and places over and against him, as the representatives of true and objective *Humor*, Sterne and Hippel. "Das Sichnachgeben des Dichters im Verlauf seiner Äußerungen muß, wie bei Sterne und Hippel, ein ganz unbefangenes, leichtes, unscheinbares Fortschlendern sein, das in seiner Unbedeutenheit gerade den höchsten Begriff von Tiefe gibt; und da es eben Einzelheiten sind, die ordnungslos emporsprudeln, muß der innere Zusammenhang um so tiefer liegen und in dem Vereinzelten als solchen den Lichtpunkt des Geistes hervortreiben."[20]

But Hegel was virtually alone in his praise of Hippel in the first half of the nineteenth century. Theodor Mundt, for example, did much to reawaken interest in Hippel with his extensive review of the *Gesamtausgabe* published by Reimer. Mundt reverses Hegel's judgment, however, and praises Jean Paul at Hippel's expense. Mundt does not mention Sterne, but the terms in which his judgment of Hippel are couched (particularly the emphasis on the lack of form in Hippel's novel) are so clear that a reference to Sterne by name would have been superfluous. "Das Ganze wird bei ihm nie zu einem Dichterwerk und noch weniger zu einem Kunstwerk, sondern artet in ein formloses Convolut von Abhandlungen aus, die ohne allen Sinn für Symmetrie und Architektonik der Darstellung an einandergereiht sind."[21]

Gervinus added to the charge of formlessness that of subjectivity. He accused Hippel of indifference to his readers and of having an overbearing interest in presenting his own personality at the expense of artistic form. One could say, writes Gervinus, that Hippel "schreibe oft wie in Gedanken, wie im Selbstgespräche, und in der That liegt bei ihm, wie bei Sterne, der Hauptreiz für den Leser in der Entdeckung des geheimen Zusammenhangs seiner Ideensprünge."[22] It is essentially this view of Hippel as an author unconcerned with his public, and interested rather in the presentation of his own personality in a favorable light, which, with some modifications, has survived unchallenged almost down to the present.

By the time Hettner wrote his history of eighteenth-century German literature, the interpretation of Hippel as a Sternean had become so established that there was no longer any need to argue for it. "Am bedeutendsten unter diesen sternisirenden Romanen sind Hippel's 'Lebensläufe nach aufsteigender Linie'."[23] Hettner, in developing Gervinus's argument, calls attention to the importance of the *Ich* in the *Sturm und Drang*, and Alexander von Oetingen, in his heavily abridged version of the *Lebensläufe*, was later to quote Hettner to the effect that the *Ich* made its presence felt throughout the work; it thrust itself into the foreground and revealed itself just as it was, without propriety and measure, and in all its oddity and blind passions.[24] Thus Hippel becomes for Oetingen a figure of the *Sturm und Drang*, but Oetingen takes Hettner's observation as an authorization for eliminating precisely what critics have always considered to be among the most Shandean aspects of the *Lebensläufe*: the digressions. The story line is all that survives. This misguided attempt to rework Hippel for the present (of 1878) would be comparable to a retelling of *Tristram Shandy* in chronological order and without digressions and extraneous narrative intrusions; in both cases the reduction of the work to the basic plot would leave out the most innovative and significant aspect of the text.

One of the few nineteenth-century critics to see more than just a Sternean influence on Hippel was Julian Schmidt. But his criticism attacks what were considered to be typically Sternean flaws: "Die *Lebensläufe* würden einer unserer gelesensten Romane sein, wenn sie nur einigermaßen componirt wären. Aber es ist ein wüstes Durcheinander, nur durch einen dünnen Faden mit einander verbunden. Zum Theil ist es wohl Mangel an künstlerischer Kraft, zum Theil Sterne's Vorbild: nicht zum kleinsten Theil aber Folge seiner skeptischen Gemüthsart, die auch die tieffsten Eindrücke mit bitterm Humor zersetzte."[25]

Only where a more nationalistic tone prevails did critics tend to play down Sterne's influence. Thus F. J. Schneider, whose extensive writings on Hippel are as a rule sensible and informative, is disappointing in his article on Hippel and Sterne. For Schneider trivializes the relationship by reducing it to a matter of details borrowed by Hippel. Schneider leaves the reader with the impression that the relationship can be characterized by the combination of minute details and broad generalizations that Hippel allegedly took over from Sterne. Schneider explains, for example, the name of Hippel's protagonist by referring to Uncle Toby's remark to Trim in *Tristram Shandy*, IV, xviii, 295: "Trim—yet had my name been *Alexander*, I could have done no more at *Namur* than my duty." Remembrance of the past, says Schneider, is awakened through signs in both works, including the map in *Tristram Shandy*, and the Bible in the *Lebensläufe*. Or, to take a final example, Schneider observes that "*Tristram Shandy* bleibt idyllisch, nur das erste Buch der *Lebensläufe* ist idyllisch."[26] Schneider rightly criticizes Johann Czerny's book on the subject of Hippel's relationship to Sterne,[27] for Czerny does little more than repeat observations on Hippel already made by others. But on this question, at least, it can be said that Schneider, too, fails to go much beyond what had by this time become commonplace.

Hermann Meyer also points out similarities in detail between the *Lebensläufe* and *Tristram Shandy*, especially with regard to the hobby horses of Tristram's and Alexander's families. Meyer considers Hippel "der begabteste 'sternisierende' Dichter vor Jean Paul" although he "misunderstood" Sterne and produced "ein wildes Gestrüpp üppig wuchernder Gefühlsergüsse und Reflexionen [. . .], in welchem der Faden der Handlung völlig verloren geht."[28]

Thus it is possible for Peter Michelsen to begin his examination of Hippel's novel at almost precisely the point where Gervinus left off.[29] The difference is that Michelsen distinguishes between *Tristram Shandy* and Bode's translation of *Tristram Shandy*, and argues that Hippel and the other Sterneans were more misled by Bode than guided by Sterne. The *Laune* of Sterne's work, its exaggerated reflections, inconsistencies and apparent formlessness were for the German audience of Bode's translation all evidence of the work's originality, a prized quality among German authors of the later eighteenth century.

Michelsen's argument is that Hippel, in attempting to imitate *Tristram Shandy*, misunderstood Sterne's intentions, and came up with a kind of rigidified and at the same time formless and anarchic echo of Sterne's novel. It was the *apparent* formlessness of *Tristram Shandy*, says Michelsen, that served as the model for the *real* formlessness of Hippel's *Lebensläufe*. Hippel's work negates order as a matter of principle, for, according to Michelsen, only the chaotic and arbitrary is true in Hippel's view (pp. 227, 310).

It is to Michelsen's credit that he deals with Hippel's stated justification for his "formlessness," something no critic in the preceding 182 years had done. Hippel's cultivation of formlessness, he says, has a definite intention, namely, "den Eindruck der Natürlichkeit zu erwecken, woraus man wiederum auf die Wahrheit des Ausgesagten schließen sollte. Daß dem Leser eingeredet wird, der Mangel an Gescheitelem, an Form, sei eine Garantie für historisch-biographische Authentizität, ist ein Kunstgriff, der die tatsächliche Fiktivität des Erzählers verschleiern soll" (p. 277). And Michelsen points out that Hippel uses documents, letters, diaries, conversations and digressions for a definite purpose: "sie alle zielen auf den Schein einer

Unmittelbarkeit ab, deren Pflege gerade in jener Zeit, der des Sturms und Drangs, im Namen der Naturgemäßheit, Mode zu werden begann" (p. 278). Michelsen continues by pointing out that this appearance of immediacy and of non-fictionality is part of the intended effect of the work (p. 279). Michelsen's analysis here is entirely correct and is central to any understanding of Hippel.

But what is perhaps most surprising about Michelsen's analysis is not that it for the first time examines Hippel's intent behind the apparent chaos that had always been noticed, but rather that Michelsen still ends up by making the same quasi-moralistic critique of the novel that most earlier critics had made. Having carefully and with critical acumen distinguished between Hippel and the intent of his novel, Michelsen in his conclusion forgets this distinction and treats the novel in good nineteenth-century critical fashion as nothing more than a mirror of the author's soul. "Das ,Ich' im *Tristram Shandy* war noch Rolle gewesen; jetzt wird das anders: das Ich soll bekennen," he says in reference to the *Lebensläufe* (p. 276). But Michelsen calls the work "unredlich", since it nonetheless remains a novel, despite all Hippel's efforts to make it appear an actual *document humain*. Michelsen apparently does not take his own exegesis of the text seriously, for he does not ask what the implications of Hippel's method of composition are, but falls back into a moralistic critique that could be taken straight from Gervinus, who argued that Hippel's appeal to the reality and authenticity of his work was no more than a fig-leaf for its meandering and unstructured composition (see Gervinus, *Geschichte*, V, 189).

According to Michelsen, the novel, in pretending to be not a novel, denies that it is what it is, and is therefore "unredlich," especially if it goes to any lengths to make its pretence of reality believable. The faulty logic of this argument is clear. One wonders why Michelsen and Gervinus do not admit the ultimately religious provenance of this type of criticism and simply condemn all novels on the moral grounds that they deceive their readers.

Michelsen's work has nonetheless determined the general

tone of contemporary Hippel scholarship. Eva Becker, for example, accepts Michelsen's interpretation of Hippel's formlessness. For her, too, Hippel, unlike Sterne and Jean Paul, did not know how to express artistic unity beneath a facade of diffuseness. "Hippel's Roman ist wirklich ein Chaos, und das nicht nur hinsichtlich der Form. Er ist das getreue Abbild eines zerbrochenen, verwirrten Weltbildes, mit dem der Autor nicht fertig geworden ist."[30] She does begin to go beyond Michelsen when she argues that there is some inner justification for Hippel's apparent formlessness. Hippel, she observes, defends his "Unform" for what she calls religious purposes. Since for Hippel all human endeavor is condemned to be incomplete, formal wholeness can present only a deceptive image of unity and completion, and this Hippel rejects as "unehrlich" (p. 216). Here at least the "formlessness" is not said to be a result of Sterne's influence, but rather is a reflection of Hippel's own convictions.[31]

Norbert Miller's study of the sentimental narrator takes up where Michelsen left off.[32] This is particularly the case with regard to the position of the narrator. Miller borrows Michelsen's description of what happens to the Sternean narrator in Hippel's hands, "Ichverhärtung," and considers it in light of the tension between chaos and order which he sees in Hippel's novel. Miller argues that to multiply narrative perspectives is to increase the distance between the reader on the one hand and the narrator and the world as it is presented in the novel on the other. In so doing he restates Michelsen's position in even more extreme form than Michelsen himself did. "[Bei Hippel] sind die Begebenheiten um das erfahrend-erzählende Ich des Helden Alexander alles andere als verbürgte, unbezweifelte Handlungen im Sinne Sternes: Hippels *Lebensläufe* zeigen die Welt als Chaos, dessen dichter, unsicherer Nebel vom Ich nicht zu durchdringen ist" (p. 292). The *Lebensläufe* represents thus not just the triumph of the *Ich* over its environment, it is also the triumph of a subjective narrator who is identical to the author, and neither of whom is able to transcend his fundamentally anarchic view of the world.

Miller argues that Sterne, though he might have pointed the way for Hippel, nevertheless avoided the pitfall of solipsism. Tristram, he says, differs from Hippel's narrator in that he is clearly distinct from the author, and not just a mask. In the *Lebensläufe*, however, though facts are not uncertain in and of themselves for Hippel's narrator, they become vague and diffuse because of the narrator's reflection on the facts.

The clarity and forcefulness of Miller's argument has the air of being the final word on the topic, but it is precisely his radical formulation of this argument that is most open to question. Can it really be said that Tristram is the more objective narrator, or that Alexander is the victim of his and his author's subjectivity? Can it not be shown that Tristram is by far the more subjective of the two, and that Hippel's whole endeavor is to reduce the role of the narrator? This would explain the multiplication of narrative perspectives, for which Miller has no explanation, other than to call them masks of the author. But what intention lies behind the use of these masks? Surely it is not to increase the distance between reader and the world as it is presented in the novel (why should Hippel wish to increase this distance anyway?), but to eliminate the distance as far as possible. The appearance of chaos is part of an attempt at objectivity that Hippel undertakes in response to Sterne's extreme narrative subjectivism.

The beginning of a reply to the position of Michelsen and Miller is to be found in Uwe Grund's careful dissertation on the *Lebensläufe*.[33] He points out that the "Ichverhärtung" Michelsen and Miller speak of expresses the superiority of the sovereign narrator as it is directed only against the critics, not against the reader. Grund examines above all those passages of the novel in which Alexander is the neutral recorder of conversations, and observes that Hippel's purpose is to make the reader think by presenting him with puzzles and leaving it up to the reader to solve them, or by offering him alternatives and coming to no conclusion of his own, again leaving this up to the reader. Grund quotes from Hippel's letter to Scheffner of 16 April 1780 (XIV, 175–6), in which Hippel laments the limits placed by the present state of society on *Handlung*, and concludes with a mixture of hope and resignation, saying that only ideas, "das Denken," can improve the world, and that books should be written to encourage the spread of ideas. Grund comments: "Es ist [. . .] die Sprachform als solche, welche die Anstrengung des 'Denkens' bewirkt. [. . . .] Die sich am 'Denken' ausrichtende Literatur sieht in der Intellektualisierung des Leseaktes ihren wichtigsten Auftrag" (p. 169, 170).

Grund's dissertation is useful as a corrective to the views of Miller and Michelsen that otherwise have gone unchallenged. But Grund's argument is itself in need of correction, for he regards Hippel's Alexander exclusively as a witty narrator, not only in the sense that Alexander surprises and entertains the reader by connecting elements that are usually thought to be disparate and unconnected—the eighteenth century's definition of wit—but also in a more modern sense: arcane wit forces the reader to think for himself if he is to understand what he is reading.

Alexander is, however, at least as much a sentimental as a witty narrator. Grund chooses to ignore the novel's sentimental aspects, calling them longwinded, their effect being "ermüdend [. . .] auf den heutigen Leser, der in einem Roman ein geschlossenes Kunstwerk zu sehen und es als Ganzes zu genießen gewohnt ist."[34] Whether true or false, this assertion serves, oddly enough, the function of justifying Grund's determination *not* to enjoy the *Lebensläufe* "als Ganzes."

Furthermore, Grund, in considering the play of the narrator's wit, argues that it is never beyond boundaries, "die auch dem Leser zugänglich sind." In this passage Grund argues against Miller, who made the unprovable assertion that Hippel himself could not have understood all of the witty references in his work. But, to return to Grund's claim, was Hippel's style readily understandable to his contemporaries in fact? What were their reactions? Grund wants to make their horizons of understanding as all-inclusive as possible, but he does not investigate any of their reactions as expressed, for example, in reviews. Indeed, he does well to avoid them, for the objection that the narrator's wit tended to go too far was a common complaint among Hippel's contemporaries. Grund thus finds himself in the embarrassing position of arguing that Hippel's contemporaries understood his wit without much difficulty (even though present-day readers can no longer do so), and yet not being able to support this claim with any examples from the early reviews of Hippel's novel.

Furthermore, when Hippel says he will write a novel in order to provoke "Denken," he has said nothing explicit about the *kind* of novel he thinks can achieve this end. Grund's interpretation works for a few passages in the novel, most notably for the difficult opening pages. But Grund does not take into consideration Hippel's audience, or at best he does so only implicitly. Hippel himself was not so rash. A necessary corrective to Grund's interpretation of Hippel's letter to Scheffner is to be found in the exchange of letters between Hippel and Friedrich Heinrich Jacobi, letters which critics have ignored since their publication early in this century. Since Jacobi did not know of Hippel's authorship, he addressed his letter "An den Verfasser der Lebensläufe in [sic] aufsteigender Linie."

> Mit dem ersten Theile der *Lebensläufe* in diesem Augenblicke zu Ende, fühle ich auf einmal den festen Muth dazu, was ich während des Lesens wohl hundertmal zu thun entbrannte.
>
> Schüchtern macht die Liebe,—aber sie macht auch kühn, die ächte, unüberwindliche, siegende.
>
> Außer dem Wort Liebe weiß ich Keines, dessen Sinn mir nicht zu gemein wäre für an Sie.
>
> Heute der erste Schritt, den ich nach Ihnen wage—wer weiß, ob Sie mir nicht irgendwo entgegen kommen? früher oder später, wir treffen uns!
>
> Vor drei Jahren legte ich Ihr Buch ziemlich gleichgültig auf die Seite, nachdem ich darin ein wenig gelesen, ein wenig geblättert hatte. Eben so zwei ganz verschiedene Leute, Asmus und Lessing. Leisewizen, Kleukern und Lavatern verdanke ich's, daß ich es wieder vornahm.
>
> Leben Sie wohl!
> Der Sie mit den heißesten
> Wünschen seines Herzens segnet,
>   ist geboren im Jahre 1743
>   den 25sten Jänner,
>   mit Namen Jacobi

getauft
Friedrich Heinrich
Schriebs am 3ten December
1780.[35]

Does this sound like Grund's conception of Hippel's ideal reader, one for whom the art of reading has been intellectualized? The answer is obvious—but what did Hippel think of this enthusiastic, *schwärmerische* reception of his work? Hippel's reply exists only in a copy made by Hamann, who here acted as middle man—more than a courier but (at least in his relationship with Hippel) something short of a confidant. Hippel's letter was written probably in 1782 or 1783, after he had completed the *Lebensläufe*, and is signed "Hr."

> Sie denken und empfinden, das haben Sie bewiesen und mehrerer Prämissen bedarf es nicht, um meiner Seits annehmen zu können, daß Sie den Geist, der mich bey diesem Buche getrieben, nicht verfehlt haben, den so viele verfehlten—
> allerdings hätte die *Hauptsache* dieses Buchs auch anders behandelt werden können, allein es bleibt die Frage: ob zu unserer Zeit eine andere Behandlung so heilsam gewesen als die, so ich einschlug?
> Wenige, wahrlich wenige, würden meine eigentliche Absicht tragen, wenn ich sie gerade zu eröfnet hätte. Uebrigens bin ich ein Todfeind vom leeren Witz und gleich leerer Speculation. Diese Todfeindschaft zwischen der Schlange und dem Weibe ist die Triebfeder, welche verschiedene Räder in diesem Buche in Bewegung gesetzt hat—Auf diese Rechnung gehören auch Styl, manche Einschaltung und Wendung.—
> Mein Plan ist zwar unterbrochen, allein für einen Mann wie Sie ist überall Licht.
>
> (Ibid., p. 40)

This letter makes clear that Hippel intended his novel to be read the way that he (and many other Enlightenment figures) read the Bible: namely in a historical-pedagogical sense. The truth stands above (or behind) the word which announces it. The text is written not for an ideal reader, but is calculated to have its effect on a contemporary reader with all his limitations, and to help raise him above these very limitations.

Hippel's novel is written also for a sentimental audience. The text is the occasion for sentimental feeling in addition to leading to "Denken," and in no sense is it supposed to lead to "Spekulation," though Grund often seems to argue the contrary. The text serves to create a community of sentimental hearts and to stimulate the mind. A reader like Jacobi feels his heart is in harmony with that of the author; through the play of wit his reason is set free, not just to follow the wit of the author but also to think issues through to the end that the author deliberately leaves unresolved.

What is unique and valuable in Grund's dissertation, however, is that he offers an alternative reading of Hippel, one that sees him no longer as an epigone of Sterne, but as an author who demands to be read and evaluated on his own terms if we are ever to come to a fuller understanding of the *Lebensläufe* as well as his other works. But a new consideration of Hippel must be careful not to fall into an extreme rejection of any influence on Sterne's part. To do so would be to read Hippel's novel without proper regard for Sterne's importance in Germany. I propose a different reading of the relationship between Sterne and Hippel, one that modifies significantly the view of Hippel as an epigone without making the untenable claim that Hippel can be understood without reference to Sterne.

NOTES

[1] Theodor Gottlieb von Hippel's *Sämmtliche Werke*, 14 vols. (Berlin: Reimer, 1828–39; rpt. Berlin/New York: de Gruyter, 1978), XIV, 82. All references to this edition. The letter is dated 9 February 1778. For the most complete account of Hippel's life and works, see Joseph Kohnen, *Theodor Gottlieb von Hippel, 1741–1796, L'homme et l'oeuvre* (Bern, Frankfurt, New York: Lang, 1983).

[2] See *Biographie des Königl. Preuß. Geheimenkriegsraths zu Königsberg, Theodor Gottlieb von Hippel, zum Theil von ihm selbst verfaßt*. (Gotha:Perthes, 1801; reprint Hildesheim: Gerstenberg, 1977), pp. 417–27.

[3] First published in *Reminiscenzen, Goethe's Mutter; nebst Briefen und Aufzeichnungen zur Charakteristik anderer merkwürdiger Männer und Frauen*. Ed. Dr. Wilhelm Dorow (Leipzig: Hinrichs, 1842), pp. 272 ff; excerpts reprinted in *Reichls Philosophischer Almanach* (Darmstadt: Reichl, 1924), pp. 214–222; not included in the *Sämmtliche Werke*. *Vor hundert Jahren, Elise von der Reckes Reisen durch Deutschland 1784–86. Nach dem Tagebuch ihrer Begleiterin Sophie Becker* (ed. G. Karo, M. Geyer,

Stuttgart: Spemann, 1884), provides an extremely interesting glimpse of Königsberg in July 1784 (pp. 11-14), but does not mention Hippel.

⁴ The first version appeared in succeeding issues of Adolf Heinrich Friedrich Schlichtegroll's *Nekrolog* 1796 (VII, ii, 171-346) and 1797 (VIII, i, 123-414) and was reprinted in one volume by Perthes in 1801. (Since copies of Schlichtegroll's original *Nekrolog* are hard to come by and since the one volume printed by Perthes is identical to the original and has recently been reprinted, I will refer to this one volume edition throughout as "Schlichtegroll".) It was Johann Friedrich Abegg who, on a trip to Königsberg a few years after Hippel's death, collected information on Hippel from his friends, information he then supplied to Schlichtegroll in Gotha. See Abegg's *Reisetagebuch von 1798*, ed. by Walter and Jolanda Abegg in cooperation with Zwi Batscha (Frankfurt: Insel, 1976). The second version of the biography, under the editorship of Hippel's nephew, appeared as volume XII of the *Sämmtliche Werke* in 1835. Generally speaking, the Schlichtegroll edition takes a critical view of Hippel, which his nephew attempts to counter. Schlichtegroll has the advantage of giving an extensive list of Hippel's published and unpublished works; the nephew's edition has the advantage of including passages from the autobiography omitted by Schlichtegroll. Both must be used together.

⁵ Also in Dorow's *Reminiscenzen*, pp. 288-299; an excerpt is also to be found in the *Handbuch der Judenfrage. Eine Zusammenstellung des wichtigsten Materials zur Beurteilung des jüdischen Volkes*, ed. Theodor Fritsch, 23rd edition (!), (Hamburg: Gleipner, 1919), pp. 63-4.

⁶ It is not surprising that Hippel's writings on women have been receiving increased attention recently. Wolfgang Max Faust annotated and wrote an afterword to the first edition of *Über die Ehe* (Stuttgart: Deutsche Verlags-Anstalt, 1972). Notos publishers, in Selb, West Germany, reprinted the fourth edition of *Über die Ehe* in 1976. *Über die bürgerliche Verbesserung der Weiber* was reissued with an afterword by Ralph-Rainer Wuthenow (Frankfurt: Syndikat, 1977). Timothy F. Sellner has written an introduction to, translated, and abridged this work as *On Improving the Status of Women* (Detroit: Wayne State Univ. Press, 1979). Juliane Dittrich-Jacobi wrote an introduction to a reprint of this work and of the *Nachlaß über weibliche Bildung* (Berlin: Voß, 1801; Vaduz/Liechtenstein: Topos, 1981); the *Nachlaß* was intended for a new edition of *Über die bürgerliche Verbesserung der Weiber*, one that never materialized. Günter de Bruyn had edited, abridged, and written a commentary on the first edition of *Über die Ehe* (Berlin: Verlag der Nation, 1985, 3rd printing). Though a start was evidently made by Franz Erdmann, in his scarce *Theodor Gottlieb v. Hippel: Über die Ehe. Eine literar-historische und sprachliche Untersuchung* (Diss. Breslau 1924), there is as yet no critical edition of *Über die Ehe*, one that takes into account all four editions. Indeed, except for *Der Mann nach der Uhr*, there is no critical edition of any of Hippel's works.

⁷ The distortions in the autobiography so angered a certain W. G. Keber that he composed an ill-tempered pamphlet entitled *Nachrichten und Bemerkungen den Geheimen Kriegsrath von Hippel betreffend. Ein Nachtrag zu seiner Biographie im Nekrolog* (Königsberg: Goebbels and Unzer, 1802). Paul Peterken's *Gesellschaftliche und fiktionale Identität. Eine Studie zu Theodor Gottlieb von Hippels Roman "Lebensläufe [. . .]"* (Stuttgart: Akademischer Verlag Hans-Dieter Heinz, 1981) argues that, at least with regard to Hippel's childhood and youth, Keber's account is a "nüchterne Berichterstattung" (p. 183). This is a decided overstatement. Keber was so motivated by anger and vengeance for imagined slights that his work can hardly be read as an unbiased

corrective to Hippel. Peterken's assertion that Scheffner's anonymous pamphlet in reply to Keber is "heute jedoch nicht mehr auffindbar" is also incorrect.

[8] There was speculation that found its way into print only after Hippel's death that it was the humiliation caused by this unhappy love that led to Hippel's ambition to renew his family's aristocratic title; in this way, Hippel would finally erase his inferior status and be eligible to marry a member of the nobility. He would retroactively undo, as it were, the injustice done to him. As has often been pointed out, however, Hippel, for all his writings on marriage, himself remained a lifelong bachelor. See Schlichtegroll, p. 271 ff.

[9] For more on these early works, see Ferdinand Joseph Schneider, *T. G. v. Hippel 1741 bis 1781 und die erste Epoche seiner literarischen Tätigkeit* (Prague: Taussig & Taussig, 1911). Schneider rescued many of Hippel's writings from oblivion, but unfortunately continued his biography only up to the year 1781, the year in which the last volume of the *Lebensläufe* appeared. (It should also be noted that Hippel's nephew broke off the collection of Hippel's letters to Scheffner in vol. XIV of the *Sämmtliche Werke* with the year 1785). Joseph Kohnen has uncovered what is surely a large percentage of what remains in existence but that Schneider missed. See his *Theodor Gottlieb von Hippel, 1741-1796, L'homme et l'oeuvre*, which supersedes Schneider and must be regarded as the standard work on Hippel.

[10] See Erich Jenisch's introduction to his critical edition of *Der Mann nach der Uhr* (Halle: Niemeyer, 1928). Four other plays, at least two of which had been performed in Königsberg during his lifetime, were found in Hippel's papers after his death. See Schlichtegroll, pp. 473-4.

[11] On the institution of the *Hofhalsgericht* as well as for an overview of the complex legal bureaucracy of eighteenth-century Prussia, see Friedrich Giese, *Preußische Rechtsgeschichte* (Berlin and Leipzig: de Gruyter, 1920).

[12] Among the critics who have much that is interesting to say on Hippel but do not deal with the influence of Sterne to any significant extent are, for example, Eichendorff, *Der deutsche Roman des 18. Jahrhunderts in seinem Verhältnis zum Christentum*; Neue Gesamtausgabe der Werke und Schriften in vier Bänden (Stuttgart, 1851), IV; Josef Nadler, *Literaturgeschichte der deutschen Stämme und Landschaften*, 2nd ed. (Regensburg, 1923), II, 541 ff.; and Dieter Kimpel's article on Hippel in Benno von Wiese, ed., *Deutsche Dichter des 18. Jahrhunderts* (Berlin: Erich Schmidt, 1981), pp. 462-481.

[13] Laurence Sterne, *The Life and Opinions of Tristram Shandy, Gentleman*, ed. James A. Work (Indianapolis: Odyssey Press, 1940), II, xi, 108. All reference to this edition.

[14] *Der Teutsche Merkur*, 1779, IV, 287.

[15] This letter is dated "den 25 Januar 1779," even though the year must be 1780. For more on the correct dating of Hippel's letters, see Johannes Sembritzki, "Hippels Briefe an Scheffner," *Euphorion*, XVIII (1911), 406-11.

[16] *Allgemeine deutsche Bibliothek*, 41 (1780), 468.

[17] Ludwig Ernst Borowski, *Ueber das Autorschiksal des Verfassers des Buchs: Ueber die Ehe—der Lebensläufe nach aufsteigender Linie u. a. m., Eine Beylage zu den benannten Schriften*, (Königsberg, Hartung, 1797).

[18] G. W. F. Hegel, "Ueber: Hamann's Schriften," in *Sämtliche Werke*, Jubiläumsausgabe, ed. Hermann Glockner (Stuttgart: Frommann & Holzboog, 1958), XX, 207.

[19] On the relationship between Hippel and Jean Paul, see Wilhelm Scherer, *Geschichte*

der Deutschen Literatur (Berlin, n. d.), pp. 733–4; Guenter G. Schmalz, "Jean Paul Friedrich Richters Urteile ueber Theodor Gottlieb von Hippel", *Proceedings of the Pacific Northwest Conference on Foreign Languages*, 30, i-ii (1979), 71–4; and Joseph Kohnen, "Ottomar und der 'Sterbegraf'", *Germanisch-Romanische Monatschrift*, 29 (1979), 185–99.

[20] Hegel, *Aesthetik*, (Berlin and Weimar: Aufbau, 1976), I, 576.

[21] Theodor Mundt, *Kritische Wälder*, (Leipzig: Melzer, 1833), p. 238.

[22] Georg Gervinus, *Geschichte der poetischen National-Literatur der Deutschen*, 3rd ed., (Leipzig: Engelmann, 1846), V, 191.

[23] Hermann Hettner, *Geschichte der deutschen Literatur im achtzehnten Jahrhundert*, (Berlin and Weimar: Aufbau, 1979), II, 313.

[24] *Hippel's Lebensläufe, eine baltische Geschichte aus dem vorigen Jahrhundert*, ed. Alexander von Oetingen, (Leipzig: Duncker & Humblot, 1878), I, 32.

[25] Julian Schmidt, *Geschichte des geistigen Lebens in Deutschland*, (Leipzig: Grunow, 1863), II, 749–50.

[26] F. J. Schneider, "Studien zu Th. G. v. Hippels *Lebensläufe*. 2. Über den Humor L. Sternes und Th. G. v. Hippels," *Euphorion* XXII (1915), 696, 697, 700.

[27] Johann Czerny, *Sterne, Hippel und Jean Paul*, (Berlin: Duncker & Humblot, 1904).

[28] Hermann Meyer, *Der Sonderling in der deutschen Dichtung*, (Munich: Hanser, 1963), pp. 57, 58.

[29] Peter Michelsen, *Laurence Sterne und der deutsche Roman des achtzehnten Jahrhunderts*, Palaestra 232, 2nd ed. (Göttingen: Vandenhoeck and Ruprecht, 1972).

[30] Eva Becker, *Der deutsche Roman um 1780*, (Stuttgart: Metzler, 1964), p. 215.

[31] See also Helga Vormus, "Theodor Gottlieb von Hippel: *Lebensläufe nach aufsteigender Linie nebst Beilagen ABC.*—Eine Interpretation," "Unordnung ist bei Hippel kein Kompositionsfehler, kein Mangel an erzählerischem Talent, sondern ein bewußtes Prinzip," *Etudes Germaniques* 21 (1966), 14. See also Jürgen Jacobs, *Prosa der Aufklärung*, "Es ist ein extrem subjektivistisches Erzählprogramm, das hier [in den *Lebensläufen*] mit Hilfe sternisierender Mittel verwirklicht ist," (Munich: Winkler, 1976), pp. 206–7.

[32] Norbert Miller, *Der empfindsame Erzähler*, (Munich: Hanser, 1968), p. 247.

[33] Uwe Grund, "Studien zur Sprachgestaltung in Th. G. v. Hippels Roman *Die Lebensläufe nach aufsteigender Linie*," Diss. Berlin 1970.

[34] p. 168. Cf. the *Allgemeine deutsche Bibliothek*'s review: "die naiven und empfindsamen Züge in dieser Liebesintrigue werden gewiß keinen Leser ermüden lassen," 41 (1780), 469.

[35] Arthur Warda, "Friedrich Heinrich Jacobi und der Verfasser der *Lebensläufe*," *Euphorion*, XV (1908), 35.

2

The Eighteenth-Century Novel and the Role of the Narrator

In order to evaluate Hippel's relationship to Sterne, it is necessary to see both authors in the context of contemporary novels and discussions of the novel. In this chapter I will emphasize the role of the narrator in eighteenth-century novels, particularly with reference to Richardson, Fielding, Sterne, and Diderot, and examine the relationship between the novel and historiography. My thesis is that the eighteenth-century novel was in part an imitation of historical writing, an imitation which was then parodied, leading finally to a return to historical techniques, this time on a new level. This survey of the theory of the novel and of novelistic practice will show that Hippel invented virtually no narrative devices, and that he was indebted in this regard not only to Sterne but also to many others. Hippel's contribution consists in the new ends to which he employed traditional means rather than in any technical innovation.

1. The Novel and Historiography in the Early Eighteenth Century

The novel was a problematic genre in the eighteenth century. The novels of the ancients belonged not to the Golden Age but rather to the period of decadence that had followed, and the genre lacked legitimacy in the eighteenth century in part because it had no respectable ancient models to follow.

Nor was the later history of the novel one to lend the genre increased respectability. The romances from the late medieval period to the seventeenth century became so preoccupied with the theme of love that the word *roman,* which originally meant a narrative in French instead of Latin, came to be virtually synonymous with love story, usually of a disreputable kind. As Huet put it, "ce que l'on apelle proprement Romans sont des fictions d'aventures amoureuses, écrites en Prose avec art, pour le plaisir & l'instruction des Lecteurs. Je dis des fictions, pour les distinguer des Histoires véritables. J'ajoute, d'avantures amoureuses, parce que l'amour doit estre le principal sujet du Roman."[1] Huet saw the novel as the sometimes invented, sometimes basically true account of a love affair.

At the same time there was another school of thought, one which saw in the novel a kind of history, written for didactic purposes. This position derived from that advanced by Aristotle in the *Poetics.* The poet, said Aristotle, had the freedom to portray things not as they happened but as they could have happened. Since poetry was wider in its scope than history, it could present the ideal portrait and the truth underlying the events. John Barclay argues in this tradition in his *Argenics* (1621): "I will compile some stately fable, in the manner of a history; in it will I fold up strange events, and mingle together arms, marriages, bloodshed, mirth, with many and various successes."[2] And the preface to Mlle. de Scudéry's *Ibrahim* (1641) proclaimed the work to be historical and one in which true resemblance is observed.

Despite the claims of authors that they were writing historical truth, however, their plots remained artificial and completely lacking in verisimilitude. In them fantasy and miraculous events took the place of history. This paradox was given theoretical expression in a work by Christian Thomasius, in which the argument is put forward that the goal of the historical novel is to make the average reader unable to distinguish truth from invention in the work, and to have the historian, who can make this distinction, find the work at least probable. The work is, however, defined as "die Historie einer gantzen Nation unter den Deckmantel vieler in einander gemischten und mit rechter Kunst verwirrten Geschichten,"[3] a definition which would seem to undercut any sense of probability.

Both *galant* and historical novels dealt with elevated heroes set in a distant time or place, and they were concerned with love intrigues and incredible adventures. At the beginning of the eighteenth century, however, there were serious attacks on the romances of the previous age. Gotthard Heidegger in his *Mythoscopia romantica; oder Discours Von den so benanten Romans* (1698), attacked the improbabilities and ill-effects of the novels of Lohenstein, Buchholtz, and Mlle. de Scudéry. Heidegger and other critics considered novels to be deceptive, composed of lies, and called them hoaxes played by the author on his readers. Morally they exerted a pernicuous influence, for their frivolity and preoccupation with the theme of love was thought to be in danger of corrupting the reader. A representative critical view is that of John Clarke, who found that romances have "a strong Tendency to corrupt and debauch the Mind with silly Mischievous Notions of Love and Honour, and other Things relating to the Conduct of Life."[4] The novel was considered at once unaesthetic and immoral, a danger to taste and to virtue. This double accusation was summed up by Diderot in his *Eloge de Richardson,* when he called the (pre-Richardsonian) novel "dangereuse pour le goût et pour les moeurs."[5]

The critical disapprobation of the novel meant that authors of novels felt constrained to justify their endeavors. The typical form this effort at legitimization took was the author's denial that he was in fact writing anything so suspect as a novel. Instead, authors claimed to be writing history. The choice of history was a logical one, for two reasons. First, history was a respected genre, represented by great classical authors. By becoming more like history, the novel automatically gained respectability. Second, the fictional aspects of ancient as well as contemporary historiography were appealing to novelists, who did not have to engage in much disguising in order to present their works as history.

History was Cicero's *magistra vitae. Veritas* had the meaning of the exemplary in his eyes, and history thus could be written for the improvement of the reader. Poetry, which was written for entertainment, seemed frivolous by comparison, and false.[6]

Since the task of historiography was to improve the reader, the historian had every right to employ rhetorical devices to make his history more persuasive. The ancient historians had had their characters deliver an oration at the high point of the action in order to give the reader the impression of being present at the event. Batteux even went so far as to justify this method on the part of historians, a claim that is somewhat inconsistent with his insistence on historical objectivity.[7] Batteux was willing to modify his position because of the effectiveness of the dramatic presentation. He wrote, "der Geschichtschreiber muß erzählen, was von den Personen, die er auf die Bühne bringt, gesagt oder gethan worden ist, und sie nicht selber reden lassen. Jedoch, da man angemerket hat, daß, je mehr die handelnden Personen selbst reden, je lebhafter und feuriger die Erzählung wird: so haben die Historienschreiber, nach dem Maße, wie sie es in der Kunst hochgebracht hatte [sic], etwas von der Einkleidung der Dichter entlehnt, und die allzu eintönige Form der Erzählung in die dramatische verwandelt" (pp. 288–9).

He went on to cite Livius and Sallust as examples, and to find the practice acceptable when the speech is important, appropriate to the situation, worthy of being preserved, and not overly long. He preferred that the speech be authentic, but he added, "Zuweilen nehmen es die Geschichtschreiber auf sich, die Reden, die gehalten worden sind, selbst zu machen, oder auch Reden zu machen, die gar nicht gehalten worden sind; und dieses darum damit sie die Bewegungsgründe zu den Unternehmungen desto deutlicher vor Augen legen können. Der Geschichtschreiber, als ein Nachahmer der Poeten, versetzt sich alsdann in die Umstände, worinn er seine handelnden Personen sieht [. . .]" (pp. 289–90). This practice Batteux termed a "Kunstgriff [. . .], der die Erzählung belebt, ohne der Wahrheit Eintrag zu thun" (p. 290).

Fielding, in his *Journal of a Voyage to Lisbon*, justified this in a passage that is not meant ironically. "Some few embellishments must be allowed to every historian; for we are not to conceive that the speeches in Livy, Sallust, or Thucydides, were literally spoken in the very words in which we now read them. It is sufficient that every fact hath its foundation in truth."[8] Fielding earlier had made fun of the dramatic historian. After quoting a love letter from the hero in *The History of the Life of the late Mr. Jonathan Wild the Great,* the narrator makes an ironical excuse for the letter, saying, "if it should be observed that the style of this letter doth not exactly correspond with that of our hero's speeches, which we have here recorded, we answer, it is sufficient if in these the historian adheres faithfully to the matter, though he embellishes the diction with some flourishes of his own eloquence, without which the excellent speeches recorded in ancient historians (particularly in Sallust) would have scarce been found in their writings. Nay, even amongst the moderns, famous as they are for elocution, it may be doubted whether those inimitable harangues published in the monthly magazines came literally from the mouths of the Hurgos, etc., as they are there inserted, or whether we may not rather suppose some historian of great eloquence hath borrowed the matter only, and adorned it with those rhetorical flowers for which many of the said Hurgos are not so extremely eminent."[9]

As Kant said much later in one of his lectures, "Wenn wir einen lateinischen Schriftsteller, einen Livius, lesen, so finden wir Reden, welche die Feldherrn an der Spitze ihrer Armeen hielten, oder wann der Feind schon in Anmarsch war und die größte Fassung des Gemüths erfordert haben. Und selbst die Weltgeschichte trägt man so vor, wie man wohl wünschen möchte, daß sie sich ereignet hätte."[10] Historians were not much concerned with rigorous documentation and objectivity, nor were they disturbed by gaps in their presentation, so long as the moral lesson was presented clearly. One of the conventions of historical writing in the eighteenth century was an open acceptance of these practices.

The novel in historical disguise, to be sure, was not an invention of the eighteenth century. The novelists of the sixteenth and seventeenth centuries had claimed for their works historical validity as well. But the *vraisemblance* they meant was in imitation of that which should be (but was not) true. They did not want to show a probable (or even possible) reality so much as a transfigured, idealized portrayal of good society. Ioan Williams points out that it is misleading to read neoclassical authors like Mlle. de Scudéry out of context, for they emphasized historical and true resemblance not in any modern sense of objectivity. They were by no means precursors of naturalism or the historical novel. They called for "the imitation of a generalized human nature rather than the conditions of ordinary life," and their history was also distorted to conform to "contemporary ideas of seemliness and propriety" (Williams, p. 4). Their novels emphasized nature only insofar as it was good, pleasing, and beautiful. For the historian, said Mary de la Rivière Manley in 1705, "ought with great care to observe the Probability of Truth, which consists in saying nothing but what may Morally be believed."[11]

The narrative techniques they developed to bolster their claims to authenticity reflected the aristocratic tastes of the audience and the authors of these novels. The novel seemed to this audience more authentic if it was placed in a historically or geographically remote setting, and particularly if it was presented as the *mémoire* of a nobleman whose historical existence seemed to guarantee the authenticity of a work by him or about him. Frequently the fictional editor would claim that the work was a translation from the work of an author living abroad who wished to preserve his incognito.

In the early eighteenth century all these techniques were developed and became more sophisticated. That is, they became more persuasive to an audience that was becoming increasingly bourgeois. Authors seriously began to imitate historical writings in their compositions, instead of being content with little more than mere assertions of historical truth.

Moreover, these narratives dealt more and more with events of the present as seen by a private, hitherto unknown man, who tells not of his public exploits but of his individual feelings and experiences. Immediacy began to be a guarantee of authenticity.

One aspect of this tendency towards the historical presentation of individual, private destinies was the increased popularity of the autobiographical novel. Implicitly responding to the charge that novels corrupted aesthetic taste, the fictional editor who claimed responsibility for publishing the work often appeared as one who purified and refined his manuscript, who made cuts where the author began to digress.[12]

It was not long before novelists succeeded to a remarkable degree in their mimicry of historians. The shift away from the *roman* and towards history can be seen most readily on the title pages of works published between 1700 and 1740, as the words novel or *roman* disappear almost completely and *histoire* and *Geschichte* begin to appear. Though theoreticians always distinguished sharply between novels and histories most novelists of the early eighteenth century did their best to create pseudo-histories. In some works of Prévost, for example, it is difficult to separate the historian from the novelist. Indeed, Prévost was both a historian as well as a novelist, and "tous les grands romans de Prévost révèlent à la lecture le goût de leur auteur pour l'histoire et ses réelles connaissances historiques."[13] Even in 1963 the Bibliothèque Nationale in Paris classified two novels of Prévost (*Histoire de Guillaume le Conquérant*, 1742, and *Voyages du Capitaine Robert Lade*, 1744) under the rubric of histories.[14]

In England, Defoe's *Robinson Crusoe* (1719) fooled readers into thinking the events described in the book had actually taken place. Defoe encouraged this belief in his Preface to the work. "The Editor believes the thing to be a just History of Fact; neither is there any Appearance of Fiction in it."[25] German authors, too, presented their novels in the guise of histories. One author took on the role of a "tugendhafften und bescheidenen Historien-Schreibers" (*Lebensgeschichte Der unvergleichlich-schönen Türckin/ wundersame Lebens- und Liebes-Geschichte* [. . .] von Menander [1733]); another asserted, "ein Historienbuch muß nach meinem Geschmack erfreuen, erbauen, und unser Herz bessern. Daher habe ich diese wahre Geschichte nach vieler Überlegung endlich zu Stande gebracht" (*Kosakische Standesperson*, 1761).[16] One author even pointed out his dual role in the preface. Johann Heinrich Gottlob von Justi in his *Vorwort* to *Die Wirkungen und Folgen sowohl der wahren, als der falschen Staatskunst in der Geschichte des Psammitichus Königes von Egypten und der damaligen Zeiten* (Frankfurt and Leipzig, 1759), defended the new genre of the pseudo-historical novel, in which the author "die Begebenheiten ausführlicher vorstellet, und diejenigen Umstände, welche die Geschichtsschreiber nur mit kurzen Worten berühren, aus seiner eigenen Erfindung hinzu füget."[17] Justi, who asserted that he had used his sources with care, made it impossible for contemporary readers to distinguish his invention, or rather expansion of the facts, from the historical record itself. One reviewer criticized this mixture of history and fiction, saying that Justi had filled "die Lücken der Geschichtschreiber mit seinen eigenen Einfällen [. . . .] Nun bin ich zwischen der Geschichte und dem Roman in der Mitte, und lese eigentlich bey wahren Namen, Begebenheiten, die der Schriftsteller nach eigenen Belieben ersonnen hat." He went on to ask, "was sollen wir nun mit einem solchen Buche anfangen," that is neither novel nor history?[18]

2. The New Evaluation of the Relationship Between Novel and History

Since history was both true and morally uplifting, the novel could cease to be an outsider in terms of genre insofar as it became historical. In practice this meant that authors began to introduce plausible narrative devices to create the impression of authenticity. Increased authenticity would make the novel more acceptable both in terms of entertaining the reader and in terms of improving him. The audience, it was widely held, was more likely to be moved by what they read if they believed it to be true than if they took it to be invented.

This development can be followed in the theoretical discussions of the novel and of history from the same period. Huet distinguished history from romance according to the degree of fictionality. Histories were, in his view, though not entirely true, nevertheless preponderantly true, with only some admixture of fictional elements. But the romance was false for the most part or even from beginning to end. Of histories, he wrote, "ces ouvrages sont véritables en gros, & faux seulement dans quelques parties: les Romans au contraire sont véritables dans quelques parties, & faux dans le gros. Les uns sont des véritez mêlées de quelques faussetez, les autres sont des faussetez mêlées de quelques véritez. Je veux dire que la vérité tient le dessus dans ces Histoires, & que la fausseté predomine tellement dans les Romans, qu'ils peuvent mesme estre entièrement faux, & en gros & en détail" (pp. 8–9).

By 1728 this relationship was still seen in roughly the same terms but with different emphases. One critic wrote, "Un récit qui ne contient rien que de vrai est une *histoire;* un tissu de fictions est une *fable;* le mélange de la fable et de l'histoire fait le *roman*. Ce qu'il y a de vrai intéresse; ce qu'il a de fiction embellit et amuse."[19] Here it is no longer the romance that is made up for the most part of fiction, but rather the fable. And the romance is seen not as the counterpart of historiography but as a genre that includes both history and fable. Since history is merely instructive or interesting, the *roman* is superior to history in that it combines the didactic with the entertaining aspects of the fable. The *roman* has come a long way towards surpassing history in its status as genre.

Batteux, like Huet, recognized that historians did not simply describe events from an unprejudiced point of view. In this respect the historian resembles the poet, who also mixes the true with the false. In Ramler's translation: "Ob es nun gleich mit dem Geschichtschreiber nicht eine gleiche Bewandniß hat, so steht er doch ebenfalls zwischen der Wahrheit und der Erdichtung in der Mitte. Er wünscht natürlicher Weise seine Leser an sich zu ziehen. [. . . .] Er lieset seine Verzeihung in den Augen der Zuhörer, die fast allemal eine rührende Wahrscheinlichkeit lieber haben, als eine trockene Wahrheit" (p. 264). But Batteux was careful to disapprove of this situation, calling it an error on the part of the historian: "allein so nahe er auch der Tugend kommt, ist er doch darinn nicht weniger ein Fehler" (p. 265). Specifically, Batteux termed it a mistake for the historian to do more than to give the reader "nach der Ordnung der Zeiten und der Oerter eine Liste von

Begebenheiten." Instead, historians have written "vollständige Abhandlungen von der Staatskunst" for the purpose of instructing the mind, educating the heart, and illuminating moral philosophy with the example of historical events. Batteux approved of these ends, but could not approve of the means, which amount to a falsification of history through the admixture of poetic devices. Batteux's historian should be neutral, without passion and ulterior purpose. "Sein ganzes Amt ist, die Sache vorzutragen, wie sie ist" (p. 295).

German critics undertook a similar reevaluation of the relationship between the two genres. Gottsched's changing responses to the novel can be measured by comparing earlier editions of his works with later ones. In the *Critische Dichtkunst* of 1730 he treated novels as a kind of heroic epic. And three years later he wrote, "Ein Roman ist zwar, in soferne er als ein Gedichte angesehen wird, mit unter die Gattungen der Poesie zu rechnen, er erlanget aber bey derselben nur eine von den untersten Stellen."[20] By 1751, however, the novel was considered by Gottsched to be a genre in its own right, not just subordinate to verse epic. He remained opposed to the poetic, exaggerated language of earlier novels, but praised the natural manner of narrating, which he associated with the historical style. "Je näher also die Schreibart in Romanen der historischen kommt, desto schöner ist sie."[21] Gottsched was an early proponent of plausibility on the part of novelists. He insisted that they study the customs of the age they dealt with in the novel, and not contradict historical fact. He criticized earlier pseudo-histories in which only the costumes and names were historically accurate.

For Bodmer, too, historical truth, though not mathematically exact, remained superior to poetic truth. "Also sind Gedicht, Fabel, und Roman einestheils, und Histoire anderntheils, nicht weiter von einander unterschieden, als daß die leztere mehr Grade der Wahrscheinlichkeit hat, indem sie mehr und bewährtere Zeugen hat, deren Aussage besser zusammenstimmet, und vollständiger ist." He added, "die poetische Wahrheit bleibet allezeit einige Grade unter der historischen; ja sie entfernet sich öfters mit Fleiß von derselben, damit sie sich durch den Schein des Falschen wunderbar mache."[22] Historical truth remained the ideal which the poet should imitate in his works.

The very success of the novel in imitating historical works soon called into question the methods of both the historians and the novelists. Critics began to reemphasize the division between fiction and fact. Breitinger permitted the historian to use "zuweilen den Pinsel des poetischen Mahlers," but only within limits and only in order to make the truth appear more clearly.[23] Other critics were more rigorous in their new concern for historical objectivity. According to Johann Jacob Mascou's *Geschichte der Teutschen* (Leipzig, 1726), p. 433: "aus der Historie einen Roman zu machen" is something the historian should avoid. And he went on to attack Prévost for his use of the manuscript fiction in the *Philosophische Feldzüge oder Geschichte des Herrn von Montcal*.[24]

Paradoxically the historiographers' traditional use of rhetoric had to be abandoned or at least reduced because of the success of the poets in engaging in the same method of narration. The novelists who sought to raise the prestige of their works by allying them with the sublime genre of History ended up giving impetus to the concern for objectivity on the part of historians. The young Lessing, in the *Briefe, die neueste Litteratur betreffend* (1759–65), pointed out a difference in type between historians and novelists: "Ich kann Ihnen nicht unrecht geben, wenn Sie behaupten, daß es um das Feld der *Geschichte* in dem ganzen Umfange der deutschen Literatur noch am schlechtesten aussehe."[25] The "schöne Geister," who could write well, had not studied history. Those who were learned were too pedantic to write well. They were further hindered by their area of research: a distant past from which few records survive. Thus, Lessing continues, "wem kann hier auch die größte Kunst zu erzählen, zu schildern, zu beurteilen, wohl viel helfen? Er müßte denn kein Gewissen machen, uns seine Vermutungen für Wahrheiten zu verkaufen, und die Lücken der Zeugnisse aus seiner Erfindung zu ergänzen. Wollen Sie ihm das wohl erlauben? O weg mit diesem poetischen Geschichtschreiber! Ich mag ihn nicht lesen, als einen Geschichtschreiber wenigstens nicht; und wenn ihn sein Vortrag noch so liebenswürdig machte!" *(Ibid.)* Lessing, it should be noted, was writing about German historians, not about Voltaire, Hume, Vico, or Gibbon.

Thus at a time when the ancient historians themselves came under attack for having embellished the truth or even for having lied, modern historians were being even more severely criticized. Kant, writing some twenty years after Lessing, argued that where ancient historians were merely without information and therefore necessarily inventive, contemporary historians were factional. "Unsere Geschichtschreiber sind noch unwahrer als die alten; denn diese schreiben nicht die Unwahrheit aus Partheilichkeit, sondern aus Mangel an Geschichten und verdrehten auch nicht die Wahrheit. Daher findet man mehr Spuren der Wahrheit bei den Alten, als bei den Geschichtschreibern der jezigen Zeit, wo die Partheilichkeit mit darauf hinaus geht, der Wahrheit aus eigenem Vortheile Abbruch zu thun."[26]

An example of the historical works that Kant might have had in mind is the one composed by Gottlieb Benedikt Schirach (1743–1804), *Biographie der Deutschen*, a collection of biographies of historical figures. Criticizing the style of the third volume of this work (1771) as being too novelistic, the reviewer for the *Frankfurter gelehrte Anzeigen* remarked, "traurig war es vor uns, daß ein Schriftsteller im Jahr 1771 sich noch Leser vorstellen kann, die dergleichen schöne Reflexionen, wie folgende, nötig haben sollen und mögen: Nun genoß *Kunigunde,* der *schöne Körper,* und die *häßliche Seele,* die Erfüllung ihrer Wünsche. [. . . .] Würklich führte Albrecht innerhalb seines Schlosses Wartburg ein *glückliches* Leben, umgeben von einer Menge *schmeichelhafter* Seelen, und *zärtlich* von der Geliebten geliebt, so wie alle diejenigen, welche in der Ehe sich tief unter ihren Stand erniedrigen und eine Person zur Dame machen, die sonst hätte Damen dienen müssen, und es täglich empfindet, wie viel der Mann ihr gab, der ihr Mann ward."[27]

Of a completely different calibre is Edward Gibbon's *Decline and Fall of the Roman Empire* (1776–88) and it would be a more than misguided effort to compare them in any systematic fashion. The following is a passage from Gibbon describing the entrance of Mohammed II into Constantinople after the fall of the city on 29 May 1453.

> From St. Sophia he proceeded to the august but desolate mansion of an hundred successors of the great Constantine; but which, in a few hours, had been stripped of the pomp of royalty. A melancholy reflection on the vicissitudes of human greatness forced itself on his mind; and he repeated an elegant distich of Persian poetry, "The spider has wove his web in the Imperial palace; and the owl hath sung her watch-song on the towers of Afrasiab."[28]

Gibbon quotes his source for this distich, but he must have known that it was, to say the least, suspect in its authenticity, that the source was following the time-honored tradition of resorting to direct quotation at significant moments in the historical account. This is nothing but the "Rede des Feldherrn an der Spitze seiner Armeen" that Kant criticized.

In short, even a monument as great as Gibbon's is far from historiography in the spirit of Ranke. It is not, of course, that Gibbon falls short of Ranke's ideals, but Gibbon's principles are different, as are his methods of presentation. The events do not seem to tell themselves, rather they are introduced and reflected upon by a narrator, a philosophical historian, who comments on the events.[29] He is essentially a moralist. As Friedrich Schiller put it in his inaugural lecture (Jena, 1789), *Was heißt und zu welchem Ende studiert man Universal-geschichte:* "Fruchtbar und weit umfassend ist das Gebiet der Geschichte; in ihrem Kreise liegt die ganze moralische Welt." Schiller asks what the result of the proper study of history should be. Addressing his audience, he says, "Licht wird sie [die Weltgeschichte] in Ihrem Verstande, und eine wohltätige Begeisterung in Ihrem Herzen entzünden. [. . . .] Ein edles Verlangen muß in uns entblühen [. . .]"[30]

"Prior to the French Revolution," Hayden White has noted, "historiography was conventionally regarded as a literary art.

More specifically, it was regarded as a branch of rhetoric and its 'fictive' nature generally recognized."[31] This can readily be seen in the passage from Schiller: his description of the historian's task is none too different from his understanding of the dramatist's task, nor from the understanding of the novelist's task held by many in the eighteenth century.

One result of the historians' new concern for objectivity and rigor was the relative decline of historiography in the hierarchy of genres. For if historians were bound to an ideal of factuality, their works tended to lose their didactic value. The modern historian was felt to be at a disadvantage because his inevitable ignorance of the inner life of his characters made moral evaluation of them difficult. As one anonymous critic put it: "In den Geschichtbüchern werden die Menschen nur unvollkommen abgeschildert. Diese verrichten viele Handlungen im verborgenen, aus welchen wieder andere Thaten entspringen, welche zuweilen einen Einfluß in die bürgerliche Gesellschaft haben. Ein aufrichtiger Geschichtschreiber weiß daher nicht von allen bekannten Handlungen die Ursachen. Diese leeren Plätze kann ein Romanschreiber erfüllen, und uns die berühmten Menschen in ihren Geheimzimmern und Schlafkammern fürstellen."[32] Thus at a time when the ancient historians themselves came under attack for having embellished the truth or even for having lied, more modern historians were attacked for spreading accounts that were accurate, to be sure, but of questionable moral value.

3. The Emancipation of the Novel

> 'Tis not *the Possible,* but *the Probable* and *Likely* which must be the Poet's Guide in *Manners.* By this he wins Attention, and moves the conscious Reader or Spectator; who judges best from *within,* by what he naturally feels and experiences in his own Heart.[33]

The high point of the mixed genre of the pseudo-historical novel soon passed. Novelists had acquired from the historians valuable narrative techniques, and had achieved the prestige of being more effective as moral educators than historians. Thus the fiction of historical authenticity soon became conventional and was recognized as such. Novelists found that it was no longer necessary to convince the audience that the story related was in fact true. For if the audience were convinced that the story *could* be true, they were equally moved. The novel no longer needed to legitimize itself in terms of historical authenticity alone. Instead, it began to justify itself increasingly on the grounds of its greater effectiveness in imparting moral principles through examples that are concrete.

The decisive breakthrough was made by Samuel Richardson in his *Pamela, or Virtue Rewarded* (1740) and *Clarissa Harlowe* (1747). Though they maintained the convention of being histories published by an editor who guaranteed their authenticity, the letter form enabled Richardson to present the events to the reader almost as they unfolded, instead of from the retrospective view of the *mémoire* author. The historical conventions were by no means given up, but the emphasis shifted away from the historically authentic, which by no means had to be probable, to the dramatically plausible and more perfect illusion of seeming to be on the scene of the events.

Richardson himself drew attention to this concern for immediacy in his Preface to *Clarissa*. "All the letters are written while the hearts of the writers must be supposed to be wholly engaged in their subjects (the events at the time generally dubious); so that they abound not only with critical situations, but with what may be called *instantaneous* descriptions and reflections (proper to be brought home to the breast of the youthful reader;) as also with affecting conversations; many of them written in the dialogue or dramatic way.

" '*Much more* lively and affecting,' says one of the principal characters (Vol. VII, Let. XXX.) 'must be the style of those who write in the height of a *present* distress, the mind tortured by the pangs of uncertainty (the events then hidden in the womb of fate;) *than* the dry, narrative, unanimated style of a person relating difficulties and danger surmounted, can be; the relater perfectly at ease; and if himself unmoved by his own story, not likely greatly to affect the reader.' "[34]

This shift from historical to dramatic presentation is perhaps made most vivid, however, in a parenthetical remark from Richardson's Postscript to *Clarissa,* in which reference is made to "The Author of the History (or rather Dramatic Narrative) of Clarissa [. . .]" (VIII, 345).

Richardson's preference for the appearance of plausibility was echoed in tentative fashion by the anonymous reviewer of a moral weekly: "Man meynt, die erdichteten Geschichten hätten nicht so viel Eindruck als diejenigen, welche wirklich geschehen sind, und welche uns die Historie an die Hand giebt. Denn wie sollte man eine Begierde in sich empfinden, einem Dinge, das niemals gewesen ist, nachzuahmen; und gesetzt, daß man auch allemal vorgiebt, es hätte sich diejenige Begebenheit, die man erzählt, wirklich zugetragen; so sehe man doch gar deutlich, daß dieses ein bloßes Vorgeben sey, und die Reden, welche zwischen Personen insgeheim vorgefallen sind, u. die Briefe, die sie gewechselt haben, ja die ganzen Einrichtungen zeigen, daß, wo nicht alles, doch vieles erdichtet sey. Allein kurz darauf zu antworten, so ist bey dem letzten blos darauf zu sehen, daß es wahrscheinlich gemacht werde, und wenn dieses geschieht, kann man nicht zweifeln, daß es sich zugetragen habe."[35] This direct endorsement of the probable over the allegedly historical is somewhat diluted, however, when the author continues by saying, "Allerdings wäre es rathsam, daß man wirklich geschehene und zwar vielen Leuten bekannte Dinge zum Grunde legte, weil daraus noch größerer Nutzen entstünde." It is as though he were not yet quite ready to do without the historical conventions.

Later critics were not so timid. In an article entitled "Ob es erlaubt sey, die so genanten Romainen oder erdichteten Geschichte zu lesen?" by G. F. Meier, the author advocates the probable without any historical props. "Denn es ist uns einerley, ob etwas wirklich geschehen sey oder nicht, wenn wir erkennen, es hätte so geschehen können."[36] And an anonymous author in *Der Gesellige* asserted, "Die Geschichte lehret nur, wie man sich wirklich verhalten habe; jene [die guten Romane] aber gehen, in so fern sie möglich und wahrscheinlich sind, von derselben ab, und zeigen uns, wie man sich verhalten könnte und sollte [. . . .]"[37] This position had already been stated by authors of romances in the seventeenth and early eighteenth centuries, of course, but the definition of what was probable had changed and now no longer included, for example, miracles and supernatural intervention.[38]

Gellert, for example, was much closer to the modern sense of probability when he wrote: "So erzählen, daß man die Sache nicht allein versteht, sondern daß man glaubt, sie selbst zu sehen, und ein Zeuge davon zu seyn, das heißt lebhaft erzählen. Dieses geschieht durch die kleinen Gemälde, die man in Erzählen von den Umständen, oder Personen, entwirft, insonderheit wenn man die Personen zuweilen selbst reden läßt, und uns dadurch mit ihrem Charakter bekannt macht."[39]

Likewise Henry Home, Lord Kames, asserted that "A dialogue makes a deeper impression than a narration: because in the former persons express their own sentiments; whereas in the latter sentiments are related at second hand."[40] Home defended the repetitions in Homer by calling them dramatic, such that they "have an air of truth, by making things appear as passing in our sight" (Ibid., p. 204).

Finally, Wieland, in the foreword to *Agathon* (1767), defended his work on the basis not so much of its historical authenticity as of its probability. The truth of this work, he wrote, "bestehet darinn, daß alles mit dem Lauf der Welt übereinstimme, daß die Character nicht willkührlich, und bloß nach der Phantasie, oder den Absichten des Verfassers gebildet, sondern aus dem unerschöpflichen Vorrath der Natur selbst hergenommen; [. . .] und also alles so gedichtet sey, daß kein hinlänglicher Grund angegeben werden könne, warum es nicht eben so wie es erzählt wird, hätte geschehen können [. . . .]"[41] Wieland then went on to give assurances that Agathon and other characters are in fact historical persons and of a kind still to be found today, "und dass (die Neben-Umstände, die Folge und besondere Bestimmung der zufälligen Begebenheiten, und was sonsten nur zur Auszierung, welche willkührlich ist, gehört, ausgenommen), alles, was das Wesentliche dieser Geschichte ausmacht, eben so historisch, und vielleicht noch um manchen Grad gewisser sey, als irgend ein Stük der glaubwürdigsten politischen Geschichtschreiber, welche wir aufzuweisen haben" (p. 2). Any improbabilities in the text he excused here by appealing to the truth of the events, and by referring to the "beglaubtesten Geschichtschreibern," among whom he mentions Plutarch, who tells of odder characters than Agathon (p. 2). Wieland thus sought to justify his novel on the basis of its probability, but immediately felt the need to support this justification by asserting the fundamental truth of the events related. And in "Ueber das Historische im Agathon," which he added to the second edition (1773), Wieland admitted that he had invented much, but was quick to point out that "man hat der Erdichtung nicht mehr verstattet, als die historischen Begebenheiten näher zu bestimmen und völliger auszumalen [. . . .]"[42]

Wieland's appeals to historical authenticity are so transparent and conventional, however, that they could scarcely have fooled anyone. The narrator of *Agathon,* like that of *Tom Jones,* used the convention of historical authenticity quite consciously in order to achieve his own ends, which have little to do with the historical record. Wieland stated his position most clearly in the "Nachtrag zur Geschichte der schönen Rosemunde" (1777), in which he unequivocably argued for the primacy of probability over factuality. He asked rhetorically, "Was gehen dem Dichter die historischen Umstände einer Begebenheit an?" It is not so important, "wie eine Sache sich wirklich zugetragen, sondern, wie sie sich hätte zutragen müssen, um [. . .] angenehm, unterhaltend odor rührend zu seyn."[43]

Thus the ritual claims to historical authenticity became less and less important as the inherent closeness to life and probability came to be emphasized. In effect, the novel emancipated itself from its model of historiography and became an independent genre in its own right.

4. Parodies of the Novel

After 1740 the novel was characterized by two tendencies. On the one hand the assertion of historical authenticity became more and more conventional; on the other hand, the novel increasingly borrowed dramatic techniques in the presentation of events. The common element in both these tendencies was the emphasis on encouraging the reader to believe in the probability of what he read. Novels now sought to create an illusion so perfect the reader would forget that what he was reading was fiction at all; they wanted to present the events as so immediate and so likely that the reader would be more thoroughly entertained and more subtly improved than had hitherto been the case.

One sign of the prevalence of these tendencies was that they were parodied.[44] Two authors in particular, Sterne and Diderot, pointed out that the novel remained a fictional construct despite all its efforts to deny this essential aspect of its nature.

A. Sterne

Richardson's innovation had set off a wave of imitators, so that the superiority of dramatic to narrative presentation became one of the commonplaces of the age, one that was soon parodied. Fielding, for example, probably had Richardson or at least a Richardsonian type of narrator in mind when he rejected "the painful and voluminous Historian, who thinks himself obliged to fill up as much Paper with the detail of Months and Years in which nothing remarkable happened, as he employs upon those notable Aeras when the greatest Scenes have been transacted on the human Stage.

"Such Histories as these do, in reality, very much resemble a Newspaper, which consists of just the same Number of Words, whether there be any News in it or not [. . .] The Writer, indeed, seems to think himself obliged to keep even Pace with Time, whose Amanuensis he is [. . .]"[45] Clarissa's letters had maintained an illusion of inclusiveness, as she wrote thousands of pages to describe a period lasting eight months. One of the disadvantages of instantaneous description, however, is that to support the fiction that he does not know what the future holds, the epistolary narrator has no perspective from which to distinguish the important and fateful from the merely accidental.

The narrator of *Tom Jones* (1749) deliberately and self-consciously takes up a different stance. He is quite willing to sacrifice the unselective completeness of the newspaper reporter to adopt the pose of the narrator who is both omniscient and a historian. "I am not writing a System, but a History, and I am not obliged to reconcile every Matter to the received Notions concerning Truth and Nature." Fielding's narrator leaves gaps where, he assures us, nothing of importance happened to his characters. He selects the essential from the biography of Jones and orders it in such a way as to bring out its meaning. "For as I am, in reality, the Founder of a new Province of Writing, so I am at liberty to make what Laws I please therein" (II, i, 77).[46] Thus Fielding's narrator encourages readers to trust their discriminating guide and allow themselves to be led by him instead of trying to make their own way through the raw data of history.[47]

Unlike Fielding, Sterne did not simply reject the Richardsonian manner of narrating a story in order to narrate as he saw fit. He rather sought to make the Richardsonian manner ridiculous by imitating it rigorously, that is, by carrying this narrative position through to its logical conclusion and thereby leading it *ad absurdum*.

Though *Tristram Shandy* is not, of course, an epistolary novel, both Sterne and Tristram are aware of the novel's dramatic nature.[48] The dramatic aspect of *Tristram Shandy* is similar to that of *Clarissa:* the narrator allows the characters to present themselves through their speech rather than characterizing them himself in a commentary. As A. A. Mendilow points out, there is little sense of past and future in *Tristram Shandy;* the work has a continual present, as does the drama.[49] And Sterne's use of dialogue increases this dramatic sense of immediacy and directness.

The parody begins when Sterne, like Richardson before him, used this dramatic technique to present an all-inclusive description of events. Tristram, like Clarissa, has made it his task to tell everything he knows about his topic; "nothing which has touched me will be thought trifling in its nature, or tedious in its telling" (I, vi, 10–11). No fact concerning his life is too slight or too remote for him to track down. "My way is ever to point out to the curious, different tracts of investigation, to come at the first springs of the events I tell [. . .]" (I, xxi, 66).[50]

Tristram's obsession with getting to the bottom of things, with arriving at first causes of events, carries him so far afield that his stated intention of writing his life and opinions becomes increasingly lost from sight. Tristram is so circumstantial in his account of his birth that he is never able to procede to relate his life.[51]

Since every event is important in this life, even the act of writing the life becomes a part of the life that must be narrated. Thus it follows that, as Tristram notes, the more he writes, the more he shall have to write. The narration of life that pretends to Richardsonian inclusiveness and circumstantiality is a hopeless endeavor, one that by its very nature cannot succeed. In showing the failure of Tristram to have his biography ever keep pace with his life, Sterne was, among other things, calling attention to the limitations of narrators like Clarissa, and making fun of the allegedly dramatic and allegedly all-inclusive manner of narrating events.

But it is not only Richardson that Sterne made fun of. Fielding, too, or rather the convention of the historian who is also omniscient, is parodied by the narrator Tristram.

The only security Fielding has for the accuracy of his history of Tom Jones is the narrator and his assurances that he is telling the reader all he needs to know. Even though most of *Tom Jones* is told in the third person, a first-person narrator appears in the opening chapter of each book, and comments on the characters and on the action for the instruction of the reader. In his role of historian he makes the reader aware of the chain of events, occasionally even going so far as to point out certain delicate motives that might have struck the reader as trivial.[52] The narrator justifies these winks to the public with the remark, "Though this Incident will probably appear of little Consequence to many of our Readers; yet, trifling as it was, it had so violent an Effect on poor *Jones,* that we thought it our Duty, to relate it. In reality, there are many little Circumstances too often omitted by injudicious Historians, from which Events of the utmost Importance arise" (V, iv, 225). Fielding's judicious historian always knows where his digressions and intrusions are leading him.[53]

If Fielding's narrator can be said to be omniscient and omnipotent within the confines of the novel, Sterne's narrator is omniscient and impotent. And he is, paradoxically, impotent as a narrator by the very fact of his omniscience. The apparently unlimited access to the facts of the story related by Tristram, the narrator, interferes with the account of the life of Tristram, the character.

Tristram is the most truly omniscient narrator perhaps in all literature; he seems to know literally everything about his topic. Of course this compulsive omniscience involves him in innumerable digressions, but that is the situation in which the omniscient narrator who is honest about his business must necessarily find himself. *Real* omniscience does not square well with the narrator's sovereign control over his narrative, in other words, with the *convention* of narrative omniscience. Sterne treats the fiction of the all-knowing narrator as though it were no fiction but the actual position of the narrator. Such a narrator is incapable of giving his story any form other than that of the fragment. His story is engulfed by the details of the world to be described.

Tristram parodies the pose of the judicious historian who is reluctant to omit a single one of those "many little circumstances." No matter how remote, they must be tracked down, examined, their relationship to the story considered. Fielding's narrator viewed the world "as a vast Machine, in which the great Wheels are originally set in Motion by those which are very minute, and almost imperceptible to any but the strongest Eyes" (V, iv. 225). Tristram parodies this way of viewing the world, for he is capable of uncovering throughout the work relationships that are imperceptible to any eyes but his.

Tristram implicitly asks, How can the historian ever claim to come to the final cause of an event or motive of a character? Tristram criticizes the pose of the judicious historian when he writes, "Could a historiographer drive on his history, as a muleteer drives on his mule,—straight forward [. . .] without ever once turning his head aside either to the right hand or to the left,—he might venture to foretell you to an hour when he should get to his journey's end;—but the thing is, morally speaking, impossible: For, if he is a man of the least spirit, he will have fifty deviations from a straight line to make with this or that party as he goes along, which he can no ways avoid" (I, xiv, 36–37). Where does the chain of explanation stop? The narrator has to select, order, intrude upon his story, but in so doing he can no longer make any claim to objectivity, to presenting events just as they happened. The omniscience of the narrator is no guarantee of his objectivity. In fact, Sterne showed, such a narrator can be most subjective and capricious.

Victor Shklovski has argued that *Tristram Shandy* is *nothing but* a parody of traditional forms.[54] The content of the novel, wrote Shklovski, consists of emphasizing form by means of destroying it. The forms of Sterne's novel are a dislocation and violation of traditional forms, so that not one of the techniques of storytelling serves the purpose it had always been made to serve. Shklovksi concluded that *Tristram Shandy* is the most typical novel ever written (Tristram himself jokingly calls it "this book of books," III, xxxi, 218), because it is made up of typical techniques, conventional elements taken out of their normal context and put into a new and unusual order.

Shklovski surely is one-sided in considering only formal aspects and excluding any treatment of the ultimately moral intent of the work. Of course Sterne's narrator trespasses against all the conventions of storytelling, or follows them only in order to parody them. But the effect of this is, for example, to make the "Confrontation with Death," which has a weighty enough ring to it, into but one more of "those whiffling vexations which come puffing across a man's canvas"[55] (VII, xvi, 496). Even the more sentimental episodes (Maria, Le Fever) are not entirely free of parodistic or ironic undertones. Though Shklovski is right to point out that Sterne is playing with forms, he fails to consider fully the effect of this play, and he is quite wrong in calling Sterne unfeeling ("gefühllos," p. 149). Sterne is criticizing his countrymen's gravity and self-importance as well as their shallow cult of the sentimental. He hopes to improve them through laughter. This is the moral root of Sterne's play, which is not so close to play-for-the-sake-of-play.

Shklovski is right, however, to emphasize that Sterne defunctionalizes forms, so that they cease to serve any purpose other than to reveal themselves for what they are. Sterne wants to jar his readers into an awareness of the fictional nature of novelistic conventions. In the words of another critic, "The trouble with Sterne's predecessors, he cannot have failed to see, was that they made segments of life too ordered and too intelligible to be true accounts, connections too simply clear to be credible. And, so viewed, *Tristram Shandy* is a deep-laid criticism of the novels of Richardson and Fielding."[56]

Tristram educates the reader by leading him astray and vexing him with the caprices of the narrator, who deliberately raises expectations only in order to disappoint them. Tristram thereby teaches the reader to distrust even an omniscient narrator.[57]

B. Diderot

Diderot's career as a novelist recapitulates many of the dominant themes in the development of the eighteenth-century novel. Early in his career Diderot was sceptical of the romance, which he attacked as an affront to morality and taste, and as preoccupied with amorous adventures. "Par un roman on a entendu jusqu'à ce jour un tissu d'événements chimériques et frivoles, dont la lecture était dangereuse pour le goût et les moeurs," wrote Diderot in the opening sentence of his *Eloge de Richardson* (1761–2).[58]

It was the example of Richardson that evidently led Diderot to reconsider his attitude towards the novel. For the attack on the romance just quoted is followed in Diderot's text by the words: "Je voudrais bien qu'on trouvât un autre nom pour les ouvrages de Richardson, qui élèvent l'esprit, qui touchent l'âme, qui respirent partout l'amour du bien, et qu'on appelle aussi des romans." The word romance was in such disrepute that Diderot wished there could be another word to designate the new type of novel that Richardson had written, one that did not transport the reader to distant lands, one that refrained from placing him either among savages or in a fairy-tale world. Instead, Richardson chose as his scene the world we live in, said Diderot, in which the characters are as *vraisemblable* as possible. The passions of the characters are like those felt by the reader himself, and the general course of events shown in the work is one that the reader is familiar with.

Though Diderot approved of Richardson's new kind of novel, he rejected the traditional alternative to the term romance, history. For Diderot was as suspicious of history as he was of romance: "l'histoire attribue à quelques individus ce qu'ils n'ont ni dit, ni fait;" and further, "l'histoire la plus vraie est pleine de mensonges" (p. 221). For Diderot the Richardsonian novel expressed a higher kind of truth than works of history were capable of expressing, for the novel, since it is not bound to the facts, is able to reproduce typical, and therefore true, aspects of life.

One way Richardson was able to write fiction that was more true than history was, according to Diderot, by means of his use of detail. Richardson presented everyday events in his novels, Diderot conceded, but he went on to argue that Richardson presented just those everyday events that would otherwise have gone unnoticed. Richardson's use of detail makes the reader aware of occurrences which, perhaps because they are so commonplace, would have escaped the reader, or at least not have struck him with such force. "Sachez que c'est à cette multitude de petites choses que tient l'illusion; il y a bien de la difficulté à les imaginer; il y a bien encore à les rendre. Le geste est quelquefois aussi sublime que le mot; et puis ce sont toutes ces vérités de détail qui préparent l'âme aux impressions fortes des grands événements," (p. 218) such as the death of Clarissa. Details serve to delay action, and awaken impatience in the reader. "Lorsque votre impatience aura été suspendue par ces délais momentanés qui lui servaient de digues, avec quelle impétuosité ne se répandra-t-elle pas au moment ou il plaira au poète de les rompre! C'est alors qu'affaissé de douleur ou transporté de joie, vous n'aurez plus la force de retenir vos larmes prêtes à couler, et de vous dire à vous-même: *Mais peut-être que cela n'est pas vrai.* Cette pensée a été éloignée de vous peu à peu; et elle est si loin qu'elle ne se présentera pas" (p. 218).

Thus Diderot defended Richardson from critics who accused his works of being overly long by justifying their length as a kind of epic retardation, or extended presentation of preparatory detail which served to make the ultimate effect on the reader all the more impressive. This early passage points in the direction Diderot was himself later to take.

But for the time being Diderot did not merely praise Richardson. He also imitated the English novelist in *La Religieuse* (1760). The narrator, Marie Suzanne Simonin, writes of her experiences as an unwilling nun in various convents. As Grimm revealed in his *Correspondance littéraire* of 1770, the novel is based on the case of a nun named Marguerite Delamarre, whose appeals to be released from the convent of Longchamp were ultimately unsuccessful. One who came to her aid was the Marquis de Croismare, a friend of Diderot and a welcome guest in the Paris salons. Without knowing her name or any details of the case he exerted himself on her behalf. Later, in 1759, when the Marquis left Paris to go into retirement on his estate near Caen, Diderot and his friends attempted to bring the Marquis back to Paris by means of a ruse: Diderot and the other conspirators composed letters purporting to be from the nun, in which she wrote to the Marquis to request assistance after her "escape" from the convent. Though the Marquis believed the letters to be genuine and wanted to be of help, he still did not return to Paris. Finally Diderot had the nun "die," and later he revealed the hoax to the Marquis when he finally did return to Paris some years later.

During the composition of the letters, Diderot became intrigued by the subject and wrote the *mémoire* now known as *La Religieuse*. Though technically a fictional *mémoire,* it is written with the immediacy of an epistolary novel. Georges May points out that *La Religieuse* tends to be not so much a *mémoire* as a private journal in the manner of *Pamela*.[59] The imperfect and preterite of the memoir writer gives way to the present of the diarist in the course of the work, so that it is written more as a continuous present than as a remembered past. This leads to some logical improbabilities in the text, since Suzanne must know in retrospect, for example, what the sexual proclivities of one of the mothers superior are. Yet in her recollection of their first meetings Suzanne shows no sign that she understands the advances of the mother superior. It is somewhat improbable that Suzanne, in the course of writing, should look back on these events with the same naivete she had had when she first met the mother superior, but this technique is effective in holding the reader's attention and encouraging the suspension of disbelief.

At this stage of its composition, in 1760, the unpublished manuscript of *La Religieuse* is a successful imitation of a Richardsonian novel. Later Diderot was to make something more of *La Religieuse*, but first he turned his attention to other matters, among them *Jacques le fataliste* (1771, published in the *Correspondance littéraire* beginning in 1778). If *La Religieuse* can be considered Diderot's novel in the manner of Richardson, then *Jacques* is his novel in the manner of Sterne. In this work Diderot, like Sterne before him, satirized the various novelistic conventions of the preceding hundred years.

One way he did so was by pretending to adhere to them himself. Diderot's narrator denies, for example, that he is engaged in writing a novel. Instead, he claims to be presenting the truth. "Il est bien évident que je ne fais point un roman, puisque je néglige ce qu'un romancier ne manquerait pas d'employer. Celui qui prendrait ce que j'écris pour la vérité serait peut-être moins dans l'erreur que celui qui le prendrait pour une fable."[60] Since he is not writing a novel, it follows he must be writing a history, or at least say he is, according to the conventions of the time; "je n'aime pas les romans, à moins que ce ne soient ceux de Richardson. Je fais l'histoire; cette histoire intéressa ou n'intéressa pas, c'est le moindre de mes soucis. Mon projet est d'être vrai [. . .]" (p. 315). In his role as historian he is reluctant to invent letters he does not possess, and makes something of a show of his scrupulous honesty: "je vois seulement qu'avec un peu d'imagination et de style rien n'est plus aisé que de filer un roman. Demeurons dans le vrai [. . .]" (Ibid.).

All of these assertions are meant as a parody of the pretensions to historical authenticity of the contemporary novel. As Vivienne Mylne has said, "the narrator's frequent appeals to 'truth' are part of Diderot's attack on what the reader thinks a novel should be and do. Thus the repeated assurances that his is no mere novel are a mocking echo of the claims so widespread among novels of the time."[61] The parodistic intent is made obvious when the narrator begins to exaggerate the historical conventions and take them literally. Near the end of the work, for example, Jacques has been imprisoned and the *maître* is in flight after having fought a duel. At this climactic moment, in which the two protagonists seem to be separated with little hope of their ever coming together again, and in which the future of both Jacques and the *maître* is doubtful, the narrator introduces the time-honored manuscript fiction. He claims that he has been working from a manuscript, and just here, the narrator informs the reader, the manuscript breaks off. There are, however, three variant endings which the narrator presents, though he will not vouch for their authenticity. The last of these provides a fairy-tale ending to Jacques's *amours,* one which reunites Jacques and his *maître* and has them settle down in the service of a lord, whose daughter, Denise, Jacques marries. Yet even this ending is undercut by a last speculation of the narrator's, who questions Denise's faithfulness.

Thus the manuscript fiction, traditionally used by the narrator to skip over unimportant or uneventful passages in the hero's life, is here used at the climax in order to frustrate the reader's expectations. These expectations are then teased by a deliberately fictional and unrealistic ending in the style of a fairy tale. Finally, this ending itself is undercut as the narrator points out that if they do live happily ever after, it will be because Jacques, in his fatalism, would be resigned even to Denise's unfaithfulness.

On another occasion as well Diderot introduces the manuscript fiction not in order to create the illusion of authenticity, its traditional use, but in order to destroy it. Jacques is just on the verge of recounting, after much preliminary detail, his *conte d'amour*. He has given so much background material, however, that his throat is sore and he is unable to continue talking. Furthermore, the narrator states, "Il y a ici une lacune vraiment déplorable dans la conversation de Jacques et de son maître" (p. 299). The narrator, "comme un honnête philologue,"[62] does his best to decipher from the manuscript what course events actually took. "Il paraît que Jacques réduit en silence par son mal de gorge suspendit l'histoire de ses amours et que son maître commença l'histoire des siennes. Ce n'est ici qu'une conjecture que je donne pour ce qu'elle vaut" (*Jacques,* p. 299).

The *maître* is an orderly man. "He wants to be able to put his finger on things, to use a language cleaned up of untidy paradoxes, to hear the conclusion of *les amours de Jacques,* for example, and not be bothered by the detours, asides, and maunderings on which his valet seems to thrive."[63] Above all, he is a conventional story teller, quite in contrast to Jacques. The account he gives of his life and love affairs imitates all the conventional, arbitrary, and artificial techniques of the romance. It is full of the tricksters, disguises, rendezvous and coincidences familiar to the readers of romance. In fact these are so familiar to Jacques that not only is he able to predict them before they are told, he also falls asleep as they are being told, much to the annoyance of his maître.[64]

The narrator's opinion of romance is, in this case, close to Diderot's. "Et puis, Lecteur, toujours des contes d'amour; un, deux, trois, quatre contes d'amour que je vous ai faits, trois ou quatre autres contes d'amour qui vous reviennent encore, ce sont beaucoup de contes d'amours. Il est vrai d'un autre côté que puisqu'on écrit pour vous il faut ou se passer de votre applaudissement, ou vous servir à votre goût, et que vous l'avez bien décidé pour les contes d'amour. Toutes vos nouvelles en vers ou en prose sont des contes d'amour; presque tous vos poëmes, élégies, églogues, idylles, chansons, épîtres, comédies, tragédies, opéras, sont des contes d'amours; presque toutes vos peintures et sculptures ne sont que des contes d'amour. Vous êtes aux contes d'amour pour toute nourriture depuis que vous existez, et vous ne vous en lassez point" (p. 238). Diderot attacks in this passage the reader's obsession with the still popular romances and their love adventure, just as in the *maître*'s story he parodies the genre by telling just such a tale at the same time as he undercuts its effect by showing its conventionality and predictability.

Jacques le fataliste is, however, a parody of more than just the romance.[65] Twenty-five years earlier, in *Les Bijoux indiscrets* (1748), Diderot had already made ironic use of such narrative techniques as the manuscript fiction and the claim to historical authenticity. Indeed the "editor" of the *Bijoux* asserted that he was working from a translation, a common convention Diderot did not bother to make fun of again in *Jacques*. Though of both works it could be said that "Diderot intentionally destroys the conventional illusion of reality in fiction,"[66] nevertheless it must be emphasized that in the intervening quarter century Diderot's scope had widened considerably. The objects of his parodistic attacks have grown to include even an author in whose style Diderot had himself written: Richardson.

It might seem unlikely that Diderot, who had praised Richardson so highly and so sincerely in the *Eloge,* and who had imitated him so well in *La Religieuse,* would change his mind about Richardson to the extent that he would be capable of parodying him. And at least one critic has seen in *Jacques* a continued support of Richardson's dramatic techniques.[67] To understand Diderot's relationship to Richardson, however, it is necessary to turn again to the *Eloge*. The importance of this work for *La Religieuse* is obvious, but it is also important for *Jacques*. The way in which Diderot praises Richardson reveals the aesthetic terms in which Diderot thinks of the novel throughout his career. "O Richardson! on prend, malgré qu'on en ait, un rôle dans tes ouvrages, on se mêle à la conversation, on approuve, on blâme, on admire, on s'irrite, on s'indigne. Combien de fois ne me suis-je pas surpris, comme il est arrivé à des enfants qu'on avait menés au spectacle pour la première fois, criant: *Ne le croyez pas, il vous trompe . . . Si vous allez là, vous êtes perdu"* (p. 213).

It should not be overlooked that in this passage Diderot views the successful creation of an illusion as something he, Diderot the reader, should resist. The apparent authenticity suggested by Richardson wins out over the deliberate attempt of the reader to maintain an awareness of the discrepancy between fiction and reality.

Richardson's success in imposing the illusion of reality on even the sceptical reader calls forth Diderot's praise of Richardson's art. It is significant, though, that even in this early and enthusiastic review Diderot returns to the question of the means by which the aesthetic illusion triumphs over the reader's resistance. In one passage of the *Eloge* Diderot imagines himself in an old castle, in which he discovers the letters of Clarissa and Pamela. That is to say, Diderot supposes them to be real for a moment and asks himself, what would the letters be like in that case? "Quel chagrin n'aurais-je pas ressenti, s'il avait eu quelque lacune entre elles!" Then he imagines himself the editor of these letters. "Croit-on que j'eusse souffert qu'une main téméraire (j'ai presque dit sacrilège) en eût supprimé une ligne?" (p. 218).

Even in a work which praises the successful creation of the illusion of reality in fiction, Diderot's concern for preserving aesthetic distance is insistent. In this passage from the *Eloge* Diderot thinks of the very tricks he was later, in *Jacques,* to play with the manuscript fiction. Here he rejects such tricks as bordering on sacrilege. He emphatically rejects anything that would disturb the illusion, but Diderot's mind constantly returns to the fact that it is after all an illusion that he is succumbing to when reading Richardson. The paradoxical position of the *Eloge* is that illusionism is insidious, even dangerous, yet the emotional impact on the reader is so great that he is overwhelmed by the success of the deception. By the time of *Jacques,* however, Diderot's scepticism had evidently increased and the initial enthusiasm for Richardson worn off somewhat.

Jacques le fataliste parodies Richardson's dramatic style by making it transparent. Richardson's stated intent was to make his readers virtuous, but he sought to improve and educate them not by means of direct address, as in a sermon, but by letting the readers draw their own conclusions from the events which are presented without authorial comment. Richardson's novels thus retain the basic purpose of communicating a morally improving body of views and sentiments to the reader, though this is disguised in the form of conversations among the characters. On one level, *Jacques,* like any Richardsonian novel, is a dramatic dialogue between the protagonists, with some interpolated stories, most of which contribute to the themes of the work, particularly the question of fatalism and the love adventures of Jacques. The narrator, however, engages in a second level of conversation with the reader and intrudes with his comments on the dialogue of the characters. His interventions, like those of the fictitious reader, deliberately undermine the illusion of immediacy that the first level seeks to establish. Once the narrator is made present as such an intrusive character in the work, however, the freedom of the reader to come to his own conclusions and draw his own inferences without the guidance of a commentator is revealed to be no more than a fiction. And Diderot's narrator intervenes to break the illusion precisely by calling attention to the importance of his role as narrator. "Vous voyez, Lecteur, que je suis en beau chemin, et qu'il ne tiendrait qu'à moi de vous faire attendre un an, deux ans, trois ans le récit des amours de Jacques [. . . .] Qu'il est facile de faire des contes!" (p. 5). Thus from the very beginning the narrator makes it clear that he is making up a story, that there is nothing authentic about the work, and that it is entirely his own invention. He returns to this point once again with almost the same words. "Vous voyez, Lecteur, combien je suis obligeant; il ne tiendrait qu'à moi [. . .] d'interrompre l'histoire du Capitaine de Jacques et de vous impatienter à mon aise; mais pour cela il faudrait mentir et je n'aime pas le mensonge, à moins qu'il ne soit utile et forcé" (p. 80).

The narrator deliberately intervenes in order to make his

reader impatient and to vex him with delays. In this case he paradoxically combines his interruption with the assertion that he is at the service of the reader and opposes all deception of the reader. Thus the function of this intrusion (to vex the reader) undermines the content of the intrusion (to assure the reader of the narrator's truthfulness and obliging nature): "nous comprenons justement que nous ne sommes pas dans un roman à l'instant précis où l'auteur feint, avec une mauvaise foi claironnante, de nous y transporter."[68]

Diderot in *Jacques le fataliste* makes the implied communication from narrator to reader explicit and develops it into a dialogue. He incorporates the tacitly understood dimension of narrator and reader into the text, makes of them characters, and thus by means of reproducing the actual situation of reader and narrator consistently undermines Richardsonian illusionism.

Jacques, like *Tristram*, parodies art by imitating life.[69] That is, each work makes fun of conventional novelistic presentations of the world by adhering to their conventions of being true to life even more faithfully than was the traditional practice. And it is precisely by means of this greater closeness to life as it is, in all its untidiness and resistance to conventional forms, that these two novelists break the illusion of reality.

Diderot acknowledged his debt to Sterne explicitly in *Jacques*. Particularly at the end Sterne's influence is evident, for the second of the three variant endings is, the narrator assures us, copied from *Tristram Shandy*. The fun Diderot has with Jacques's wound to the knee is similar to that had by Sterne with Trim's wounded knee (VIII, xxii, 573–5). But the similarities extend beyond these details and encompass the themes of the works, particularly the theme of narrative omniscience. The two central narrators of *Jacques* are the narrator and Jacques himself. They attempt to tell the story of Jacques's love adventure, just as Tristram attempted to tell the story of his own life. In both works the narrative goal is continually put off to some later date. Thus near the end of *Jacques* the impatient reader asks, "Et les amours de Jacques?—Jacques a dit cent fois qu'il était écrit là-haut qu'il n'en finirait pas l'histoire, et je vois que

Jacques avait raison" (p. 373). In each work the delays are brought about by the unavoidable subjectivity of the narrator.

In principle any narrator is inhibited in presenting events just as they occurred. He is inhibited first by his own subjectivity, and second by the subjective interests of his audience. Jacques makes this clear at one point in his conversation with his *maître*.

> Le Maître.—[. . .] dis la chose comme elle est.
> Jacques.—Cela n'est pas aisé. N'a-t-on pas son caractère, son intérêt, son goût, ses passions, d'après quoi l'on exagère ou l'on atténue? Dis la chose comme elle est! . . . Cela n'arrive peut-être pas deux fois en un jour dans toute une grande ville. Et celui que vous écoute est-il mieux disposé que celui qui parle? Non. D'où il doit arriver que deux fois à peine en un jour dans toute une grande ville on soit entendu comme on dit.
> Le Maître.—Que diable, Jacques, voilà des maximes à proscrire l'usage de la langue et des oreilles, à ne rien dire, à ne rien écouter et à ne rien croire! Cependant dis comme toi, je t'écouterai comme moi, et je t'en croirai comme je pourrai.
>
> (pp. 70–1)

This passage ridicules the naive assumptions of Richardson (and almost all other authors of the time) on the possibility of reliable, unbiased communication, and makes explicit the skepticism towards narrative objectivity which Sterne had already represented implicitly in the figure of Tristram Shandy.[70]

When Tristram cannot decide which narrative path to follow he turns to the reader with the question, "What would your worships have me do?" (IX, xxiii, 207). At one point in *Jacques* the narrator offers the reader two variants on the course of events and leaves it up to the reader to decide which he prefers to believe. The effect of this demonstrative surrender of the narrator's omniscient position is, of course, to underline the fact of his omniscience: for even when the narrator claims to be ignorant of the true course of events, it is manifestly *his* decision to pretend to this ignorance.

There is, however, one difference between *Tristram* and *Jacques*. In Sterne's novel it is Tristram's hobby-horsical urge to communicate everything he knows and to record everything that passes through his mind that leads to the open-ended character of the work. In *Jacques* the same narrative situation as in *Tristram* is generalized, so that it no longer can be accounted for solely with reference to the oddity of the narrator.[71] Diderot splits up the single narrator of *Tristram* and replaces him with a variety of narrators, including Jacques, the *maître,* the hostess and others in addition to the work's unnamed, first-person narrator. Yet none of them is capable of bringing a story to a convincing conclusion. Their stories seem to lead nowhere as their apparent conclusions are relativized and thrown into a different, ambiguous light by further information. This contributes to what one critic has called "la désintégration systématique du dialogue et du récit."[72] In Diderot, this breakdown is caused not by the ruling passion of an idiosyncratic narrator, but is a condition of all narration.

In *Les Deux Amis de Bourbonne* (1770) Diderot distinguished among three kinds of stories. The first of them is the *conte plaisant,* in which there is no pretense of imitation of nature, no assertion of truth for the events related, no illusionism. The fable would be an example of the *conte plaisant.* The second kind of tale Diderot called the *conte merveilleux,* in which miraculous, supernatural and fantastic events occur. An example of this would be the homeric epic. Diderot's final category is the *conte historique,* or the realistic tale. Here the traditional Aristotelian split between history and fiction is overcome, for the narrator of the *conte historique* is both historian and poet in equal measure.[73] It is the task of this type of narrator to be "en même temps historien et poète, véridique et menteur."[74] The *conteur historique* wants to be believed, to awaken the reader's interests and emotions, but he does so without "éloquence" and without "poésie," for they inspire disbelief. The technique the *conteur historique* uses to win the reader's belief is the careful presentation of detail. The details must be related to the events in the story, and they must be so simple and natural that the reader is forced to accept them as real. In words that echo the *Eloge de Richardson,* Diderot says, "vous serez forcé de vous dire en vous même: Ma foi, cela est vrai; on n'invente pas ces choses-là" (Ibid.). These details make the story believable because they do not contribute to a portrait of ideal beauty, as in the works of contemporary historical narrators; on the contrary, they reveal the little flaws and defects of character to be found in everyday life.

It is evidently with these considerations in mind that Diderot returned to *La Religieuse* in 1780. At this time Diderot combined the manuscript of 1760, which contained only the *mémoire* of Suzanne, with Grimm's account of the work's genesis in the *Correspondance littéraire* of 1770, and published both together in installments of the *Correspondance littéraire* between 1780–82. Grimm's text, which has come to be known as the *Préface annexe*, also underwent revision by Diderot, who considerably shortened Grimm's account, reducing the 189 lines of the original to just 79.[75] When talking of the conspirators engaged in deceiving the Marquis, Diderot substituted "Mr. Diderot," "Mr. D. . .," "l'auteur des mémoires," and sometimes "je" where Grimm had written "nous" (Ibid., p. 16). For example, "nous autres enfants de Bélial" of Grimm's version becomes "cet enfant de Bélial," that is, Diderot himself. It must be remembered that all these revisions take place silently, as it were, with no indication that Grimm had not written every word of this version of the *Préface annexe*. Yet there are unmistakably two voices speaking in the *Préface annexe*. Grimm asserted of *La Religieuse,* for example, "que ce roman n'a jamais existé que par lambeaux et en est resté là," but this is followed by the remark, "Et j'ajouterai, moi qui connais un peu M. Diderot, que ce roman, il l'a achevé" (p. 17). This second narrative voice, one that corrects the first narrator, is that of Diderot, as Herbert Dieckmann was the first to establish.[76] Among the other changes, Diderot incorporated a letter from Grimm's text into the text of the novel. Grimm had termed the whole affair a "plaisanterie," a word Diderot dropped in favor of "mystification." Diderot even revised some of Croismare's authentic letters to Suzanne.

The most significant change, however, is Diderot's addition, at the end of the *Préface annexe,* of the "Question aux gens de lettres," in which Diderot describes the many morning hours he spent composing some moving, pathetic letters, "bien romanesque." He then went on to spend many an hour editing the letters, eliminating everything exaggerated in them, aiming instead for extreme simplicity and "la dernière vraisemblance." The first set of letters, he says, is beautiful, the second is true. The first wins our admiration, the second creates the illusion of reality. The question to the men of letters is: which set of letters is the better? This question is not answered in the text. The reader is left to read *La Religieuse* and decide for himself. But the context in which the question is asked suggests the answer Diderot would have given, or rather, the differing answers he would have given at different stages in his development. In 1760 Diderot would have found the beautiful and moving memoir of Suzanne more effective, though he was aware of certain improbabilities in her account. In 1760 Diderot was willing to let a somewhat unlikely accumulation of "romanesque" misfortunes befall Suzanne in a short period in order to arouse the reader's sympathy.

Twenty years later, however, Diderot evidently changed his views. The earlier primacy of the pathetic, dramatic and the "romanesque" was parodied in *Jacques,* which in turn gave way, in the revised version of *La Religieuse,* to the primacy of the illusion of reality, and to a return to the historical techniques, this time applied with more subtlety than ever before. The relationship between the text of *La Religieuse* and the *Préface annexe* is apparently one of fiction and historical report. And indeed, this is precisely the relationship between the 1760 version of *La Religieuse* and Grimm's account. But under Diderot's hands both texts were rewritten in 1780–82 so that the *Préface annexe,* though it retains the appearance of a historical report, becomes itself part of the fiction. Herbert Dieckmann points out that "The *Préface Annexe* can no longer be considered as a document which gives the biographical and historical background of *La Religieuse,* the 'true story' behind the 'fiction' of the novel [. . .] The *Préface Annexe* is part of the novel, it is as much invention and fable as the novel itself. Diderot subjected it to the same 'literary' revision to which he subjected *La Religieuse* and the more he revised it in style and content, the more he transformed it into a work of art" (Ibid., p. 31).

Diderot had implied as much in his "Question aux gens de lettres." There he posed the question as to the superiority of one method over the other without coming to any explicit decision, but he left no doubt that *both* sets of letters were composed by him, were something he had created. The "Question" made it clear that though one set of letters gives the greater *illusion* of reality, it is no less a fiction than the one that is "bien romanesque." Georges May has written that the *Préface annexe* "ne doit plus être tenu, comme on l'avait cru, pour un exposé historique et documentaire destiné avant tout à restituer les événements du passé dans leur authenticité scrupuleuse. Seule la trame est historique; les nombreuses broderies superposées ultérieurement représentent, elles, la part de la poésie, du romanesque, de l'imaginaire. Le texte définitif qui en resulte est donc fait d'une combinaison de réalité et de fiction analogue à celle qu'on retrouve dans le roman même auquel il doit être annexé" ("Introduction de Préface," p. 8). In other words, the *Préface annexe* is, like *La Religieuse* itself, based on historical events and documents. Each work attempts to create the illusion of reality that is essential for an effective work of art. The original version of *La Religieuse* attempted to do so by Richardsonian, dramatic means. The *Préface annexe* does so by a return to historical techniques.[77]

The *Préface annexe* destroys the illusion of *La Religieuse,* but in so doing it maintains its own validity and authenticity on a separate level. The historical pose itself is not undercut or made fun of, as it was in *Jacques*. Instead, the old conventions of authenticity are given new life in that the pose is no longer just that: a pose, to be taken up or dropped as it suits the narrator. It is based rather on actual documents, details provided by the historical events themselves and invested with new believability by the narrator who incorporates them into his text. Just as Diderot had proposed in the analysis of the *conte historique*, the narrator is successful in creating the illusion of reality when he writes neither pure fiction nor pure history, but a work made up of equal parts of both.

The problem with the parody of conventional forms, both in *Tristram* and *Jacques le fataliste,* is that, to be sure, the parody exaggerated existing conventions to show up their insufficiency, but in declaring the bankruptcy of the old forms the parodistic imitation itself was incapable of putting forward any alternative way of telling a story from beginning to end. Faced with this dilemma, Diderot's response was to work in actual historical detail in order to make the reader say to himself: this is so convincing it cannot be fiction. Diderot's revision of *La Religieuse* anticipates Hippel's return to historical authenticity, this time with a new emphasis on private history, which convinces not because it is common knowledge or verifiable, but because of its use of details taken from real life, details that retain their air of historical contingency and locate these works somewhere between history and the novel.

NOTES

[1] Pierre Daniel Huet, *Traité de l'Origine des Romans,* Sammlung Metzler, 54 (1670; rpt. Stuttgart: Metzler, 1966), pp. 4–5.

[2] Quoted by Wolfgang G. Deppe, *History versus Romance,* Neue Beiträge zur englischen Philologie, VI (Münster: Aschendorff, 1965), p. 43.

[3] *Freymütige Lustige und Ernsthaffte jedoch Vernunfft- und Gesetz-mäßige Gedancken Oder Monats-Gespräche* [. . .] Januar 1688, p. 42 ff, quoted in *Theorie und Technik des Romans im 17. und 18. Jahrhundert,* ed. Dieter Kimpel, (Tübingen: Niemeyer, 1970), I, 44.

[4] *An Essay upon Study,* (1730), pp. 250–51, quoted in Ioan Williams, *Novel and Romance 1700–1800.* (New York: Barnes & Noble, 1970), p. 6.

[5] *Oeuvres complètes,* ed. Assezat et Tourneux, (Paris: Garnier, 1875–77), V, 212–13.

[6] See Klaus Heitmann, "Das Verhältnis von Dichtung und Geschichtsschreibung in älterer Theorie," *Archiv für Kulturgeschichte,* 52 (1970), 244–79.

[7] *Einleitung in die schönen Wissenschaften,* trans. and with supplements by Karl Wilhelm Ramler, 4th ed., (Leipzig: Weidmann, 1774), IV, 264 ("Von der historischen Erzählung").

[8] "Author's Preface," p. 188, (in same edition as *Jonathan Wild,* see following note).

[9] *Jonathan Wild,* Everyman's Library ed., (London: Dent; New York: Dutton, 1932), III, vi, 101. The definitive Wesleyan edition volumes containing these two works have not yet been published. The *Journal* was written in 1754, *Jonathan Wild* in 1743. See also Michael Hays, "Dramatic Literature as History: Some Suggestions about Theory and

Method," *Literature and History:* ed. Harry R. Garvin, *Bucknell Review* 23, Nr. 2 (1977).

[10] Kant, *Menschenkunde oder philosophische Anthropologie,* ed. Fr. Ch. Starke (Leipzig: Expedition des europäischen Aufsehers, 1831; rpt. Hildesheim: Olms, 1976), pp. 30–31.

[11] *The Secret History of Queen Zarah,* quoted in *English Theories of the Novel,* (Tübingen: Niemeyer, 1970), II, 7.

[12] See Philip Stewart, *Imitation and Illusion in the French Memoir-Novel, 1700–1750,* (New Haven and London: Yale University Press, 1969).

[13] See Georges May, *Le Dilemme du roman au XVIIIe siècle* (New Haven and Paris: Yale Univ. Press, 1963); and Vivienne Mylne, *The Eighteenth-Century French Novel* (Cambridge: Cambridge Univ. Press, 1981).

[14] May, *Le Dilemme du roman,* p. 157. May notes that the proscription of novels by the government in 1738 forced novels for a time to be published abroad or to disguise themselves as history.

[15] Williams, p. 56.

[16] Quoted in Ernst Weber, *Die poetologische Selbstreflexion im deutschen Roman des 18ten. Jahrhunderts, Studien zur Poetik und Geschichte der Literatur,* 34 (Stuttgart: Kohlhammer, 1974), 51.

[17] Lieselotte E. Kurth, "Historiographie und historischer Roman: Kritik und Theorie im 18. Jahrhundert," *Modern Language Notes,* 79 (1964), 347.

[18] Ibid., pp. 348–49. The review, by Thomas Abbt, first appeared in *Briefe, die neueste Litteratur betreffend* 12 (1761), 255–84.

[19] Gabriel Seigneux de Corrivon, "Lettre à Mme D** sur les romans," *Bibliothèque francoise, ou Histoire Littéraire de la France* (Amsterdam: Jean Frederic Bernard), 12 (1728), art. 3, p. 47, quoted in Stewart, p. 29.

[20] *Beyträge Zur Critischen Historie Der Deutschen Sprache, Poesie und Beredsamkeit* [. . .] Sechstes Stück, (Leipzig, 1733), p. 274 (review of Ziegler's *Asiatische Banise*), quoted in *Romantheorie,* ed. Eberhard Lämmert et al., (Cologne: Kiepenheuer & Witsch, 1971), p. 71; hereafter cited as Lämmert.

[21] *Versuch einer Critischen Dichtkunst* [. . .] Teil 2, I. Abschnitt, V. Hauptstück: Von milesischen Fabeln, Ritterbüchern und Romanen, (Leipzig, 1751), p. 528, quoted in Lämmert, p. 95.

[22] *Critische Betrachtungen über die Poetischen Gemählde Der Dichter* [. . .] 19. Abschnitt. Von den Characteren in dem prosaischen Gedichte von der Syrischen Aramina, (Zürich, Leipzig, 1741), p. 549, quoted in Lämmert, p. 77.

[23] *Critische Dichtkunst,* (Zürich: Orell, 1740; rpt. Stuttgart: Metzler, 1966), I, 33.

[24] Kurth, "Historiographie und historischer Roman," pp. 340–1.

[25] *Briefe, die neueste Litteratur betreffend,* III (1759), 52nd letter (Stuttgart: Reclam, 1972), p. 177.

[26] *Menschenkunde,* p. 31.

[27] *Frankfurter Gelehrte Anzeigen 1772,* selected and ed. Hans-Dietrich Dahnke, Peter Müller (Leipzig: Reclam, 1971), p. 57.

[28] I am indebted to Jeffrey Smitten for bringing this passage to my attention. See his unpublished paper "Time and Discourse in Gibbon's *History.*"

[29] Here I am following Smitten's presentation.

[30] Schiller, *Sämtliche Werke* (Munich: Hanser, 1968), IV, 703.

³¹ "The Fictions of Factual Representation," in *The Literature of Fact*, ed. Angus Fletcher (New York: Columbia Univ. Press, 1976), pp. 23-24.

³² "Einige Gedanken und Regeln von den deutschen Romanen," *Critische Versuch ausgefertiget durch Einige Mitglieder der Deutschen Gesellschaft in Greifswald*, II (1744), quoted in Kimpel, *Theorie und Technik des Romans*, p. 75.

³³ Anthony Earl of Shaftesbury, *Characteristics of Men, Manners, Opinions, Times*, 3rd ed. (London, 1723), III, 260,—note.

³⁴ Samuel Richardson, *The History of Clarissa Harlowe*, (New York, 1902; rpt. New York: AMS Press, 1970), I, xli-xlii.

³⁵ *Der Zeitvertreiber, eine moralische Wochenschrift*, 41 (Leipzig, 1745), 328, quoted in Lämmert, pp. 84-5.

³⁶ *Der Gesellige, eine moralische Wochenschrift*, V, No. 220, (Halle, 1750) p. 115, quoted in Lämmert, p. 87.

³⁷ "Beurtheilung des Romainenlesens," Ibid., p. 351, quoted in Wilhelm Voßkamp, *Romantheorie in Deutschland von Martin Opitz bis Friedrich von Blanckenburg*, (Stuttgart: Metzler, 1973), p. 191.

³⁸ This was made clear by Johann Carl Dähnert's review of *Amusemens d'un Prisonnier*: "Es ist kein Einwurf wider diese Bücher, daß es nicht immer wirkliche Geschichte sind, die sie vortragen. In den mehresten liegen wahre Geschichte zum Grunde, und wo eine Romane nicht Hexen- und Gespenstermährchen enthält, so wird es nicht schwer seyn, an allen Orten Urbilder zu finden, davon sie als Abrisse gelten können," *Critische Nachrichten durch Johann Carl Dähnert*, II, No. 11, (Greifswald, 1751), p. 82, quoted in Lämmert, p. 90.

³⁹ *Abhandlung von dem guten Geschmack in Briefen* (1751), quoted in Kimpel, *Theorie und Technik*, I, 83.

⁴⁰ *Elements of Criticism* (London: Millar; Edinburgh: Kincaid & Bell, 1762), III, 220.

⁴¹ *Geschichte des Agathon*, (Frankfurt and Leipzig, 1776; rpt. Berlin: Akademie Verlag, 1961), p. 1.

⁴² Wieland, *Romane*, ed. Friedrich Beissner (Munich: Winkler, 1964), p. 28.

⁴³ Quoted in Kurth, "Historiographie und historischer Roman," p. 357.

⁴⁴ See Howard Anderson, "Answers to the Author of *Clarissa*: Theme and Narrative Technique in *Tom Jones* and *Tristram Shandy*," *Philological Quarterly* 51 (1972), 859-73.

⁴⁵ *Tom Jones, the History of a Foundling*, ed. M. C. Battestin, F. Bowers (Middletown, CT: Wesleyan Univ. Press, 1975), II, i. 76.

⁴⁶ "Fielding spielt mit der Fiktion des Historikers, weil er sie als Beweismittel im Grunde nicht braucht," Dietrich Rolle, *Fielding und Sterne*, (Münster: Aschendorff, 1963), pp. 84-5.

⁴⁷ As Ian Watt says, the narrator's prose "immediately informs us that exploratory operations have long since been accomplished, that we are to be spared that labour, and presented instead with a sifted and clarified report of the finding." *The Rise of the Novel*, (Berkeley and Los Angeles: Univ. of California Press, 1957), p. 30. For the view that Fielding's narrator is not omniscient, see Leo Braudy, *Narrative Form in History and Fiction* (Princeton: Princeton Univ. Press, 1970), pp. 144-80.

⁴⁸ Tristram himself refers to his narrative as "a work of this dramatic cast," IV, x, 281.

⁴⁹ *Time and the Novel*, (New York: Humanities Press, 1972), p. 182.

⁵⁰ Henry Fluchère calls Tristram "the director of the show, for whom every character, however episodic, and every detail of his behaviour, however trifling, and every twist of

circumstance is important," *Laurence Sterne: From Tristram to Yorick,* trans. and abr. Barbara Bray, (London: Oxford University Press, 1965), p. 338.

⁵¹ As Wayne Booth puts it, "in a sense *Tristram Shandy* is an elaborate evasion of the promise given in the title." "The Self-Conscious Narrator in Comic Fiction before *Tristram Shandy,*" *PMLA,* LXVII (1952), 169.

⁵² See Deppe, *History versus Romance,* p. 71.

⁵³ "He never doubts his own ability to tell his story" and is "never overwhelmed by his problems". Booth, "The Self-Conscious Narrator," p. 177.

⁵⁴ *Theorie der Prosa,* ed. and trans. Gisela Drohla, (Frankfurt a. M. Fischer, 1966), pp. 131–62.

⁵⁵ OED quotes just this passage from *Tristram* in its definition of "whiffling": "moving lightly as if driven by gusts of wind."

⁵⁶ B. H. Lehman, "Of Time, Personality, and the Author. A Study of *Tristram Shandy:* Comedy," *Essays on the Eighteenth Century Novel,* ed. Robert Donald Spector. (Bloomington: Indiana Univ. Press, 1965), p. 179.

⁵⁷ Narrative omniscience should be on Mendilow's list of conventions flouted by Sterne when he writes, "Sterne was very deeply interested in the problems these conventions raise, namely the relationship between reality and fictional illusion. Above all, he wished to arouse his readers to the realization that these are conventions, that they should not be taken for reality [. . .]" Mendilow is referring to conventions of plot, chronology and causality in his *Time and the Novel* (p. 166). Likewise John Traugott's assertion that "To say that Sterne was self-conscious is, I think, to say little. What he really seems to have wanted is self-consciousness from the reader," applies not just to Tristram's use of rhetoric. See Traugott's *Tristram Shandy's World,* (Berkeley and Los Angeles: University of California Press, 1954), p. 109.

⁵⁸ *Oeuvres complètes,* V, 212–13.

⁵⁹ *Diderot et* La Religieuse, (New Haven: Yale University Press; Paris: Presse universitaire de France, 1954), pp. 206–7, 217.

⁶⁰ *Jaques [sic] le fataliste et son maître,* Edition critique, (Paris and Geneva: Libraire Droz, 1976), p. 18.

⁶¹ Mylne, *Eighteenth-Century French Novel,* p. 215.

⁶² Robert Mauzi, "La Parodie romanesque dans *Jacques le Fataliste,*" *Diderot Studies* VI (1964), 93.

⁶³ Stephen Werner, "Diderot's Great Scroll: Narrative Art in *Jacques le Fataliste,*" *Studies on Voltaire and the Eighteenth Century* 128 (1975), 28.

⁶⁴ See Rainer Warning, *"Jacques le fataliste,"* Der Französische Roman, ed. Klaus Heitman, (Düsseldorf: Bagel, 1975), I, 201–33.

⁶⁵ "Diderots Beitrag zum Roman der Aufklärung ist Aufklärung des Lesers über den Umgang mit Fiktionen." (Ibid., p. 216).

⁶⁶ Irwin L. Greenberg, "Narrative Technique and Literary Intent in Diderot's *Les Bijoux indiscrets* and *Jacques le fataliste,*" *Studies on Voltaire* 79 (1971), 97.

⁶⁷ Mauzi, "La Parodie romanesque," p. 127 ff.

⁶⁸ Mauzi, "La Parodie romanesque," pp. 99–100.

⁶⁹ Neither Rainer Warning's *Tristram Shandy und Jacques le Fataliste,* Theorie und Geschichte der Literatur und der schönen Künste, 4 (Munich: Fink, 1965), nor Alice Fredman, *Diderot and Sterne,* (New York, Columbia University Press, 1955), compare the narrative techniques of the two authors in any detail.

⁷⁰ "Diderot agreed with Sterne that the order of reality could only be described

subjectively, and that the validity of the description depended on an acknowledgement of its subjective nature," Ernest Simon, "Fatalism, the Hobby-Horse and the Esthetics of the Novel," *Diderot Studies* XVI (1973), 271.

[71] This difference in structure has been most recently pointed out by Milan Kundera in his introduction to his own play, *Jacques and his Master*, trans. Michael Henry Hein (New York: Harper + Row, 1985).

[72] Mauzi, "Parodie romanesque," p. 118.

[73] Marlou Switten, "*L'histoire* and *la poesie* in Diderot's writing on the novel," *Romanic Review*, 47 (1956), 250–69.

[74] Diderot, *Oeuvres*, V, 277.

[75] *La Religieuse*, "Introduction de Préface de *La Religieuse*," text Herbert Dieckmann, notes Georges May, (Paris: Hermann, 1975), p. 16, n. 5.

[76] "The Préface Annexe of *La Religieuse*," *Diderot Studies* II (1952), 17.

[77] René Godenne has pointed out that even the hoax played on Croismare has a literary tradition behind it. See "Les Nouvellistes des Années 1680–1750 et *La Religieuse*," *Diderot Studies* XVI (1973), 55–68. This, too, underscores the fictional aspects of the *Préface annexe*.

3

Sterne and Hippel: The Relationship Reconsidered

Some of the traditional interpretations of the relationship between Sterne and Hippel have a point when they criticize Hippel's *Laune*. Contemporary critics complained that Hippel failed to be amusing because his allusions were too far-fetched, and therefore unclear—and these critics found the same error in *Tristram Shandy*. Modern critics are more convincing in their argument that Hippel tried for the same effects, but was never as successful as Sterne.[1] It has become typical, however, to explain the stylistic shortcomings and overextended *Laune* of Hippel by referring to his extreme subjectivity. His primary concern, so the argument goes, was to use the novel as a vehicle for presenting his *Ich*. Since the *Ich* is the only real character, all the other characters are but mouthpieces, or puppets, of the author. The *Ich* is furthermore the only constitutive principle, and, since Hippel held a chaotic worldview, the work is necessarily formless. Its chaos reflects Hippel's chaotic subjectivity. This criticism was first made by Hippel's contemporaries, who accused the author of too little concern for his audience, and it survives in the arguments of those critics who accuse Hippel of too much subjectivity. Hippel's contemporaries attributed his faults to Sterne's baneful influence, whereas latter-day critics argue that Hippel, like so many German authors in the eighteenth century, misunderstood Sterne.

And some support for such criticisms is to be found in the *Lebensläufe*. It is only with some effort that the hero's life does get told, for Hippel, like Sterne, seemed less interested in his semiautobiographical story than in the long digressions and asides. Rather than tell his course of life Alexander prefers to record the morbid observations of the *Sterbegraf*, "ein besonderer Mann. Seine Hauptbeschäftigung war, Leute sterben zu sehen" (II, 429). Or Alexander quotes from Kant's lecture notes—which later was to lead to suspicions that Kant was the author of the *Lebensläufe*. Or Alexander notes down a comic *Leichenabdankung*, a "schmackhafter Vergleich" of man's life with a meal (II, 441–55). Such picturesque asides tend to support, on the surface at least, the contention that Hippel was imitating the Sternean, digressive, *launige*, style.

When viewed as an imitation of *Tristram Shandy*, it is clear that Hippel's novel falls short of its model. Perhaps every novel in Sterne's manner is condemned to be the work of an epigone. *Tristram Shandy* had already stretched the conventions of the novel to the limit. Sterne was so inventive with his technique of dislocating both the reader and traditional narrative structures that he left little room for any novelists after him to play with these conventions in an original fashion. The inferiority of Hippel's *Lebensläufe* is grounded, however, not solely in the inimitability of Sterne's novel. There are also historical reasons. The differences between Sterne's novels and those of Hippel reflect the different stages of development of English and German literature in the eighteenth century. When *Tristram Shandy* began to appear, English literature was already a literature of international importance. Its influence was particularly strong in Germany, which in the 1750s was just beginning to create a national literature. As Herder wrote in 1796, "Wir wachten auf, da es allenthalben Mittag war und bei einigen Nationen sich gar schon die Sonne neigte. Kurz, *wir kamen zu spät. Und weil wir so spät kamen, ahmten wir nach* [. . . .]"[2] Michelsen develops this point when he writes that the difference between Sterne's urbanity and wit and the crudeness and clumsiness of his followers, translators and imitators in Germany is the difference between high society and provincialism.[3] Michelsen is right: Sterne's inimitability, Hippel's historical disadvantage, perhaps a lack of talent on Hippel's part, all these reasons help to explain the difference in quality between the two authors' novels. But the most important (and obvious) reason has never been properly evaluated: Hippel's aims were, despite certain similarities, essentially different from Sterne's.

Tristram Shandy is of course a comic novel, but it is also a first-person novel, and it is this aspect of Sterne's work that can be seen as the more important for Hippel.[4] *Tristram Shandy*, as Michelsen says (p. 14), had shown how a novel could consist of nothing but digressions. As Tristram himself writes, "Digressions, incontestably, are the sunshine;—they are the life, the soul of reading!—take them out of this book, for instance,—you might as well take the book along with them [. . .]" (I, xxii, 73). Hippel can be considered the first German author who did not simply imitate this trait of Sterne's but regarded it as a challenge. Tristram is an example of an omniscient narrator carried to an extreme: he knows everything about his topic, and has made it his task to tell everything. (Henri Fluchère speaks of Tristram's "determination not to let the smallest particle of reality escape.")[5] He playfully creates a narrator who is led so far afield by his own curiosity and claim to omniscience in matters relating to his life that he can never get around to describing that life. This quite deliberate failure of Tristram's narrative is Sterne's indictment of traditional narrative conventions.

Sterne calls the pose of the omniscient narrator into question, he carries it to its logical conclusion, but in leading it *ad absurdum* he puts forward no other narrative pose. The fiction underlying the first person novel is that the narrator himself is the author of the novel. Until *Tristram Shandy* the omniscience of this narrator-author was an often—if for the most part tacitly—accepted pre-condition of the first person novel.[6] Sterne made this assumption explicit and in so doing made it problematic. Hippel's novel can be understood as an attempt to deal with this problem, to make the world tellable again after Sterne had shown that omniscience must impede the telling of a story. Hippel's solution is to develop the position of the narrator further.

The immediate context for Hippel's views on narration is to be found in contemporary German discussions of the novel. These discussions followed the trend of critical thought current in France and to some extent England. In all three countries there took place in the course of the century a shift in emphasis away from novelistic factuality, *Wahrhaftigkeit*, the *vrai*, towards plausibility, *Wahrscheinlichkeit, vraisemblance*. The shift, however, was not a simple substitution of fiction for truth. In the first place the old concept of factuality had little to do with truth. The claim of the novelist that his story had actually taken place was no more than a convention allowing the author to tell the most improbable and fantastic events. In the second place the principle of probability was not understood as being radically different from that of factuality. Rather, probability meant being true to life as life was seen by the typical reader. The events in a *wahrhaftige Geschichte* were improbable but were claimed by the author to be true. The events in a *wahrscheinliche Geschichte*, if they were not in fact true, could be true, and were plausible. The common element of the two terms is that they measure themselves against the reality they claim to imitate. The *wahrhaftige Geschichte* claims for itself a historical truth, the *wahrscheinliche* a poetic truth. The difference is one of degree.

It is nonetheless a critical one in terms of effect upon the audience. Throughout the century one moral justification of the novel remained constant: it improved the reader by presenting moral truths more persuasively than did philosophical or historical works. What changed in the course of the century was the evaluation of the means available to the novelist in pursuing this end. Gradually it was accepted that the more probable a work of fiction was, the more believable, and the more believable, the greater the effect on the reader.

In 1774 two theoretical works appeared that attempted to establish some rules according to which the illusion of reality could best be achieved in the novel: Blanckenburg's *Versuch über den Roman* and Engel's *Über Handlung, Gespräch und Erzählung*. For Blanckenburg, believability is more important in a novel than historical accuracy. One way of making the novel believable is to choose middle characters as protagonists, ones with flaws and shortcomings that make them less than perfect heroes, but who are thereby closer to the average reader. Moreover, these middle characters should be described not in a quasi-historical record of their heroic deeds, but rather their inner, private character should be presented. Readers would have to see "das ganze *innere* Seyn der handelnden Personen, mit all' den sie in Bewegung setzenden *Ursachen* in dem Werk des *Dichters*" according to Blanckenburg, "wenn der Dichter sich nicht in dem bloßen Erzähler verwandeln soll."[7]

This does not, however, lead to an obsession with the inner state of being of the hero. Blanckenburg is careful to assert that there be no direct presentation of the hero's inner condition, and that this be presented indirectly, as it is reflected in the protagonist's environment. For Blanckenburg's protagonists are above all "handelnde Personen," and are by no means introspective. To increase the immediacy of the protagonist's actions, the author should present them dramatically. Blanckenburg prefers seeing an event unfold before the reader's eyes to having it merely told him. He writes, "Der Eindruck ist sehr verschieden, den es macht, wenn wir eine Wirkung vor unsern Augen erfolgen sehen, oder wenn wir sie erzählt hören. Und diesen flachen, kahlen Eindruck, der die bloße *Erzählung* der Begebenheit macht, und der unser Leidenschaften gar nicht erregt, kann nun der Romanendichter vermeiden, wenn er diese Erzählung in Handlung zu verwandeln weis" (p. 494).

But Blanckenburg is too aware of the difference between drama and novel to assert that the novel can take over a technique of the stage without making any adjustments. "Das Schauspiel kann uns, nach der Natur seiner Gattung, nichts, als schon *fertige* und *gebildete* Charaktere zeigen," he asserts (p. 390). The novel, on the other hand, shows how a character comes into being, not how it reveals itself in connection with a single event or occurrence, as in the drama. "Hierinn liegt auch der eigentliche Unterschied zwischen Drama und Roman" (Ibid.).

Thus *Handlung* in Blanckenburg's usage takes on the meaning of *Hervorbringen*. *Handlung* is for Blanckenburg the development of a character in which the development is shown from within. It is the "abwechselnder Zustand innerer Gemüthsfassung, innerliche Bewegung" (p. 56). In *Agathon*, for example, Wieland's narrator, rather than telling the reader that Agathon has fallen in love with Danae (that would be *Erzählung*), instead lets the reader see this love developing. This sense of *Handlung* is particularly appropriate to the novel, which, in contrast to the drama, has broad resources of time and space with which to work, thus making development possible. But Blanckenburg, without making an explicit distinction, also uses *Handlung* to mean the vivid presentation of events, such that the reader is under the illusion that they are occurring before his very eyes. "Freylich werden wir die Sache immer nicht so lebhaft vor uns sehen können, als im Drama, aber um so mehr der Romanendichter *Raum* und *Zeit* in seinem Werke hat, um so ehe wird er uns, an statt von seinen Personen zu erzählen, daß sie lieben oder hassen, *Handlungen* der Liebe und des Hasses zeigen;—und um so mehr wird er dann auch unsere Theilnehmung erregen" (p. 498). In this passage *Handlung* is closer in meaning to "a dramatic presentation of events" than to "development of character from within."

Blanckenburg does want to make the novel more dramatic, and he encourages novelists to compete with the dramatic poets (p. 99). But Blanckenburg seems reluctant to assert that novels should become dramatic through and through and consist only of dialogue. Instead, he is content to allow a mixture of forms. "Man hat es versucht, indem man die Personen selbst schreiben läßt, den Roman so dramatisch zu machen, als möglich [. . . .] Der Wahn wenigstens, daß man die verschiedenen Gattungen nicht mit einander vermischen müsse, und der wohl mit der Lehre, von den drey berühmten Einheiten einerley Urheber hat, sollte den Dichter nicht davon abhalten" (p. 515). Blanckenburg's usage of *Handlung* is ambiguous. Where he uses it in its novelistic sense, he prepares the way for the *Entwicklungsroman*. Where he uses the term in its dramatic sense, he continues the traditional usage that Hippel was to develop.

Blanckenburg also calls for limiting the role of the author-narrator. Paraphrasing Lessing's *Emilia Galotti* (I, iv), Blanckenburg asserts, "Das größte Lob, das er [der Dichter] erhalten kann, ist,—daß wir ihn über seinem Werke vergessen haben."[8] And somewhat later he adds, "Der Dichter selbst gehört gar nicht mit ins Ganze seines Werks; er wäre was außerordentliches, das gleichsam in den Gang desselben hineingriffe. Der Künstler, der all' Augenblicke über seiner Uhr stellen muß, hat wahrlich keine gute Uhr gemacht" (pp. 339–40). Only under certain conditions may the narrator appear in the work. The Sternean narrator may do so, but his remarks must be explanatory in nature and not be commonplace. "Außer dem Reiz, den die launichte Erzählung gewährt, hat der Schriftsteller dieser Art vielleicht vorzüglich das Recht, vor seinen Personen hervorzutreten, und uns mit Bemerkungen und Aufklärungen über die Reihe der Begebenheiten zu unterhalten. Alltägliche Dinge aber werden wir freylich auch von ihm nicht hören wollen" (pp. 526–7).

The narrator may also make moral observations on his characters, but these must be necessary to a correct understanding of the characters and not be extraneous. "Auf diese Art nun kann der Dichter in eigner Person moralisieren. Nicht alltägliche Bemerkungen, die jeder selbst machen kann, wenn er es verdient, daß der Dichter als Leser an ihn denkt,—nicht entbehrliche Zusätze und Digressionen, die man wegschneiden kann, ohne die mindeste Lücke im Werk und in unsern Vorstellungen gewahr zu werden, soll der Dichter einflicken" (p. 406).

Engel, like Blanckenburg, favors the dramatic over the narrative presentation of events. But Engel goes further than Blanckenburg in recommending that *Handlung* in the novel be presented entirely in dialogue. He proposes that "die Erzehlung von dem jedesmaligen Zustande einer handelnden Seele, und von dem ganzen Zusammenhange aller in ihr vorgehender Veränderungen, keine so specielle und vollständige Idee geben kann, als das Gespräch"[9] and, "daß die dialogische Form zur Schilderung von Charakteren unendlich fähiger, als die erzehlende sey" (p. 246). Engel distinguishes his dramatic dialogue from the philosophical dialogue on the one hand and, on the other hand, from one which contains "bloß Discurs, bloß Charaktergemälde ohne eigentliche Handlung, wirkliche Erzehlung unter der Form des Gesprächs." He recommends Socrates as a model, whose dialogues are "voll wahrer, jetziger Handlung; die Hauptperson docirt nicht." He further proposes that the author present "Entwicklung auf der Stelle, die so sehr in den Dialogen der meisten Neuern fehlt, weil die Herren fast immer Dogmatiker sind, die ihr festgesetztes System haben" (p. 213).

The inner life of the character, as in Blanckenburg, is to be developed through *Handlung*, and this implies the withdrawal of the narrator, who is as little able to comment on the events and characters as is the dramatic poet when his characters are on stage.

Though Hippel, who by the way never mentions Blanckenburg or Engel, shows little interest in setting up a chain of *Ursachen* to explain the character of his protagonist as recommended by Blanckenburg, it could be said that Hippel in effect substitutes the *Ich* for Blanckenburg's *Inneres*. But in keeping with Blanckenburg's emphasis on the activity of the characters, Hippel rarely relates what Alexander is thinking and feeling; rather, Alexander is confronted with a series of variations on his own experience of the death of the beloved. The formative effect such confrontation must have on his character is sometimes given expression in his own words, but often it is left up to the reader to draw his own conclusions. The *Ich* is important not in its own right, but in its relationship to the world.

Hippel's definition of *Handlung* is, however, not ambiguous, as is Blanckenburg's. Hippel continues to use the word as it had been used in Henry Home's *Elements of Criticism*. Though Home does not use the word *Handlung* in the passages from his work quoted by Blanckenburg, it is clearly Home's implicit definition, and not Blanckenburg's ambiguous definition, to which Hippel returns. Home writes, "No person of reflection but must be sensible, that an incident makes a stronger impression on an eyewitness, than when heard at second hand. Writers of genius, sensible that the eye is the best avenue to the heart, represent everything as passing in our sight; and from readers or hearers, transform us, as it were, into spectators. A skilful writer conceals himself, and presents his personages. In a word, everything becomes dramatic as much as possible" (*Elements of Criticism*, III, 197).[10]

Hippel's *Handlung* combines dramatic techniques with historical ones. Much of the novel is presented in dialogue, and thus has dramatic immediacy, but the conversations are also authentic, for the narrator asserts with more truth than was usually the case that they actually have taken place. Hippel thus hopes to write a work that is both plausible and real, both *vraisemblable* and *vrai*, *wahrscheinlich* and *wahr*. In combining these two methods Hippel seeks to heighten the poetic truth of a work by making it *in fact* an imitation of reality. For Hippel, *Wahrhaftigkeit* is no longer just a convention. It is a principle of composition that he takes literally. Thus at the beginning of the second volume of the *Lebensläufe* Alexander announces his intention not to pretend to an omniscience he cannot have.

> Auch selbst, wenn ich im gemeinen Leben erzählen höre, seh' ich—ich sehe den Erzähler steif an, recht, als schien ich es zu bedauern, daß ich diese Geschichte nicht im Original gesehen; ich verlange, der Erzähler soll sie nachhandeln; soll, was und wie es geschehen, leibhaftig zeigen. Je mehr ein Erzähler zu sehen ist, je mehr freu' ich mich, je mehr find' ich die Kopie getroffen. Oft hab' ich gedacht, daß es eine Geschichte geben könne (ob einen Roman, weiß ich nicht), wo man nicht höre, sondern sehe, durch und durch sehe, wo nicht Erzählung, sondern Handlung wäre, wo man alles, oder wenigstens mehr sehe, als höre.— Man sieht freilich den Erzähler im gemeinen Leben, allein die Wahrheit zu sagen, man hört ihn mehr, und es würd' Affektation seyn, wenn er mehr zu sehen, als zu hören wäre. Ein Erzähler, wenn er im Druck erscheint, wie wenig ist er zu sehen! wie weit weniger, als im gemeinen Leben!———Dergleichen *Geschichte,* wo, wie meine Mutter sagen würde, *gewandelt* und *gehandelt* wird, wird man sie eine *redende*, eine *Geschichte mit eigenen Worten* nennen, meinethalben! Daß eine Geschichte *durchweg in Gesprächen*, eine in *Frag' und Antworten* ein ganz ander Ding sey, versteht sich. Wären in einer redenden Geschichte auch nur ausgerissene Lebensblätter, wie leicht würden sie zusammenzusetzen seyn.—Man würde dem Leser noch obenein eben hiedurch

unvermerkt Gelegenheit zu mehrerer Anstrengung geben, und ihn zum Mitarbeiter an seinem Werke machen.———Daß ich es bei dieser Geschichte zu diesem Ziel nicht angelegt, bescheid' ich mich von selbst, und ich bin schon zufrieden, wenn mein Lebenslauf nur hier und da Darstellung enthält, und wenn sich in dem Schlusse des ersten Bandes die Personen selbst zu erkennen und zu verstehen gegeben. *Rede* und *du bist*, könnte das Motto zu diesen Gesprächen seyn; es liegt eine besondere Natur in der Rede.———

(II,1-2)

    This passage is of central importance to Hippel's work, for it introduces a number of concepts that are fundamental to his understanding of the novel. At the beginning and end of this quotation the narrator expresses his longing for immediacy not just in the novel but also "im gemeinen Leben." He always values a direct sense impression more highly than information that is second-hand. This is the principle that underlies his apparently inconsistent remarks on the relative merits of seeing and hearing. When a story is told in person ("im gemeinen Leben"), the emphasis is on sight. The best storyteller should, like an actor, perform and not just relate what he tells. He should appeal not just to the ear but also to the eye. At best, however, such a performance is but a poor substitute for the events themselves, which Hippel would prefer to see as they happened, without having to rely on someone to report them. When Hippel praises the narrator as performer, he singles out for praise precisely that kind of narration in which the narrator does not interpret the story, but rather recreates them before the eyes of his audience. This narrator draws attention not to himself but to the events, so that he becomes as it were a transparent medium through which the events can be seen without distortion.

    But this praise of the narrator could easily be misunderstood. When Hippel says, "Je mehr ein Erzähler zu sehen ist, je mehr freu ich mich," it could seem that he advocates that the narrator call attention to himself. To correct any such misunderstanding, Hippel seems to reverse himself and suddenly consider hearing more important than seeing, and calls it "Affektation" when the narrator is more seen than heard. But the thrust of his argument is consistent throughout: the events themselves are of prime importance, and the narrator is little more than a necessary evil. The audience should see not the narrator but see through the narrator to the events. If the narrator's presence diverts the audience from the story, then they should not look at him but instead listen to what he says. Indeed this is almost a necessity when the narrator tells his story not in person but "im Druck."

The implication for the novel of this concern to emphasize the events at the expense of the narrator is that a work must strive to give at least the illusion of immediacy. Thus a novel should not be "Erzählung," that is, it should not be told, narrated, mediated, rather it should be "Handlung [. . .], wo man alles oder wenigstens mehr sehe, als höre." The narrator's other term for "Handlung" is "Darstellung," which he mentions near the end of this passage. "Darstellung" is perhaps the better term since it suggests the presentation of events as on a stage, whereas "Handlung" suggests more the events themselves, which could be presented any way the author wishes.

The narrator implicitly distinguishes between his proposal of a novel as "Darstellung" and experiments such as those undertaken by Engel with the *Dialogroman* when he speaks of a "Geschichte *durchweg in Gesprächen*, [. . .] in *Frag'* und *Antworten*" and calls it "ein ganz ander Ding." Hippel's narrator proposes a more radical break with novels of the past, for the very elements of his novel cease to be fictive and are rather "ausgerissene [und wieder zusammengesetzte] Lebensblätter."

To be sure, the narrator admits that it is open to question whether or not such a work would be a novel, and he claims to have attained his ideal in this work "nur hier und da." But the *Darstellungsroman* is clearly the goal he is striving for. He recommends such a novel because it forces the reader to participate. The reader, confronted with "ausgerissene Lebensblätter," tries to put them together himself as he reads. By putting them into some context that will make them meaningful for him, the reader is placed in the same position as the narrator-author. In this fashion a community of interests is established between the author and his public such that they can be considered his "Mitarbeiter."

Near the end of the *Lebensläufe*, the narrator observes that "wer es genau nimmt, wird finden, daß alles in der Welt Roman sey. Hat je ein großer Herr das gemeine Leben, so wie es da gemein ist, gesehen? Wer kennt die Stadt, den Berg, das Thal aus der Beschreibung, wenn er an Stell' und Ort kommt? [. . .] Seht ihr aber, ihr Romanhelden! seht ihr nicht in meinem Buche das gemeine Leben? Ist der Geist wahr, wie er denn wahr und wahrhaftig ist, was kümmert euch der Leib?" (III, pt. 2, 413–14). In spite of his assertion that 'everything is a novel' Hippel refuses even here to admit that he is writing a novel. Hippel means that 'everything is a novel' only in a specific sense ("wer es genau nimmt"), that is, only in the sense that everything told is a novel insofar as it is narrated. Thus everything is a novel only in a formal sense, and the form of a work is merely its "Leib." What is decisive is the "Geist" of a work, that is, the extent to which it presents "das gemeine Leben, [. . .] die Stadt, den Berg, das Thal" directly, immediately, and without narrative interference.

The absence of interference implies, however, that "das gemeine Leben" be presented in its totality. Since the novel can reflect all aspects of the world, it begins itself to take on some of the totality of the world. This tendency towards open-endedness in the novel can lead to extreme subjectivity, as the *Ich* of the author-narrator becomes the only element holding together the myriad aspects of the world presented in the novel. And indeed it has become one of the commonplaces of Hippel's critics to read the *Lebensläufe* in this way.

This critique fails, however, to evaluate properly another element that Hippel took over from the theoretical discussion of his day, namely the importance of authenticity. Here Hippel goes one step beyond his contemporaries. The novel should not only present itself and be read as a history, it should also become history. Not, of course, the kind of historiography that had been practiced until well into the eighteenth century, and whose authority had at least in part been shaken by the ease with which it had been imitated by the lowly novel. Both the novel and historiography were open to the charges of being deceptive and of lacking veracity.[11] By rejecting both genres, the way was left open for something new, for which Hippel had no name but that can be understood as a radical extension of earlier, traditional techniques. Thus Hippel uses the memoir fiction throughout the *Lebensläufe*, so that practically every event has its own narrator, one who has first-hand experience of what he relates. And Hippel continues the historical techniques of presenting documents and having the editor comment on them.

But in Hippel's novel these documents are no longer merely alleged to be real, they in fact to some extent are real. Hippel mixes novelistic and historical methods, and thus responds to Sterne in much the same manner as had Diderot. Both Hippel and Diderot return to the conventional historical pose and attempt to make it convincing again through the fictionalization of real documents. Unlike Diderot, however, who upholds the authenticity of the historical part of his narrative by having it point out the fictional nature of the novelistic body of *La Religieuse*, Hippel attempts to win the audience's belief for the whole of his work and refuses to separate the historical from the fictional. Thus the rough-hewn, *ex tempore* character of the "Préface annexe," which contrasts so markedly with the linear, direct development of the rest of *La Religieuse*, becomes a prevailing narrative characteristic of the whole of the *Lebensläufe*. The apparent chaos and formlessness of the world presented in the *Lebensläufe* is the result not of extreme subjectivity but of extreme objectivity, as the narrator refrains from interfering with the world and instead presents it unretouched and in its totality.

Hippel was prepared to go great lengths in order to turn his work into "Lebensblätter." At the beginning of the *Lebensläufe* the narrator is about to introduce himself but after the first word is abruptly cut short by a critic: "Ich-Halt!" But the narrator makes his appearance only in order to withdraw from the stage (taking the critic with him) and permit an unmediated confrontation of world and reader.

The guiding hand of the narrator is for Hippel a deceiving hand, and one that he banishes from the presentation of the world in the novel. Hippel's radical (and remarkably modern) cure for the Shandean disease of the omniscient narrator run wild is to create the narrator who knows little, but who can speak reliably.[12] The subjectivity of the narrator must necessarily color the perception of reality. Hippel's aim is to reduce this subjective element to a minimum in order to keep the world (and not just the narrator's *impressions* of it) tellable. He wants to present actions, not opinions concerning actions, to paraphrase the quote from Epictetus which Sterne used as the motto for *Tristram Shandy*: "It is not actions, but opinions concerning actions, which disturb men" (trans. J. A. Work). The monolithic narrator of Sterne's work (Victor Lange has called Tristram "dieser monomanische Erzähler," and asserted that Sterne created "den *monologischen Roman*"[13]) is split into fragments by Hippel, each one of them a miniature monolith—but the sum of their narratives can claim the greatest possible reliability in their presentation of the fictional world. Each one is reliable (as far as he can be), and tells all he knows (but that is necessarily not much).

The narrator Alexander could better be called the editor and copyist. He lets the characters present themselves directly, without interference from the narrator, in that they write letters of advice to Alexander. This technique is used with great frequency in the first volume of the *Lebensläufe*. Thus Alexander's father lectures to him on education (pp. 132–38), Mine, Alexander's girlfriend, writes to him (pp. 160–77), and his mother writes him a "Denkzettel" (pp. 206–40). The pages between Mine's letters and the mother's "Denkzettel" are filled completely with the mother's narrative of her husband's background. Alexander interrupts her and abridges her tale only occasionally. Later, at Herr v. G.'s, he wants to make his readers better acquainted "mit den Charakteren dieses hochwohlgebornen curischen Hauses und seiner Art [. . .], oder wie es mir eben einfällt, sie sich selbst bekannt machen lassen. Ich will versuchen, diesen Tag nachzuschreiben [. . .]" (p. 244).

The rest of the volume is taken up with a conversation in the garden of the estate of Herr v. G. The narrator does not suddenly become a playwright, although the printed page looks as if it were taken from a play: each character is identified before his speech by name (Alexander is called "ich"), no one stands above or outside the dialogue. Alexander does not become a dramatist but rather a protocolist.

It is in the following three volumes, however, that documentation replaces narration almost completely. Up until now Alexander has, for the most part, been able to act as narrator because he has been recording his own experiences (experiences that are reminiscent of Hippel's own youth). For much of the rest of the novel this will not be the case. In volume II the quotation of documents begins in earnest. These documents and conversations, it must be emphasized, give the impression of being recorded virtually word-for-word, with Alexander making only minor alterations. "Eine Erzählung, der man das Studirte, das Geflissene, das Geordnete ansieht, ist unausstehlich.—So wie es in der Welt geht, so muß es auch in der Geschichte gehen.—Bald so, bald so" (II, 50-51). In this fashion Alexander presents then Hermann's stories of his daughter Mine (pp. 18–29), Mine's letter (pp. 70–75), the conversation between Alexander and Benjamin, Mine's brother (pp. 77–81), and the conversation between the pastor and Herr v. G. (pp. 88–96). Later he remarks, "Ich bemühe mich auch hier, Lebensläufer zu seyn, und diese Abschrift ist dem Original ähnlich.—Wir fielen von einem aufs andere. Wir scheitelten die Haare nicht. Würd' ich nicht einen Roman schreiben, wenn ich nicht auch von einem aufs andere fallen und die Haare scheiteln sollte? Ein Roman! fern sey er von mir!" (II, 152) (This observation is made in the midst of Alexander's entrance examination at the university, an episode I shall examine at some length in the next chapter.)

Most of volume II is taken up with the pursuit and death of Mine, the victim of a conspiracy involving, among others, Herr v. E. (a lecherous nobleman whom Mine refuses to marry), her father, and officers of the law in Courland and Prussia. The actual narrator of Mine's last days is a clergyman in the Prussian city of L—, "von dem ich dieses alles haarklein habe," as Alexander says (II, 341). The state of Mine's soul is expressed in her letters to Alexander (pp. 242–250). The exchange of legal documents leading to the temporary arrest of Mine takes up pages 290–306, and the *Promemoria* of the arresting officer and his interrogation take up pages 316–323. The clergyman's narration, a kind of document itself, contains other documents as well: the report and letter of resignation of Nathanael, the arresting officer, who is so moved by Mine's suffering that he gives up his post, and Mine's *Depositum* (pp. 341–43, 359–69).

Observations on death, an important subject throughout the *Lebensläufe*, become most prominent after Mine's death. The last pages of volume II and much of volume III, part 1, are given over to the *Sterbegraf*. He, Alexander, and the clergyman discuss death, and their conversation is repeated at length at the opening of volume III, part 2. One of the patients the Count entertains at his castle is the "Krippenritterin," whose story Alexander retells with the preface, "Ich will ihre Geschichte *in tertia persona* geben, ohne zu bemerken, ob ich die Umstände von ihr selbst oder vom Grafen empfangen" (III, pt. 1, 73–4).

The speculations of the Count are given much room (pp. 107–159), and are only now and then interrupted by the narrator's commentary: "Der Graf hätte so ohne End' und Ziel reden können. Es war Zephyr, den er mir zuwehte—wirklicher Zepher, sanfte Empfindung, womit er mich anfächelte" (III, pt. 1, 104). "So vortrefflich unordentlich war diese Rede. Es war kein Kunst-, sondern ein Naturstück" (Ibid., pp. 137–38). "Was ich meinen Lesern von der Wildnißrede gegeben, sollte eine Nachfolge des Originals seyn; ich wollte nicht den Hauch der Natur von der Pflaume wegwischen, sondern so wie sie da ist, mit diesem Naturathem, der mir wie ein Heiligenschein vorkommt, wollt' ich sie [. . .]" (Ibid.).

If the Count's hobby-horse is the subject of death, his counterpart is the clergyman, who is writing a book on sins against the Holy Ghost. Their hobby-horses are not antithetical, but their styles are. The clergyman says of the Count's disorderly manner of speculation. "Es ist, sagte er, so etwas Beängstigendes, so was von Todesnoth darin. Eben das, sagt' ich, hat mich entzückt bis zur Halle des Himmels. Dies in der Rede zu treffen, zu copiren, war unmöglich.—Ich liebe, fuhr der Prediger fort, eine genaue Bindung der Perioden, eine gewisse Baukunst im Vortrage, und so viel Fenster wie möglich in jedem Stock. Zwar halte ich es für keine Sünde wider den heiligen Geist—", and thus he returns to riding his hobby-horse (III, pt. 1, 160–61). This passage is significant for two reasons. First, it suggests that the Count's and Alexander's disorderly style is, at least in this section of the work, justifiable on aesthetic grounds. If the lack of order itself has something of death about it, then it is the appropriate vehicle of expression for the mourning and distraught Alexander. Second, this passage also indicates that Alexander will overcome his depression and closeness to death. For it is the clergyman's emphasis on systematization that, for Hippel, is deadening. Alexander's greater sympathy for the living and natural paradoxically leads him to defend the Count, who, for all his preoccupation with death, has more in common with life in his speculations and activities than does the clergyman in his book.

Near the opening of volume III, part 2, Alexander quotes from a letter from his father (pp. 17–21), and comments, "Um es authentisch meinen Lesern mitzutheilen, schreib ich es aus dem Original aus, das noch da vor mir liegt" (III, pt. 2, 21). A letter from his mother tells of the death of Alexander's father (Ibid., pp. 27–29). Another narrator is introduced to tell of the mother's death. She had "eine alte Priesterwittwe, anstatt einer Diakonin, zu sich genommen, und *von ihr hab' ich empfangen*, was ich meinen Lesern erzähle, und zwar so, als wär ich Augenzeuge gewesen" (III, pt. 2, 45). "Meine Leser wissen, wie sehr ich für eigene Worte bin!" (Ibid, pp. 61). This description is followed by a *Todtenlied* (pp.83–85) and by Alexander's reminiscences of his mother's maxims and views, utterly without order, simply listed one after the other, giving the impression that the narrator prints them in the sequence that they occur to him.

The narrator faithfully records the conversations of the Professor (possibly Kant) and an officer (pp. 217–21). In his despair over Mine's death Alexander decides to join the Russian army in their war against the Turks. This episode is ended when Empress Catherine the Great, in a letter given on page 256, raises Alexander into the nobility. Alexander returns to Courland and woos the daughter of Herr v. G., Tine, whom he had saved from drowning during his first visit at the estate of Herr v. G. in volume II. They are united not only by their love for each other, but also by their love for Mine. Tine offers an evaluation of her husband (pp. 375–82, and p. 445, where her remarks are called "Alexandrien"). They retire to an estate in the country and Mine gives birth to their son Leopold, as the story apparently comes to an end. But after turning a blank page (an obviously Sternean technique) the reader finds that the story continues into the present: Leopold dies, Mine is unable ever to give birth again, and Alexander resolves to leave the estate to dedicate himself, at least temporarily, to some kind of work, not defined, in public service. Thus the work ends as a diary.

The narrator closest to Hippel, the *Ich* of the opening passage, is absent from the work to a significant degree, reports only what he can say with certainty about himself, and otherwise lets the characters speak for themselves in letters, dialogues, prayer, or he retreats behind impersonal documents: protocols of meetings and judicial writings. He appears not at all in the three *Beilagen* A, B, and C. "A" follows the death of Mine in volume II, and is a translation of Latvian folksongs into German prose. Most of them deal with the themes of love, nature and death. "B," the comic counterpart to "A," follows immediately upon it in volume II, and is the *Leichenabdankung* for Mine delivered by the organist in L—. His tolerance of flies parodies that of Uncle Toby: "Kann sie ein so großer Herr, als der liebe Gott ist, in seiner Welt leiden, so können sie doch wohl in meiner Stube seyn? Ich hab' es von einem sehr vornehmen Herrn, der bei seinem Feste auch für seine Fliegen und Mücken Wein eingießen läßt, um alles was um ihn lebt und schwebt, zu sättigen und zu tränken mit Wohlgefallen" (II, 446).[14] "C," in the middle of volume III, part 2, is a book of letters written by Alexander's friend Gottfried to Alexander's mother dealing with questions of tolerance for Jews and "Ketzer" in Courland and Königsberg.

Perhaps the best way to illustrate the different narrative techniques of Sterne and Hippel is to compare their treatment of a common theme. It is one of Sterne's concerns to poke fun at social ills in his novel. His targets include useless pedantry (the Sorbonne's decree on prenatal baptism and Ernulfus's curse), artificiality (Walter Shandy's ornate, rhetorical lament on the death of Tristram's brother), the imbalance of wit and judgment, and false sentimentality. For the most part Sterne is content to attack these ills merely by presenting them *in extenso*. He does not ridicule them himself so much as he simply presents them and lets them reveal their own absurdity to the reader.

The situation is distinctly different in the *Lebensläufe*. Hippel's criticisms of society are made explicit by the narrator, are more closely linked to the class structure of that society, and are not couched in the universal terms used by Sterne, who is interested in the comic aspects of the human condition *per se*. Hippel satirizes, for example, the snobbery of the *Junkers*. The noble ladies of the *Tischgesellschaft* at Herr v. G.'s are certain that the afterworld will not be a classless society. "Sie lebten mit der Idee in Todfeindschaft, daß sie dort mit Kammerzofen in Einem Paar gehen, und in Gemeinschaft der Güter leben sollten, und dachten in ihrem Innersten: Stände müßten seyn" (I, 355–56). For Gottlob v. G., the son of Herr v. G. and a passionate hunter, powder and shot are more important than the rescue of his betrothed, Tine, who has to be saved from drowning by Alexander (II, 33–36). Later Gottlob says, "Eins bekenn' ich—ein Hund gilt mir für zwei Bauern. Hunde sind aber auch Geschöpfe, die wenigstens *Wackers* verdienten zu seyn. (Aufseher über die Bauern.)" (Ibid., p. 39).

Hippel criticizes in these passages the way considerations of class membership take precedence over natural human emotions. The nobility's inverted sense of priorities prevents them from being capable of expressing spontaneous, sympathetic feelings. Thus Herr v. W. undergoes an "unbeschreiblichen" inner struggle before he can bring himself to congratulate

Alexander for the rescue of his daughter. "Meinetwegen war er in erschrecklicher Verlegenheit; denn so sehr dieser Vorfall zu einem neuen Feste Anlaß zu geben schien, so blieb es ihm doch bedenklich, weil ich nicht von Adel war" (II, 41). It is this distorted perception, one that values anything that has to do with the nobility, no matter how lowly, over any other non-noble human concerns, that allows the nobility to be so cruel and inhuman.

The limitations of the nobility are caricatured most strongly in the figures of the hunters v. X. Y. and Z. Alexander satirically endows them with enlightened, humanistic attributes: they consider themselves music lovers—their favorite instrument is the hunting horn. And they are animal lovers as well—when it comes to their hunting dogs. These, however, and their pipes and the affairs of state of Courland are the only topics which they are capable of discussing.[15]

Nor is Hippel blind to the class pretensions of the bourgeoisie. Herr Herrmann, Mine's father, "rümpfte, wiewohl, da er nicht einmal die Hunde der Herren von X. Y. Z. zu duzen sich unterfangen hätte, wenn er mit diesen Hunden conversiren sollen—nur unter der Serviette die Nase" (I, 353). "Er wußt' aus vieljähriger Erfahrung, was der Adel in Curland zu bedeuten habe [. . .] Er dacht' an alle Ehrenerklärungen und Maulschläge, die er zu übernehmen nothgedrungen worden [. . .]" (II, 9).[16] Later, in order to excuse his "Hoffnarrenführung," Herrmann paraphrases 2 Corinthians 11:19 in his attack on the nobility: "Traget die Narren, weil ihr klug seyd." He is answered, however, by Alexander with: "Allein macht euch nicht selbst zum Narren" (II, 14).

Many of Hippel's criticisms are, as in *Tristam Shandy*, contained in digressions or episodes. But the status of these departures from the main events of the plot is quite different in Hippel's novel. Sterne's criticisms of society are contained in digressions that have at best a remote connection to the development of Tristram. In fact, the story of Tristram's development cannot be told because of the digressions. Virtually the only unifying link in Tristram's digressions is the fact that they all take place in his mind. Thus an examination of when, where, and how he digresses would lead to an understanding of the workings of his mind, would reveal if not his life, then at least his patterns of thought, the associations of words and ideas by which his mind proceeds.

Hippel's digressions are much more carefully tied to the development of the main character than are Sterne's. His digressions are important not because they acquaint the reader with the workings of Alexander's mind, but because they show the events that contribute to his education. The digressions in the *Lebensläufe* are all in some way formative, they tell of events that Alexander experiences and that are significant in his development.

In general, these digressions take the form of variations on a theme. Frequently that theme is the decisive and pernicious role played by money, property, or class in human relationships. This thematic unity allows Alexander as narrator to treat the character Alexander as just one of many characters. Alexander's experiences with Mine and Tine are typical of two possible solutions to the recurrent theme of the problems faced by young lovers who want to marry.[17] As a rule the problems are caused by the parents, who oppose a *mésalliance* or favor marriage to a different and (in their eyes) socially more advantageous partner. If their opposition is successful, one of the lovers dies (sometimes both), so that they may be united after death. This tragic ending predominates throughout the *Lebensläufe*; it is typified by Mine's fate, and is loosely modelled after the sufferings and death of Richardson's Clarissa. In the alternate, comic ending, the lovers overcome all obstacles and eventually are able to marry. It is with such a marriage to Tine that Alexander closes his account of his past life.

If one overlooks the diary entries that are added, as it were, after the end of the work, it can be said that the comic variant acts as a frame to the story, for the theme first appears in volume I in its comic form. In the account by Alexander's mother of her relationship with her husband, she says that their first contact with each other suffered under his refusal to tell her and her mother anything about his background, not even what part of the country he came from. Subsequently he turned his attention to the youngest daughter of Pastor L—, and, as Alexander's mother says, in the process lost his reputation for celibacy. Eventually, though, he returned to her, they were married, and Alexander, their only child, was born. For the daughter of Pastor L—, too, the affair ended "wie sich die Komödien alle schließen, mit der Heirath" (I, 201), for she married a Herr von—, a man well above her station.

The tone of this incident is humorous, even Sternean, for the problems here are caused not by the restrictions of parents or society, but by the quirks of the characters themselves, particularly the stubborn refusal of Alexander's father to reveal his background, a quality reminiscent of the hobby-horses of Sterne's characters. But Hippel does not long maintain this tone. Instead, he prefers the other variant, the one ending with death or with a leave-taking, in which the conflict is brought about by larger social forces.

The first tragic episode is the story of 'the man with one glove,' which Alexander overhears at Herr v. G.'s. An old man comes begging at v. G.'s door; he is a proud man reduced to beggary because he had loaned his savings to a Cavalier, who promptly spent it all in amusing himself and did not repay the loan. The old man is supported by his daughter and son-in-law for two years, until they lose their cottage in a storm. With but a week to live, the old man goes begging for money to pay for his funeral. This money is to be his surprise gift to his daughter and her husband, and v. G. generously gives him all he needs. The old man refuses all other offers of aid except for one glass of wine, his last on earth, as he says, and which he drinks with v. G. He also accepts one glove, which gives this episode its name.

Immediately after Alexander overhears this moving scene in volume I, news comes to Alexander's father of 'our acquaintance,' who has accidentally shot his only son. The acquaintance tells his story in a long *Beilage* in volume II. He and Charlotte were once in love. Charlotte is the neither rich nor beautiful, but virtuous *Cammermädchen* of v.—, who seeks to seduce her. She resists him successfully, and he is embarrassed when seen on his knees before her by another servant girl, who then tells v.——'s wife what she has seen. This saves Charlotte from v.——, who attempts to make good by giving her presents. But these only confirm 'our acquaintance's' jealous suspicions, and he marries another woman, Luise, who dies after the birth of their son. Charlotte meanwhile continues in her love for 'our acquaintance,' even turning away a rich suitor. Finally, in desperation, she marries another man, but she is still unhappy and the marriage is childless. She dies, and all are moved to tears—except for 'our acquaintance.' His conscience is awakened only when he accidentally kills his son. He becomes aware then of his guilt vis-à-vis Charlotte, and dies.

In both the story of the man with one glove and of "unser Bekannte" the tragic events are set in motion by the thoughtlessness and arrogance of members of the aristocracy in dealing with honorable but defenceless members of the middle class. To this extent they both anticipate Mine's fate, and indeed Alexander remarks that, during the story of 'our acquaintance,' "[es] fiel mir alle Augenblicke *Mine* ein" (II, 68).

When Alexander departs from Courland to attend the university in Königsberg, his first stop in Prussia is in a town in which an old man is being buried, and Alexander immediately (but erroneously) takes it to be the man with one glove. The man, who is unknown in the town, has left behind a notebook, in which he tells how he was reduced to ruin. He was a merchant who fell on hard times, and went to Königsberg "um seinen Verkehr durch einige neue Waaren zu verstärken" (II, 122). However, when his relatives learned of his impoverished situation, they demanded the return of what they had already lent him, thus leaving him penniless. He set out from Königsberg on foot and died in the Prussian town before the border with Courland. Here too Alexander thinks of Mine, saying, "wie hätte wohl ein Vorfall, der mich zum Stehen, zum Denken bringen konnte, nichte zugleich Minen und ihn in einem Paar darstellen sollen?" (II, 133).

Aside from the tragic ending to both cases, the key connecting link between the death of the old man and Mine's death is the central role played in each by money. Herrmann, Mine's father, wants to marry Magdalene, called Dene, servant girl of Frau v. E. Frau v. E. is bound by the will of her late husband to retain Dene in her service until they are parted by death. They must remain together despite their distaste for each other, unless Dene marries, in which case (hopes Frau v. E.) the will could be changed. Dene is willing to marry Herrmann, and he too becomes love-sick in his own fashion; "Herrmann litte zusehens; denn er war in das Geld der Dene sterblich verliebt" (II, 194).

But it is not only the motif of greed that is repeated in the story of Mine, *Standesdünkel* plays a significant role as well. Herrmann opposes the marriage of his daughter to Alexander because of the lowly, or at least nebulous, background of Alexander's father. Alexander's mother, too, opposes the marriage, and refuses to come to the aid of Mine when she could still have been saved. She opposes the marriage because Mine's father is but a *Litteratus*, "welches in Curland eben keinen Gelehrten sondern ein unseelig Mittelding von Edelmann und Bauer bedeutet" (I, 13). Herrmann allies himself with the powerful Herr v. E. against his own daughter because of the promises v. E. is able to make him. "Hat der Herr v. E. Pastorate zu vergeben? fragte Mine bitter.—Das nicht, allein die Connexion der Edelleute unter einander—" replies Herrmann (II, 222).

Herr v. E. is the profligate and dissipated son of Frau v. E.; he returns from Paris and falls passionately in love with Mine, who remains true to Alexander. He, however, is far away in Königsberg, and learns of her fate only when he is no longer able to help. Mine escapes from Courland into Prussia, where she is pursued by Prussian court officials acting in response to charges invented by v. E.'s lawyers. She dies before she can be taken into custody.

Variations on this story are most frequent in volume III, part 1. This is no accident, for Alexander in his grief at the death of Mine deliberately seeks out cemeteries and visits the *Sterbegraf* as a way of reminding himself of Mine. But it would be an oversimplification to say that Alexander is obsessed with death, as though death were interesting to him merely for its own sake. For the experience of death contributes to Alexander's education. As Alexander notes, Mine "nahm ein feierliches Versprechen vom Prediger, mir ihren Tod auf das aller, allergenauesten zu erzählen." And he continues by quoting Mine's words to the clergyman concerning her death, "Ist er schrecklich, ist er sanft, wie er war. Alles, alles ihm [Alexander]! Er braucht Lebenslehren [. . .]" (II, 349).

At the castle of the *Sterbegraf* Alexander learns the ultimate fate of the youngest daughter of Pastor L———, the daughter that Alexander's father had decided not to marry after all in volume I. She had married v.—, who had mistakenly expected a large dowry from the match. The dowry he received, however, was "nicht hochadelich zugeschnitten [. . . .] Er entschloß sich also zum Incognito, wo es, wenn nur eine reiche Weste hervorsticht, aufs Kleid nicht ankommt. Der Ritter beschonte seinen adelichen Namen und legte sich wohlbedächtig einen unadelichen bei. Das junge Paar lebt' also in bürgerlichen Ueberkleidern in —— einem preußischen Städtchen, und verzehrten bei einer friedlichen Ehe alles, was es hatte" (III, pt. 1, 76).

Thereafter the *Ritter* becomes a language and dance instructor at the university in Königsberg, kills a man in a duel ("Für einen Mann, der Sprach— und Tanzmeister zusammen in einer Person war, ist es sehr bescheiden, daß er nur Einen, und nicht für jede Kunst wenigstens Einen, ums Leben gebracht" [Ibid., 78]), and enters into a *Liebeshandel* with both a mother and her daughter (Ibid., p. 79). In other words he returns to the libertine mores of the aristocracy, whereas his wife remains loyal and uncomplaining, and even manages to take care of the two children. Finally, however, they are reduced to starvation by the *Ritter*, who kicks away his son when the boy pleads for food for his mother one midnight upon his father's return home. The *Ritter* turns them out of the house, and the *Ritterin* falls in debt to a former language student of her husband's. He would start an affair with her, and send her gifts. Unsuspecting at first, she returns the gifts as soon as she sees through his designs, but she still is in debt to him. Her appeal for aid to a wealthy man is refused, for he will help her only if she can put up some security or if someone will guarantee his loan. Things go better for her and her children when they are taken in by friends in the heiligen Geiststraße, who give her the money to repay her debt (Ibid., p. 83). But when the friends suddenly move away the *Ritterin* and her children are left utterly without means and the son and daughter die.

Appended to her story is the anecdote concerning the landlord, the *Leinweber*. He had been treated rudely by the *Ritter*: "Mit einer Frau und einem Leinweber getraut er's sich schon anzubinden" (Ibid., p. 86). But he is moved from anger towards his tenants to pity at the sight of the *Ritterin* with tears in her eyes as she comes to ask for an extension on the rent. He even proposes that she never again have to pay rent—but the excitement of the moment is so great that he puts his hands on the table, one on top of the other (a detail the narrator is careful to note in his effort to make the scene realistic), rests his head slowly on both, and dies. But the end of his story is not the end of hers, for the heirs refuse to recognize his promise, as stated in their legal note, a document quoted by the narrator.

Finally she is threatened with divorce by her husband, who wants to marry the daughter of the mother/daughter pair he is having an affair with. Judicial corruption allows the success of this plot, which echoes the scheme of the lawyers and v. E. against Mine. The *Ritterin* is then taken in by the *Sterbegraf*, and awaits her end in a room of his castle.

Later, in Königsberg, Alexander seeks out a cemetery and converses with the *Todesgräber*, who tells a story of two lovers buried next to each other in the cemetery. The middleclass parents of the girl had wanted her to agree to a match with a man above her station instead of marrying the man she loved and who loved her in return, and who was of her own class. The girl refused to follow the wishes of her parents, became ill, and recovered when her parents changed their minds and relented.

Nonetheless the girl died, and was soon followed by her lover. Over their graves two linden trees have grown together, their branches intertwined.

The custodian then tells a second story, simply entitled *Die Geschichte*. He remarks in his preface, "daß mehr Leute an der Liebe sterben, als an den Blattern. Die Schuld hievon gehört auf die Rechnung des Zwangs, den man den Menschen auflegt. Man hat so viel über die Klöster geschrieen; allein wahrlich jeder Staat macht recht geflissentlich ein großes Kloster aus sich!—" (Ibid., p. 193). Then the story begins. Hans, a simple, free peasant, and Grete, daughter of a farmer, fall in love and are to be married. But through a misunderstanding Hans comes to believe that he will not inherit the property of Grete's father as expected. Hans has already become obsessed with plans for improving the property when he comes to suspect that Grete's brother-in-law will lay claim to it. "Das liebe Eigenthum; es hat mehr Unheil, als dies, angerichtet," says the narrator (Ibid., p. 195). Hans in addition suspects that Grete is being unfaithful to him with her brother-in-law, and Hans stabs her nearly to death. Though Grete recovers, Hans is condemned by the courts to be hanged, but is pardoned by the king, who listens to Grete's plea on behalf of Hans. They marry, but on their way to find a new home in a different part of the country Hans falls ill and dies of a fever, and Grete must be committed to an *Irrhaus*.

In the next variation on this theme, Alexander begins to play a more active role than that of listener. He returns to the pastor who had taken in Mine during her last days, and attends the wedding of Gretchen, the pastor's daughter, with Nathanael, the good-hearted but misguided officer who had attempted to arrest Mine just before her death. Her fate had led to a change of heart in Nathanael, as he resigned his post and later proposed to Gretchen. When Alexander arrives before the wedding, the situation threatens to turn into a repetition of the story of Hans and Grete. Nathanael plays a role similar to that of Hans; he is jealous of Alexander, who is thus in a situation like that of the brother-in-law in the earlier story. Nathanael's suspicions subside only when Alexander takes his leave shortly after the wedding and after a visit to Mine's grave.

Alexander plays an active role in a situation of this kind only in the last volume of the work. He returns to the country home of v. G., where Tine v. G. is to be married to Gottlob v. W. Gottlob, however, has remained an indifferent suitor ever since Alexander's rescue of Tine, and is content to return to his favorite pastime, hunting. The love just beginning to be expressed between Alexander and Tine is soon challenged by v. K., who crassly attempts to buy her affections. The situation is made even more reminiscent of the one between Mine and v. E. when Tine's father joins in supporting v. K.'s efforts, just as Herrmann had helped v. E. Tine, however, resolutely rejects v. K., and once it becomes clear that Alexander is now a member of the nobility, the familiar triangular relationship at last finds a solution that makes the lovers happy, as Alexander and Tine are married.

But even this marriage, the closest approach to a *mésalliance* that turns out well in the novel, is not without difficulties. For though Alexander has been ennobled by Catherine the Great and has discovered his nobility of blood, Frau v. G. refuses to attend his wedding with Tine v. W., "weil mein adliches Blut durch das poetische Blut meiner Mutter Schaden gelitten, und weil meines Vaters Adel dadurch, daß er die Kanzel bestiegen, einen unauslöschlichen Fettfleck erhalten" (Ibid., p. 374). "Käme es auf sie an, sie würde unsere Ehe noch bis diesen Augenblick ungültig erklären" (Ibid., p. 390). Tine's father has a similar view; "Herr v. W. wollte seine Tochter auf keine Weise einem Major geben, dessen Vater Pastor in Curland gewesen" (Ibid., p. 338).

Thus the story told by Alexander the narrator takes place on two levels. The first level consists of the course of life of the protagonist Alexander, the story of where he goes and what he does. The second level consists of digressions and episodes, which are tied to the life of Alexander in that he is told or overhears them. There is, however, a deeper connection between the two levels than the mere accident of Alexander's presence when these stories are told. For the stories that he hears apply to situations that he in the course of the work finds himself in; they help him mature, until finally he is able to experience such a situation himself and bear up reasonably well in adversity. It might seem at times as though the first level is completely submerged by the second, as though Alexander were living no life of his own, but merely experiencing and listening to all that takes place around him. Indeed, relatively little is told of his life after his childhood years, but all the educational forces working upon him are presented in detail, until finally he too enters into life, and becomes an active participant in the events of the novel.

This entrance into life is presented in the novel as a continuation of and variation on the preceding episodes. Alexander's life becomes one episode among many similar ones. Throughout these episodes Hippel opposes any form of class consciousness or class privilege that takes precedence over natural feelings of sympathy and over considerations of the rights of man. He attacks this consciousness as well as the inordinate influence of money and property on human behavior, and he takes his examples both from the nobility and the middle class. This is the common theme on which his episodes and digressions elaborate.

By having limited narrators present these digressions, Hippel achieves what is perhaps his ultimate aim, namely to let the world itself speak directly to the reader with as little interference as possible from an omniscient narrator.[18] Hippel does not deny the narrator's subjectivity, which Sterne had so emphasized. But he shows one way in which this subjectivity need not impair either the tellability or the objectivity of the novel. Hippel carries the *limitation* of the narrator so far that it turns into an epic technique of its own. As in the case of *Tristram Shandy* the apparent chaos of Hippel's novel is not a result of dilettantism or inability to control the métier, as critics have traditionally maintained, but is part of the intention of the work. Hippel might sometimes look as though he is imitating Sterne, but in essence Hippel runs directly counter to his supposed model.

Notes

[1] See especially Norbert Miller, *Der empfindsame Erzähler*, p. 444.

[2] Johann Gottfried Herder, *Briefe zu [sic] Beförderung der Humanität*, Achte Sammlung, Nr. 100, (Berlin and Weimar: Aufbau; 1971) II, 113.

[3] See the second chapter of Michelsen's *Laurence Sterne und der deutsche Roman des 18. Jahrhunderts*, "Welt und Provinz," pp. 50–73.

[4] See Franz Stanzel, *Die typischen Erzählsituationen im Roman*, Wiener Beiträge zur englischen Philologie, 63 (1955); Bertil Romberg, *Studies in the Narrative Technique of the First-Person Novel*, (Stockholm: Almqvist & Wiksell, 1962); and of course Wayne Booth, *The Rhetoric of Fiction* (Chicago and London: Univ. of Chicago Press, 1961).

[5] *Laurence Sterne: From Tristram to Yorick: An Interpretation of Tristam Shandy*, p. 40.

[6] Booth, *Rhetoric of Fiction*, pp. 224–26.

[7] Friedrich von Blanckenburg, *Versuch über den Roman*, (Leipzig and Liegnitz: Siegert, 1774; rpt. Stuttgart: Metzler; 1965), p. 265.

[8] Ibid., p. 525. In Lessing's drama the Prince says, 'O, Sie wissen es ja wohl, Conti, daß man den Künstler dann erst recht lobt, wenn man über sein Werk sein Lob vergißt." The paraphrase is pointed out by Kurt Wölfel in his essay on Blanckenburg's *Versuch* in *Deutsche Romantheorien*, ed. R. Grimm, (Frankfurt: Athenäum, 1974), p. 49.

[9] J. J. Engel, *Über Handlung, Gespräch und Erzählung*, from the *Neue Bibliothek der schönen Wissenschaften und der freyen Künste* 16 (1774; rpt. Stuttgart: Metzler, 1964), p. 245.

[10] In Blanckenburg's *Versuch*: "Jeder Mensch von einigem Nachdenken muß gemerkt haben, daß ein Vorfall einen weit stärkern Eindruck auf einen Augenzeugen macht, als auf dieselbe Person, wenn sie von einem dritten ihn erst erfährt. Scribenten von Genie, welche wissen, daß das [sic] der beste Zugang zum Herzen ist, stellen jedes Ding so vor, als ob es vor unsern Augen vorgienge, und verwandeln uns gleichsam aus Lesern und Zuhörern in Zuschauer. Ein geschickter Scribent verbirgt sich und laßt nur [sic] seine Personen sehen; mit einem Wort, *alles wird dramatisch, so sehr es nur immer möglich ist*" (pp. 449–500).

[11] Hippel quotes with obvious agreement his father's view, "daß einem Sonntagskinde ein Volk aus der Sprache recht aus dem Grunde kennen zu lernen weit leichter wäre, als aus allen Historienbüchern, in die der Geschichtsschreiber jederzeit seine eigne Geschichte, seine eigne Denkart und überhaupt sein eignes Ich zu verwickeln und zu verweben pflegt" (XII, 43).

[12] Joseph Brodsky has recently written, "A humble man may also hope that the cumulative effect of many personal perspectives, of many stories told the way it was, may in the end amount to historical truth." (*Times Literary Supplement*, May 17, 1985, pp. 543–44). Hippel might well have approved of this as an answer to his question, "Was ist Wahrheit?"

[13] Victor Lange, "Erzählformen im Roman des achtzehnten Jahrhunderts," *Anglia*, 76 (1958), 140, 141.

[14] For Uncle Toby's tolerance, see *Tristram Shandy*, II, xii, 113. It is interesting, in considering the role of documents in the *Lebensläufe*, to conjecture on just how much of the work Hippel originally conceived as *Beilagen*. In his first reference to it Hippel calls the work *Lebensläufe* etc. "mit Beilagen A.B.C.D.E.F.G.H." See his letter to Scheffner written at the end of July 1775 (XIV, 4).

[15] Such comments on the nobility make it clear why Hippel was so anxious to preserve his anonymity. As he wrote to Grot, a friend in St. Petersburg, on 21 March 1792, "In gewissen Fällen, und besonders wenn Schriftsteller in Aemtern sind, die in außerordentlichen Connexionen mit Menschen stehen, die nicht gleich denken, ist die Anonymität eine herrliche und fast nothwendige Sache," (XII, 224). Hippel was more direct in an earlier letter to Scheffner: "Es ist doch gut, daß ich Welt unbekannt und Gott bekannt als Autor walle. Was hätte ich sonst für Bücklinge zu machen—wie mich zu krümmen und gerad zu halten," *Briefe an und von J. G. Scheffner,* ed. Artur Warda, (Munich: Duncker & Humblot, 1918) I, 293. The letter is dated 17 December 1788.

[16] Compare Sophie Becker's diary entries in *Vor hundert Jahren*: the son of *Kanzler* Korff said that "Unter dem hohen Adel, welchen die Reichsgrafen und die Oberräte bilden, soll [. . .] ein unerträglicher Stolz herrschen" (13). "Der hiesige Bürger ist selbst an seiner Erniedrigung schuld. Die Prediger kommen zu einem Grafen nie ohne Kragen und Mantel, ihre Frauen küssen der gnädigen Frau die Hand und Schürze" (p. 14).

[17] See Hippel's letter to Scheffner, 26 March 1778, "Es gibt wahrlich in der Welt zweierlei *Liebe*, wovon die eine ihr Brautbette auf dem Kirchhofe findet. Diese ist nicht für diese Welt. Die andere—ach! die hat so viel Subdivisiones, daß mir drüber der Kopf schwindelt" (XIV, 90–91). See also F. J. Schneider, *Theodor Gottlieb von Hippel in den Jahren von 1741 bis 1781 und die erste Epoche seiner literarischen Tätigkeit,* pp. 106–07.

[18] Gervinus says that it was Hippel's maxim and practice, "das Selbstangeschaute unmittelbar darzustellen," *Geschichte der poetischen National-Literarur,* V, 686. Hippel's ideal is mimesis in the original meaning of the word (a copying out of the characters' very words) as opposed to diegesis (in which the narrator restates the events in his own words). See Gérard Genette, *Narrative Discourse,* trans. Jane E. Lewin (Ithaca, NY: Cornell Univ. Press, 1980), and Seymour Chatman, *Story and Discourse* (Ithaca and London: Cornell Univ. Press, 1978).

4

Kant and the Use of Documents in the *Lebensläufe*

1. Documents in Hippel's Works.
In its use of invented documents, Hippel's *Lebensläufe* becomes less a novel and more a history. Since, however, narrators are for Hippel as suspect in fiction as in history, perhaps it is more accurate to say that the *Lebensläufe* becomes not a history but an encyclopedic collection of raw materials (such as diaries, letters, and confessions) arranged around the hero's autobiography.

Above and beyond these invented documents, however, is a second layer of documentation, one that Hippel worked into the novel in a way that shows clearly how deep his concern was to avoid engaging in any falsification: for Hippel quoted not only from invented documents, he also took his notes from conversation, lectures, and judge's bench, and worked them into a first draft. This was his method in all his works, not just the *Lebensläufe*. He passed the manuscript around to a select group of friends for them to make their additions and criticisms. Hippel always had the final word as to what went into the work, but most of Hippel's works can still be considered to be to some extent the product of a collective.[1] Two examples illustrate this point. In Hippel's biography the assertion is made that numbers 3, 6, and 9 of the *Freymäurerreden* were not by Hippel; later, *Stadtsrath* Jensch, a friend of Hippel's, asserted that he was the author of many passages in Hippel's work on the improvement of women.[2] Probably many of the apercus strewn throughout Hippel's works are not by Hippel at all, but were overheard by him in conversation.[3]

There may be many documents relating to Hippel's life that he rewrote and presented in the *Lebensläufe*. One of the figures is based at least in part on Hippel's sister-in-law. As he was working on the last volume Hippel wrote to Scheffner on 20 May 1781, "Meine Schwester hat mich in eine gewisse ländliche ädelsanfte Empfindung zurückgestimmt, wo ich mich wie in der Dämmerung fühle. - Mit dem lieben Tage! - Ich brauchte sie just in meinem Roman. Sie mußte sitzen, ohne daß sie es wußte, daß sie saß" (XIV, 218, letter of 20 May 1781).

It is likely that Alexander's relationship with Mine is based on Hippel's life as well. Schneider maintained that Hippel's relationship with von Schrötter's daughter was probably the basis of the Alexander-Mine episode in the *Lebensläufe*, and suggested that Mine's letters in the novel may be based on letters sent to Hippel by von Schrötter's daughter.[4]

It is, however, impossible to confirm such speculations, for the primary documents apparently have been destroyed. After Hippel's death, his friends found in his papers fragments of conversations he had had with them. Hippel, they discovered, had the habit of jotting down remarks he thought interesting, complete with the date and name of his conversation partner. Though it should not be forgotten that Hippel was chief of police as well as mayor, these notes were probably intended as nothing more than raw material for future works. Hippel's friends destroyed most of the notes, and much of what survived their anger has since been lost.[5]

Even during Hippel's lifetime it was argued (not, of course, on the basis of documents, but rather because of alleged stylistic traits) that Lenz, Lichtenberg, or Leisewitz authored various works of Hippel. On Lenz: Schlichtegroll quotes from the *Intelligenz Blatt der Allgemeinen Litteratur Zeitung* 1791, St. 46, "man versicherte mir zwar, Lenz, der Verf. des *Menoza*, sey auch Vf. der *Lebensläufe*, und der Beweis dafür sey das Zeugniß eines wahrhaften Mannes, dem *Lenz* selbst einige Bogen aus diesem meinem Lieblingsbuch in Mscpt. vorgelesen habe; allein andere widersprechen dieser Versicherung" (p. 443). On Lichtenberg: see Hippel's letter to Scheffner of 6 June 1777

(XIV, 50), "Herr *Lavater* hat dem Herrn Professor *Lichtenberg* als Verfasser des Buches Über die Ehe viel Ehre bewiesen, Stellen heraus genommen und unter eine *Lichtenbergs* gesetzt. – So was, liebster Freund, ist mir mehr werth, als Alles. –" Boroswki, later the author of Kant's biography, notes that Hippel "schwieg selbst da, da man sein Buch: Ueber d. Ehe Jahre lang auf die Rechnung des vortreflichsten originellen Kopfs Deutschlands, Lichtenbergs, nämlich, setzte."[6] On Leisewitz: Hippel, in his letter to Scheffner of 12 September 1779 (XIV, 155), refers to a review of the *Lebensläufe* and says, "Die eine Recension hatt' ich schon gelesen. Herr *Leisewitz* hat im folgenden Stück dies Werklein gänzlich von sich abgelehnt unter den Ausdrücken: daß er zu viel Liebe zur Religionen und Tugend hätte u. Darüber verzage nicht."[7]

2. Kant and the *Lebensläufe*.

Today it is possible only in Kant's case to see to any degree just how much Hippel made use of the words and thoughts of his friends. For as it happens, one of the documents Hippel quoted from was a notebook containing lectures delivered by Kant. It has long been known that there are Kantian passages in Hippel's novel.[8] They were first pointed out in an anonymous article in the *Allgemeine deutsche Bibliothek*.[9] The reviewer says that the anonymous author of the *Lebensläufe* has borrowed heavily from Kant's lectures on anthropology and metaphysics "ohne für einen Abschreiber gehalten zu werden." Since Kant's lectures had, of course, not yet appeared in print, it followed, according to the reviewer, that whoever wrote the *Lebensläufe* must have attended Kant's lectures.[10] Shortly thereafter, on 10 April 1781, Hippel wrote to Scheffner, "Welch ein Narr müßt ich seyn, leugnen zu wollen, daß Kant mein Lehrer gewesen. Allein den Geist dieses Buch zu kennen, ist genug, um einzusehen, daß der Herr *Gla-* mir zu viel thut. Was für ein gefährlicher Mensch ist der? Das *Kant*sche Werk kommt diese Ostern gewiß heraus, und da wird sich denn auch von dieser Seite zeigen, ob ich solch eine hämische Behandlung verdient habe. – Als ob es auf Stellung bey Definitionen, als ob es auf Definitionen selbst ankäme! als ob nicht nur ein Gott und eine Wahrheit sey, und als ob in meinem ganzen Buche nicht eitel praktische hausbackene Philosophie wäre!" (XIV, 212-13).[11]

Shortly after Hippel's death in 1796, with his authorship still a secret to all but a few, some began to suspect on the basis of Kantian passages in the *Lebensläufe* that Kant himself was the author of Hippel's work. G. Flemming, a student in Göttingen, announced his "Entdeckung. *Kant* - Verfasser der *Lebensläufe nach aufsteigender Linie*; der *Kreuz- und Queerzüge* [sic] *des Ritters von A-Z*; des Buches über die Ehe und eines andern über die bürgerliche Verbesserung der Weiber."[12] Flemming, however, never kept his promise to prove his assertion at a later date.

For this extreme position was modified after a few months by an author who is probably J. A. Bergk, who later was to deal with Hippel in his work, *Die Kunst, Bücher zu lesen* (Jena, 1799); Bergk was also the editor of early editions of Kant's anthropological writings, parts of which he published in the 1830s under the pseudonym of Fr. Chr. Starke.[13] Borowski refers to him as "Hr. B—gk aus Zeitz" and gives as source the "Allg. Lit. Anz. Oct. 796. Nu. 30 S. 328" (Borowski, p. 58). "B—gk" argues that Kant had written not the whole of the *Lebensläufe* but only its philosophical parts.

Such speculation led Kant to publish his "Erklärung wegen der v. Hippelschen Autorschaft" in the *Allgemeine Litteratur Anzeiger*, 1797, Nr. 2, pp. 15-6, and in the *Allgemeine Litteratur Zeitung*, 1797, Nr. 9, p. 72:

> Oeffentlich aufgefordert, zuerst von Hn. M. Flemming, nachher durch den Allg. Lit. Anz. 796. N. 30. S. 327 u. f. wegen der Zumuthung, ich sey der Verfasser der anonymischen dem sel. v. Hippel zugeschriebenen Werke, des Buchs über die Ehe und der Lebensläufe nach aufsteigender Linie, erkläre ich hiemit, daß ich nicht der Verfasser derselben, weder allein noch in Gemeinschaft mit ihm sey.
>
> Wie es aber zugegangen, ohne hiezu ein Plagiat annehmen zu dürfen, daß doch in diesen ihm zugeschriebenen Werken so manche Stellen buchstäblich mit denen überein kommen, die viel später in meinen auf die Critik der reinen Vernunft folgenden Schriften, als meine eigene Gedanken noch zu seiner Lebenszeit vorgetragen werden können; das

läßt sich auch ohne jene den sel. Mann beleidigende und auch ohne meine Ansprüche schmälernde Hypothese gar wohl begreiflich machen.

Sie sind nach und nach fragmentarisch in die Hefte meiner Zuhörer geflossen, mit Hinsicht von meiner Seite auf ein System, was ich in meinem Kopfe trug aber nur allererst in dem Zeitraum von 1770 bis 1780 zu Stande bringen konnte. Diese Hefte, welche Bruchstücke, die unter andern meinen Vorlesungen der Logik, der Moral, des Naturrechts u. s. w. vornämlich denen der Anthropologie, wie es ganz gewöhnlich bei einem freien Vortrage des Lehrers zugeht, sehr mangelhaft nachgeschrieben worden, fielen in des sel. Mannes Hände und wurden in der Folge von ihm gesucht, weil sie großentheils neben trocknen Wissenschaften auch manches Populäre enthielten, was der aufgeweckte Mann in seine launigten Schriften mischen konnte, und so, durch die Zuthat des Nachgedachten dem Gerichte des Witzes einen schärferen Geschmack zu geben, die Absicht haben mochte.

Nun kann, was in Vorlesungen als öffentlich zu Kauf gestellte Waare feil stehet, von einem Jeden benuzt werden, ohne sich deshalb nach dem Fabrikanten erkundigen zu dürfen, und so konnte mein Freund, der sich nie mit der Philosophie sonderlich befaßt hat, jene ihm in die Hände gekommene Materialien gleichsam zur Würze für den Gaumen seiner Leser brauchen, ohne diesen Rechenschaft geben zu dürfen, ob sie aus des Nachbars Garten oder aus Indien oder aus seinem eigenen genommen wären. Daraus ist auch erklärlich, wie dieser mein vertrauter Freund in unserm engen Umgange doch über seine Schriftstellerei in jenen Büchern nie ein Wort fallen lassen, ich selber aber aus gewöhnlicher Delikatesse ihn nie auf diese Materie bringen mögen. So löset sich das Räthsel auf und einem jeden wird das Seine zu Theil.

Königsberg, den 6. Decbr. 1796.

                                                  Immanuel Kant.

Kant's letter effectively ended the question of plagiarism.[14] However, Kant's opinion that Hippel never particularly concerned himself with philosophy must be put in perspective.[15] Certainly it is true that Hippel had difficulty penetrating Kant's philosophical language, and Hippel often criticized Kant for weakening the practical impact of his philosophy by being too abstract in his thought and expression. Thus Hippel wrote to Scheffner on 17 July 1781: "Haben Sie schon *Kants* Kritik der reinen Vernunft gelesen? Eine Dunkelheit darin, die ihres gleichen sucht! – Mir ist's zu hoch, und so etwas auszuklauben, was kann es helfen?" (XIV, 223). But not all of Kant's works were so difficult for Hippel. In his autobiography he wrote of his student years, "Ich studirte Mathematik und Philosophie mit außerordentlichem Eifer [. . . .] *Kant* fing damals erst zu lesen an, und ich besuchte seine Schule nicht eher, als bis ich den ganzen sogenannten philosophischen Cursus bey *Buck* gehört hatte."[16] And from his sickbed in Danzig Hippel wrote to Kant on 5 December 1793: "Wie sehr ich mich nach Ihrem lehrreichen Umgang sehne, der mir, das wissen Sie selbst, mehr gilt als Alles was Königsberg hat, darf ich Ihnen nicht sagen, da Sie überzeugt sind, wie innigst ich Sie verehre. [. . . .] Die Religion innerhalb der Grentzen der bloßen Vernunft, habe ich mir in meiner Kranckheit vorlesen lassen, und tausendmahl gewünscht, daß man jezt in Franckreich dieses Buch lesen möchte, welches hier in Danzig: den Namen Kants Religion, führt. Der unsterbliche Nahme: Immanuel Kant darf wahrlich kein Bedenken tragen dieser Schrift vorgesezt zu seyn, die sehr viel Gutes stiften kann und wird."[17]

Probably Schlichtegroll's view is the most satisfactory summary of the relationship between Kant and Hippel. After observing that Hippel had first "ernstlich die *Wolf*ische Philosophie studirt," he continued, "Als die Kantischen Schriften, die eine Revolution in der Philosophie bewirkt haben, erschienen, studirte er auch diese, und verschmolz die darinn vorgetragenen Ideen mit den schon in ihm durch seine mannichfaltige Lectüre und sein originelles Selbstdenken vorräthigen." Schlichtegroll added, "Diese Hauptsätze der Kantischen Philosophie scheinen in der That seine Ueberzeugung gewesen zu seyn; aber, wie schon erinnert ist, nicht ängstlich nachgesagt und nachgedacht, sondern mit Freyheit, und amalgamiert mit seinen vielen eignen Vorstellungen."[18]

Hippel's purpose in quoting from Kant is touched on by Kant himself in his "Erklärung" of 6 December 1796. Hippel, Kant said, probably wanted to add the spice of thought (or afterthought) to the main course of wit in his whimsical writings. Hippel's intent was to whet the appetite of the reader, awaken his attention by means of mixing together the more popular aspects of Kant's philosophy with the products of Hippel's fancy.

Kant implied that Hippel's purpose was to divert the reader with unexpected philosophical passages. Hippel would probably have emphasized more the intent to instruct the reader, to educate him by presenting philosophy in a language more easily understood than Kant's. In his letter to Scheffner of 10 April 1781, Hippel said the *Lebensläufe* is full of "praktische hausbackene Philosophie," and this expresses his concern for the practical aspect of his presentation of Kant. As Hippel wrote later in the *Kreuz- und Querzüge*, "Der Dichter, ein höherer Chemicus der Seelen, verwandelt die tieffste, abstracteste Philosophie in die Sprache des gemeinen Lebens. Durch diese höhere Seelenchemie findet der Dichter zuweilen den Stein der Weisen, den die Philosophie immer sucht" (VIII, 261).

Certainly, as Borowski said, Hippel's intent was not to plagiarize but to popularize. Hippel, he asserted, obviously felt "das Bestreben, so manche aus der Schule unsers *Kant* und aus den Heften desselben aufgefaßte Ideen mehr zu popularisiren und auf diese Art weiter zu verbreiten, als sie damals noch, da *Kant* sein System und viele dahin einschlagende Sentiments nur noch in seinem Kopf herumtrug und nur in seinen Vorlesungen einen Vorschmack von demjenigen gab, was er dem Publikum in der Folge als Nahrung für Denker geben wollte, verbreitet waren. Auf diesen eben jezt angeführten Zweck—das sagte er mir einmal in einer mir denkwürdig bleibenden Abendstunde, wirkte er in seinen Lebensläufen hin, ohne es je ahnen zu können oder zu dürfen, daß dieses Bestreben ihm einst den Vorwurf eines Plagiats zuziehen könnte."[19] Borowski rightly emphasizes the point that before publication of the *Kritik der reinen Vernunft* Hippel made Kant's ideas accessible to a larger audience than Kant was reaching in his lectures.

One of Hippel's particular concerns was to show the agreement of Kant's philosophy with the Bible.[20] Hippel believed that there was no antagonism between the two because Christianity was fundamentally a religion based on reason.[21] In Hippel's view, Christ had imposed no duties that reason itself had not dictated; "so stimmet zwar Vernunft und Offenbarung darin überein, wenn sie vorschreiben: Handle aus Achtung gegen das allgemeine Gesetz, wie H. *Kant* und mit ihm seine Schüler sich ausdrücken, oder: Thue alles um Gottes willen, wie die Schrift saget; allein die Religion setzt gerades Weges hinzu, was die Vernunft als höchst wahrscheinlich angiebet: 'Die Zweifel, die dir aufsteigen, wird dir die Künftigkeit lösen' " (*Biographie*, p. 120).

The only major difference Hippel saw between the two was that Kant's thought was expressed in a system, unlike the philosophy of Jesus. "Die Absicht des Stifters der christlichen Religion war nun zwar freilich nicht, ein System (wie mein Freund *Kant*) aus der Vernunft vorzutragen" (Ibid., pp. 167–68). But this is all to the advantage of Christianity, for systematization in Hippel's view works against the practicality and durability of a philosophy. As Hippel wrote to Scheffner on 10 December 1780, "Christus hat die Religion sehr verständlich als eine vernünftige lautere Milch zurückgelassen. Daß sie so verdunkelt und verkünstelt worden, dafür kann die Lehre Christi nicht. Gott kann zu Menschen nicht anders sprechen, als durch Handlungen, und so kann ihm auch nur geantwortet werden" (XIV, 202). Indeed, the Bible's lack of system is one of its advantages. "Wie viel Weisheit muß in der Lehre Jesu liegen, da bey aller ihrer Einfachheit sie sich doch zu allen Vernunftanstrengungen paßt!" (Schlichtegroll, p. 162). Any systematized philosophy is, in contrast, condemned to lose its effectiveness in the course of time. "Die *Kantische* Philosophie hat ein gleiches Schicksal erfahren [. . .]" (Ibid.).

Hippel's popularization of Kant therefore takes the form of de-systematizing Kant's philosophy and thereby making it easier to understand. In its present form, Hippel says in reference to the *Kritik der reinen Vernunft*, this is not possible: "Gott gebe, daß dies Buch zum moralischen Leben viel beitrage, zur Volksverbesserung wird es schwerlich, wenigstens in *dem* Kleide nicht gereichen," he writes to Scheffner on 27 May 1785 (XIV, 357–58). Hippel's corrective tendency towards popularization and de-systematization is evident in his most extensive quotation from Kant. In all that has been written on Hippel and Kant it is surprising that so far there has been no comparison of texts showing just where Hippel borrowed from Kant and how much he borrowed. Though it has long been obvious that the examination scene in volume II of the *Lebensläufe* is full of Kantian views and that the figure of "Se. Spektabilität," the "Professor Großvater," is based on Kant, there has never been a line-by-line comparison of this scene with any passages in Kant's work. This is an understandable lapse in earlier scholarship, for it was only in 1961 that Kant's *Vorlesungen über philosophische Enzyklopädie* was published.[22]

This text, it can now be shown in detail, is the source used by Hippel when he wrote the examination scene.[23] The importance of Kant's text for Hippel is twofold. First the sheer amount of material borrowed by Hippel is impressive. Even some of the illustrative details, which one would naively assume to have been Hippel's contribution, are taken over from Kant. Thus Hippel's implicit comparison of philosophy with alchemy ("Sie macht Gold," p. 143, all references to the Appendix) was probably suggested by Kant's example of how *Erkenntnis* can be made clear ("z. E. wenn man vom Golde sagt, daß es nicht rostet"). That one can speak with someone and later not be able to remember what the person was wearing, and the example of *Taschenspielerei* in the discussion of error (p. 144), are, surprising though it may seem, observations made by Kant himself. And it is only a short step from Kant's definition of error as a "Mischung" of sense perception with understanding to Hippel's analogy between the senses and understanding on the one hand and wine and water on the other ("Wer hat Wein ohne Wasser getrunken?" p. 143). The extensive nature of Hippel's borrowing supports the view that documentation, the use of historical raw material (here in the form of unpublished lecture notes) is more important for Hippel than originality.

Kant's text, however, is important for Hippel also in a second sense. Hippel not only borrowed much, he also borrowed selectively. Hippel did not choose his text haphazardly, nor did he in all places copy it slavishly. Hippel's additions and changes show him to be as it were engaged in a discussion with Kant, agreeing with him for the most part but also disagreeing at times.

When in agreement with Kant, Hippel sought to clarify Kant's text by expanding it and by adding passages from the Bible that were familiar to his audience. The first example of this is to be found in the distinction between natural and artificial philosophers (p. 134). In order to illustrate this distinction Hippel makes three Biblical references. It can be said of artificial philosophers that knowledge puffs them up.[24] On the other hand, the natural philosopher does not leave one stone upon another in his search for truth (Matthew 24: 2). Because of this the natural philosopher is able to find the way to truth, and to life, and can say to his disciples, "because I live ye shall live also" (John 14: 19).

In a second passage (p. 137) Hippel supports Kant's attack on spirit seers by comparing them to men who wait for something they have not heard, nor perceived by the ear, neither hath the eye seen (Isaiah 64: 4). Later (p. 140) Kant criticizes arguments that seek to explain natural events by reference to God, and Hippel quotes two passages from the Bible that support this injunction against the misuse of God's name, "Thou shalt not take the name of the Lord thy God in vain" (Exodus 20: 7), and those who seek to explain all things through God must be told, "let your communication be, Yea, yea; Nay, nay; for whatsoever is more than these cometh of evil," (Matthew 5: 37). When Kant praises oral over written presentation (p. 146), Hippel introduces his comments with a reference to Romans 10: 17, that "faith cometh by hearing, and hearing by the word of God." The intent of all these examples is clear: as Hippel at one point indicates ("damit ich mich deutlich und christlich ausdrücke," p. 140), when he wants to express a Kantian concept clearly, he often resorts to Biblical language or images.

The major disagreement Hippel has with Kant's text is not a matter of content but one of style. In Hippel's view Kant's philosophy could be useful to humanity if it were expressed clearly and non-systematically. Though Kant himself preferred philosophy that served the interests of mankind to what could be called school philosophy, Hippel hints in the opening passage of his quotation that Kant's philosophy too could be considered scholastic. When Hippel contrasts *Kunst-* and *Naturphilosophie*, he is in obvious agreement with Kant. Though these terms are Hippel's, not Kant's, they both attack *Kunstphilosophie* as sterile, dogmatic, a matter of rules and not a guide for action. Even the philosophers themselves do not live according to their stated beliefs. And Hippel and Kant agree in their praise of the *Naturphilosoph*, who does not possess philosophy but rather philosophizes, does not impart knowledge but teaches a method of reflection and inquiry. But whereas Kant half admits that he belongs to the *Kunstphilosophen* ("Was uns anbelangt, wir verstehen Scherz" p. 132), Hippel is careful to maintain his distance from this group (" 'die Herren werden doch wohl Spaß verstehen?' "). In Hippel's text there is no talk of "wir."

Thus Hippel establishes a perspective slightly different from that of Kant. Kant's views, if popularized, can serve as a *Naturphilosophie*, a philosophy with practical application to everyday life. But whenever Kant becomes a difficult, systematic *Kunstphilosoph*, Hippel feels free to criticize, for example, Kant's style (p. 136). Though Hippel quotes many of Kant's justifications he still opposes long prolegomena. Hippel uses a Biblical reference to support his own position and to criticize Kant. The passage from the 37th Psalm that Hippel alludes to is important not for what it says but for its direct, brief, simple style, so in contrast to Kant's. Hippel also implicitly criticizes the systematic approach of Kant by making his own approach decidedly unsystematic. He follows Kant's general order, but feels free to jump from topic to topic with little or no warning. In the discussion of metaphysics (pp. 147–48), Hippel abridges Kant's argument to such an extent that it becomes nearly unintelligible to anyone not already familiar with Kant's philosophy. Hippel's critical intent is hinted at in his interjection, "Wir waren im Begriff, uns recht viel Metaphysik ins Auge zu streuen [. . . .]" The mosquito that pesters the professor in his discussion of *Vernünftelei* underscores Hippel's view that it is the professor himself who is guilty of this flaw he attacks in others.

In addition to pure popularization and criticism there is a third aspect of Kant's text that is important for Hippel. For Hippel sometimes uses the lecture notes as a starting point for his own observations. Furthermore, where Hippel goes beyond Kant's views to make his own contribution, Hippel, with remarkable consistency, works out the implications of Kant's positions for the theory of the novel.

One of Hippel's fundamental concerns in writing the *Lebensläufe* is to present *das gemeine Leben*, and the very first addition he makes to Kant's text asserts, "Die Fenster im Auditorio, wo natürliche Weisheit gelehrt wird, gehen alle ins gemeine Leben." The view that philosophy should have practical benefits for daily life is implied in Kant, but it is significant that it is just this aspect of Kant that appeals to Hippel and that he develops. The essential difference, Hippel says, between *Kunst-* and *Naturphilosophie* is that the former remains closed in itself, is a matter for academics alone, whereas the latter is immediately applicable to ordinary life. Hippel's intent in quoting so much from Kant is to save a *Naturphilosophie* from becoming a *Kunstphilosophie* through the difficulty of Kant's philosophical language.

It is only natural, then, for Hippel (p. 133) to make a transition from *Naturphilosophie* ("der Mann ist ein Philosoph natürlicher Art") to a discussion of bookwriting ("dies Buch hat Geist und Leben, allein alsdann denkt man, der Verfasser, ein Philosoph der besagten Art, hat es geschrieben"). Hippel lays Kant aside for a moment in order to examine the relationship between author and work, saying that the type of book reflects the type of author-philosopher. By implication Hippel's novel itself becomes one of the themes of the book here, in the sense that the intent of a work, the effect hoped for by its author, becomes itself a subject of discussion. Hippel himself is a "Philosoph der besagten Art," and by propagating *Naturphilosophie* the *Lebensläufe* has some of the "Geist und Leben" of its author.

A further implication of this relationship between author and book is that the reader should be able to make deductions about the author from the book. The emphasis here is not, however, on the primacy of the author over his book, but rather on the transparency of the book itself. The book should refer out from itself, it should encourage the reader to see through the work to the author and thus to something that is real and in the world and not just a literary fiction. What is important as the object of investigation is not dry, bookish knowledge, nor even the author.[25] Rather, the work should encourage the reader to become active, as the conclusion to Hippel's digression shows: "Allein in Wahrheit, man sollt auf ein lebendiges Erkenntnis dringen [. . .]" (p. 134).

Hippel returns to the theme of an author's relationship to his work in a later passage (p. 146). Hippel is in complete agreement with Kant that the reader should attempt to grasp the soul of the book he is reading. "Man muß beim Lesen die Seele des Buches suchen und der Idee nachspüren, welche der Autor gehabt hat, alsdann hat man das Buch ganz." That is to say, the reader should inquire not after the author's identity, but rather the author's idea in writing the book. It would be a misreading of Hippel (and Kant) to see in these passages an apology for the primacy of the *Ich* of the author or the narrator over the work.

Hippel also finds support for his preference for the spoken over the written word in Kant. Hippel writes (p. 146) "Ein mündlicher Vortrag verrät die Art zu denken. Sie zeigt den Lehrer unangekleidet. Beim Hören denkt man immer mehr als beim Lesen." Hippel writes in a similar vein to Scheffner, "Das Schreiben hat wahrlich was profanes an sich. Gott hat alles gesagt, die Engel schreiben nicht, und welch ein Unterschied, mein theuerster brüderlicher Freund! zwischen sagen und schreiben! [. . . .] Schreiben ist eine Unvollkommenheit, ein Nothfall, ein - kurz, was so groß wie unsere Kunst ist, muß gesagt werden," letter of 26 March 1778 (XIV, 89).

The spoken word is more thought-provoking than the written word, it is livelier and closer to the event reported. The conclusion Hippel draws from this in writing his novel is that the written word should be made to imitate as closely as possible the spoken word, thus making of the novel a collection of conversations. To paraphrase Hippel it might be said that this tendency to make the written word approach the spoken word in terms of immediacy is the soul of Hippel's book, the idea of its author.

Certainly the entire scene with *Se. Spektabilität* is constructed in accordance with this idea. Alexander interrupts, for example (p. 135), his account of the entrance examination to remind the reader that the conversation is like a picnic to which each guest contributes his own share, with no order imposed on it by a chef. For: "Ich bemühe mich auch hier, Lebensläufer zu sein, und diese Abschrift ist dem Original ähnlich. - Wir fielen von einem aufs andere. Wir scheitelten die Haare nicht. Würde ich nicht einen Roman schreiben, wenn ich nicht auch von einem aufs andere fallen und die Haare scheiteln sollte? Ein Roman! fern sei er von mir! - " The copy is, of course, not similar to the original document, Kant's lecture, but is similar in its disorderliness and absence of novelistic fastidiousness to the conversation from which it is supposedly taken. Where his document is insufficiently lively, Hippel is by no means averse to rearranging it to make it conform more closely to conversational style.[26]

But perhaps the most important part of Kant's text is for Hippel the discussion of inner and outer senses and the definitions of truth, error and appearance. Kant distinguishes between inner and outer senses, each of which has its own proper objects of knowledge. According to Kant, of course, man cannot know noumena, or things in themselves. Thus the scope of the outer senses is limited. The inner senses, on the other hand, provide accurate and reliable information about man's soul. God alone can know objects immediately, for they are contained within him; Kant here says we can know only ourselves in this fashion.

This is potentially of great importance for Hippel, since it justifies the individual's concern with his soul as the only object immediately knowable to him. This passage of Kant's provides a philosophical basis for Hippel's novel, for Kant here restricts the object of immediate and infallible human knowledge, and thus also of the omniscient narrator, to the condition of his own soul. Only the autobiographical narrator has even the possibility of being omniscient.

It can be argued that Hippel was fortunate in the text he chose. For in his published works Kant was to hold a position different from the one held in the lecture notes used by Hippel. In all his published works that touched on *Seelenlehre* Kant was to say that the soul cannot be known through introspection, that the *appearances* of the soul can be known, but the *Seelenlehre* itself is empty. In the *Kritik der reinen Vernunft*, for example, Kant argues that in and of itself the soul is as unknowable as the noumena; "diese Vorstellung," Kant says, speaking of the *Ich*, has "keinen Inhalt."[27] Hippel, in using the *Vorlesungen über philosophische Enzyklopädie*, finds one of the passages in Kant that seems to leave the door to self-knowledge open.[28]

Thus it is understandable why Hippel departs from Kant's text (p. 137) to praise *Gnothi sauton*. To be sure, Hippel is also careful to avoid seeming to endorse mystical "Geisterseherei," and his language is here like that of Kant's *Träume eines Geistersehers*. But afterwards he returns to the theme with the words that, though God has all things before him *originaliter*, men can know only themselves in this fashion. And just before the passage on metaphysics (p. 147) Hippel again departs from Kant to praise self-knowledge: "Wohl dem, der sich von allem entkleiden kann, was nicht er selbst (das letzte Hemde nicht ausgenommen) ist! [. . . .] wohl dem, der Wesen vom Schein, Schatten vom Licht absondert [. . . .]"

Hippel is well aware of the difficulty of knowing oneself. Even if the Self is the only object which man can know the way God knows all things, the emphasis must be placed on "can." There is a *possibility* that man can be truthful about himself to himself, but it is no more than a possibility. Self-love of course stands in the way, but in Kant's text the real enemies of truth are *Irrtum* and *Schein*. For Kant argues (p. 143) that *Verstand* plays as large a role when it is misled by error (and of course by *Schein*) as it does in determining the truth. Kant on the one hand thus opens up the realm in which truth and omniscience are possible, namely, the realm of self-knowledge, but on the other hand he shows how difficult it is, even in this realm, to distinguish truth from *Irrtum* and *Schein*.

If, as Kant had shown, truth is so hard to distinguish from error (or from mere appearance, or even from probability), then Hippel's whole endeavor is called into question. Hippel in fact comes across the very question in Kant's lecture that he had asked in his letter to Scheffner, "*Was ist Wahrheit?* Es gibt viele Fragen, welche deswegen nicht beantwortet werden können, weil sie ganz ungestimmt sind" (p. 141). Hippel knows no better answer in his paraphrase: "Wenn also gefragt wird, was ist Wahrheit? reine gediegene Wahrheit? so kann man nicht besser drauf antworten, als: Wahrheit ist Wahrheit."[29]

One final difference between Kant's text and Hippel's makes it clear that Hippel, far from merely copying Kant, was well aware of the implications of Kant's teaching for the novel. For when Kant writes, "Zum Irren gehört ebensogut Verstand als zur Wahrheit" (p. 143), Hippel repeats this view with the parenthetical remark, "(Heil mir und meinem Buche!)."

In the lecture notes used by Hippel Kant's specific utterances on the novel are not very adventurous. Thus Kant says that "Romane, wo man Sentiments findet und Komödien von Shakespeares Art, wo der Verfasser verborgene Winkel im Menschen entdeckt, Charakter schildert etc., sind nützlich".[30] Hippel does not even bother to quote this passage. Instead, Hippel develops his own views whenever the lecture touches—even remotely—on problems that he too had become familiar with in the course of writing a novel. Hippel was asking some of the same questions as Kant: how is it possible to present truth, and what kinds of knowledge are infallible? Hippel's responses show him to have been alert to the implications in Kant for the theory of the novel, particularly problems in the relationship between author and work, problems in distinguishing truth from error and mere appearance.

Hippel finds in Kant confirmation of his skepticism vis-à-vis the omniscient narrator, for Kant argues in this lecture that we can have immediate knowledge only of ourselves. This agrees with Hippel's rejection of the narrator who tells more than he himself has experienced. Kant provides a philosophical basis for Alexander's reluctance to narrate events that concern others and for his preference to let them talk for themselves. Since one can know only his own soul, all truth that can possibly be perceived is to be found in the endeavor to know oneself. Otherwise one can be sure only of tautologies that they are true (see the discussion of the *principium contradictionis* on p. 142).

Thus Hippel attempts to avoid the inevitable falsification of reality when narrated by an omniscient *Ich* in three ways: first through the use of numerous limited narrators and through the use of documents that are historically indubitable; second by recording reality in its fullness, copying down events just as they occur without altering them through later edition; third by having the *Ich* come to know itself not through the unreliable method of introspection but by means of activity and experience in the world.

Hippel does not draw the conclusions from Kant's lecture that he could have drawn. Kant's argument here that only the self can be known immediately could be read as an invitation to solipsism on the part of the narrator. Would not the introspective narrator, who reports only on the workings of his soul, be the most honest narrator? Critics who attack Hippel's subjectivity could assert that Hippel did indeed take up this position.

But Hippel was much too conscious of the difficulty of knowing oneself to hope to arrive at truth by means of contemplation. As Hippel was later to argue in his autobiography, it is not easy really to know oneself. "Denn in der That, der Mensch liegt sich nicht so nahe, als es Leute glauben, die mit sich zwar herumspringen; allein nicht Schritt zu halten verstehen. Nosce te ipsum - ist eine philosophische Aufgabe, schwerer als zehn pythagorische Theoreme. Jeder Mensch, der über sich nachdenkt, findet einen Knauel unauflöslicher Räthsel, an die er, ohne unwahr zu werden, sich nicht wagen mag; dieß demüthiget seine Vernunft. Er findet Hang zum Eigennutz und Eigendünkel, so daß wenn er mit einem andern in Collision kömmt, er immer recht, der andere aber immer unrecht behält, und dieß demüthigt sein Herz" (Schlichtegroll, p. 232). Later in the same work Hippel expresses a view that is reminiscent of the passage from Epictetus that Sterne had made the motto for *Tristram Shandy*:

"das Mißvergnügen liegt nicht in den Gegenständen, sondern in der Art, wie man sich diese Gegenstände vorstellet und in uns selbst. Nicht auf die Sache im Ganzen, sondern auf das, was wir uns aus derselben vorzustellen eben aufgelegt sind, kommt es an [. . .]" (Ibid., p. 256).[31]

In his search for a way in which the self can know itself and speak honestly of itself, Hippel apparently distinguishes two possibilities. If one is to speak of oneself at all, one can do so either in terms of "Ich" or of "Ich selbst." We have a choice, Hippel writes, "entweder gar nicht oder nur verblümt von uns zu reden, wenn gleich wir dazu auch alle Fähigkeiten besitzen. Daß Fähigkeiten dazu gehören, wenn man das Kapitel *Ich* und das Kapitel *Ich selbst* aufschlägt, ist außer Streit," (Ibid., p. 233). Hippel is evidently making a distinction here, one that he does not elucidate. We can speculate that perhaps the *Ich* is the Self as object, seen from without, just like every other object. *Ich selbst* on the other hand is the Self as subject, egotistical, introspective. The way of *Ich selbst*, the ego's affirmation of its own subjectivity, is the way taken by what Hippel calls the genius. "Es ist gewiß, daß sogenannte Genies sich mehr als andere mit sich selbst beschäftigen. Man könnte fast ein Genie auf diese Art definieren. Die besten von ihnen reden von sich; die weniger guten suchen sich auf eine andere Art mit sich abzugeben und was zu gut zu thun, z.B. die Hofnarren" (Ibid., p. 234). The genius is the man who knows himself as he is. He may be egotistical, but he is justified in speaking of himself because he knows himself so well. That is, as long as he is in fact a genius, and not just a court jester.

But there is another way in which one can speak of oneself. It is not the genius's subjective *Ich selbst*, but rather the more modest and objective way of the *Ich*. Hippel explains, "Meine Absicht war zu bemerken, daß der Mensch, um es theils mit sich, theils mit andern nicht zu verderben, am besten thäte, es auf sein ganzes Ich nie anzulegen; das hat noch niemand von sich abgeschattet; daß er so nach nur gewisse Seiten von sich beherzige und verständige, und diese gewisse Seiten Preiß gebe; daß er sich im Handeln, d.h., in wirklicher Beschäftigung mit andern zeichne, also in einer Reisebeschreibung, in einem cursu academico, in einigen seiner Helden-, Liebes- und Staatsactionen; daß er sich wohl überzeuge, wie die Contemplation und Beschaulichkeit der geradeste Weg sey, sich zu verfehlen. Wer lange und unabläßig auf einen Ort siehet, wird am Ende nichts gewahr; es wird Dämmerung oder völlig Nacht vor unsern Augen" (Ibid., pp. 234–35). Here Hippel rejects introspection as a path to self-knowledge. One comes to know oneself only by means of activity and interaction with others. As Kant writes in the *Kritik der reinen Vernunft*, "es bleibt uns nichts übrig, als unsere Seele an dem Leitfaden der Erfahrung zu studieren."[32]

This is, of course, precisely the means by which Alexander in the *Lebensläufe* develops as a character. His education consists in seeing others in situations like the ones he himself is in, so that by observing others he is prepared when the time comes for him to become active himself. His education takes place in the course of a journey, "in einem cursu academico," in his heroic deeds in war and in his love relationships.[33]

3. Documents and the Problem of Self-Knowledge in *Tristram Shandy*

It may be instructive to compare an example of Sterne's use of a document with Hippel's. Tristram too quotes from documents in his parody of the historical pretensions of the contemporary novel. His documents are relieved of their traditional function of upholding the work's authenticity, and serve instead to usurp the line of narration. They become interesting and diverting in themselves; they are told simply for their own sake, or because Tristram or one of the other characters finds them curious. And they do indeed make up an unusual collection, but they fail (as they are meant to fail) to make the novel more believable. The reviewer of volumes III and IV of *Tristram Shandy* clearly missed the point when he wrote in the April 1761 edition of *The Critical Review* that Ernulphus's curse "bears the marks of authenticity," for the presentation of the curse in its entirety, with the original Latin text on facing pages, is so exaggerated and pedantic in its authenticity that its effect is not to be more believable but rather to call attention to itself as a document.[34] The self-referential gesture undermines the illusion of authenticity, most especially so when it ostentatiously emphasizes its own claim to being an authentic document.

But some of the documents in *Tristram Shandy* have more than merely parodistic function, and, as in the *Lebensläufe*, deal with the theme of self-knowledge. The opening quotation from Epictetus shows Sterne's awareness of the dilemma, and the entire work can be read as an illustration of the problem of subjectivity: each character is ruled by his hobby-horse, which distorts the perception of reality by relentlessly interpreting the world from a single narrow perspective. Tristram himself is a prime example of this willful, subjective point of view, as he announces at the outset his intention to ignore Horace's narrative rules, "for in writing what I have set about, I shall confine myself neither to his rules, nor to any man's rules that ever lived" (I, iv, 8).

One of Sterne's documents is in some respects remarkably similar to the Kant lecture used by Hippel. It is Yorick's sermon, which is read aloud by Trim in II, xvii, 120–43. It might seem at first that this is a completely fictional document. In fact, however, the sermon was actually published under Sterne's name in 1750. Following its appearance in *Tristram Shandy* it was printed again, now for the third time, in the collected *Sermons of Mr. Yorick* in 1766. Thus the sermon was in fact already well into its career in print at the point where Toby asserts, "it does not appear that the sermon is printed, or ever likely to be" (II, xvii, 126).[35]

It is perhaps worthy of note that this sermon, itself a document, makes liberal use of the sermons of Swift, Richard Bentley, and Dr. Smith.[36] The quotations are not acknowledged, which led, as it was later to do in the case of Hippel's borrowing from Kant, to charges of plagiarism. What is of interest in the present case is the consideration that Sterne's sermon is incorporated into *Tristram Shandy* quite ostentatiously as an extraneous document, one that as it were falls whole and unchanged out of Stevinus's work on fortification, where Yorick had absent-mindedly left it, directly into "this cyclopaedia of arts and sciences" that is *Tristram Shandy* (II, xvii, 122); yet this sermon itself incorporates within itself parts of other sermons, which are worked into Sterne's (or Yorick's) sermon in such a way that they appear to be an integral part of the text. This one sermon serves as a model of two contrasting methods by which documents can be quoted.

The theme of the sermon is the problem of moral knowledge, specifically the question of whether or not the conscience is a sufficient guide in determining individual morality.[37] The conclusion reached is that a guilty conscience is indeed a reliable indication of a moral shortcoming, but that a good conscience is no guarantee of moral purity. For a good conscience means little if a man is not religious as well, since religion provides the believer with a means of measuring behavior that is independent and cannot be made silent, as can the private and internal moral sense. Religion alone, however, if it is not accompanied by a moral sense, is also insufficient as a guide to right behavior. Thus religion and morality, like wit and judgment, must go hand-in-hand, for neither alone is an adequate guarantee of the justness of a clear conscience.

At the end of the sermon Walter Shandy praises it for being "dramatic" (p. 141). Among the aspects of the sermon that could broadly be considered dramatic are its arresting opening, which seems to question the authority of a passage from Scriptures; the sequence of examples illustrating moral depravity, in which each example is more horrifying than the one before, so that the sermon is kept from being a dry moral discourse by making the characters seem alive and real.

The sermon is also dramatic in another sense. The elaborate description of Trim's rhetorical pose during his delivery of the sermon emphasizes the declamatory aspect of the work, as though it were being spoken upon the stage to an audience. And indeed Walter and Uncle Toby, who generally approve of the sermon, and Doctor Slop, who objects to the sermon's anti-Roman views, all react to the sermon much as an audience would to a staged play. This is made clear by their frequent short interjections during the reading, and by their lengthier discussions that interrupt Trim's performance. A kind of dialogue is set up between the audience and Yorick, who in the course of his sermon answers the questions they raise.

The most interesting reaction to the sermon is, however, that of Trim. For Trim is not only the sermon's reader, not just the sole actor in this dramatic performance, but also a member of the audience who reacts to what he is reading. In a digression within the first long discussion that interrupts the sermon immediately after Trim had read its first sentence, Trim reveals that his brother is a prisoner of the Inquisition. The thought of his brother's persecution brings tears to Trim's eyes, and moves the rest of the audience to sympathetic silence. To put these melancholy thoughts out of Trim's mind, Walter Shandy suggests that Trim continue with the sermon. The remedy proves successful, as no more is thought of Trim's brother until near the end of the sermon, when the Inquisition is the example used to illustrate the ill effects of "religion not strictly governed by morality" (p. 137). At this point the moving description of the fate of the prisoners of the Inquisition (which, incidentally, in some of its strongest passages is borrowed from a sermon of Richard Bentley[38]) again moves Trim to think of his brother and implore God's help for him. Soon Trim is in tears again, as he curses the Inquisition and drops the sermon in mid-sentence, which calls forth the remark, "Why, Trim, said my father, this is not a history,—'tis a sermon thou art reading; prithee begin the sentence again" (p. 138). Trim reads on, but he soon is stamping his feet in outrage. Finally he interrupts the reading himself and says, "I would not read another line of it, quoth Trim, for all this world;—I fear, an' please your Honours, all this is in Portugal, where my poor brother Tom is. I tell thee, Trim, again, quoth my father, 'tis not an historical account,—'tis a description."[39] Trim is unable to continue his reading, and Walter Shandy reads the few paragraphs remaining to the end.

Trim's reaction is the naive one of taking a general, fictitious illustration and applying it to a specific, personal case. His reaction parodies the reaction of all readers who mistake fiction, or "description," for "history." Though it is clear that Trim deserves our sympathy and receives the sympathy of the others present at the reading, nonetheless it is equally clear that his reaction is a misguided one, and one from which the reader should learn. For Trim has forgotten the gap that always exists between fiction and reality.

Thus the sermon, which at first seemed to be nothing more than an extended digression, ends by stating one of the themes that is central to the entire work: the identification of history and fiction, the failure to remember the differences between them that necessarily obtain, comes to hinder and ultimately put an end to narration.[40] Too great an involvement in fiction leads to a breakdown of narrative ability. Distance from the text, an awareness of fiction's fictionality, is necessary if narration is to succeed. It is a lesson that Tristram, as narrator, could well afford to learn.

On closer inspection, the sermon reveals itself to be bound up with the larger themes of *Tristram Shandy* in another way as well. In the sermon the question of whether or not self-knowledge is possible is not so much an epistemological as a moral question. The soul, since it is internal, can be known without reliance on the (potentially unreliable) senses. Theoretically at least, the soul can be known immediately: everyone "must be privy to his own thoughts and desires [. . .] and know certainly the true springs and motives, which, in general, have governed the actions of his life" (p. 125–6). Paraphrasing Ecclesiastes 8: 17, the sermon continues: "In other matters we may be deceived by false appearances; and as the wise man complains, hardly do we guess aright at the things that are upon the earth, and with labour do we find the things that are before us. But here the mind has all the evidence and facts within herself;—is conscious of the web she has wove;—knows its texture and fineness, and the exact share which every passion has had in working upon the several designs which virtue or vice had plann'd before her" (p. 126).

The soul is knowable, for Sterne, but this knowledge is made difficult by self-love and interest. As Cash puts it, "the problem is not what the mind *can* know, but what it will *bother* to know" (p. 398). The problem is the same for Hippel. The difference is that Hippel does not turn to religion as a codified, objective system of moral laws as a solution to the dilemma. Instead, he recommends activity, *Handlung*, as the best road to self-knowledge, though he remains skeptical that even in this way secure self-knowledge is possible. In other words, Hippel sees the most promising if not absolutely certain answer to this question not in religion and morality, not in Sterne's combination of public and private moral guides; Hippel's tentative solution is rather in the widest sense political. It is concerned with arriving at self-knowledge by means of knowing others and by means of activity that, at least in Hippel's own life, includes an energetic career as public servant as well as author.

NOTES

[1] Schlichtegroll, pp. 443, 463–65.

[2] Jensch's statement is recorded by Johann Friedrich Abegg, *Reisetagebuch von 1798*, p. 199. F. J. Schneider, in his biography *Th. G. v. Hippel* argued that, when Nr. 9 of the *Freymäurerreden* ("Von den Pflichten eines Freimaurers gegen das schöne Geschlecht") is compared stylistically and thematically with Hippel's later work *Über die bürgerliche Verbesserung der Weiber*, there can be no doubt that Hippel is the author of Nr. 9. Schneider overlooks the possibility that Jensch was author of both works, at least in part.

[3] Joseph Kohnen compares IV, 155, of the *Lebensläufe* with the opening words of Hamann's *Rhapsodie*. For other comparisons, see further "Hippel und Hamann," in *Johann Georg Hamann*, Acta des internationalen Hamann-Colloquiums in Lüneburg 1976, (Frankfurt a. M.: Klostermann, 1979) p. 36, note 49. Rudolf Rocholl made a similar comparison. "Hamanns Humor übrigens hat mit Hippel's 'Lebensläufen' viele Verwandtschaft. Liest man einen Satz wie: - "er, der nicht Lust hat an Cavallerie oder Stärke des Rosses, noch Wohlgefallen an Infanterie und Jemandes Beinen, sieht nur auf die, die seinen Namen fürchten", so glaubt man, Hamann habe ihn geschrieben, er steht aber in den 'Lebensläufen', Ausg. v. 1778. Bd. 1. S. 15." See "Johann Georg Hamann," (Ein Vortrag, gehalten im evangelischen Verein zu Hannover: Carl Meyer, 1869), in *Johann Georg Hamann*, Wege der Forschung, ed. Reiner Wild, (Darmstadt: Wissenschaftliche Buchgesellschaft, 1978) p. 116, n. 13.

[4] Schneider, *Theodor Gottlieb von Hippel in den Jahren 1741 bis 1781*, p. 114.

[5] Schneider's efforts to recover Hippel's *Nachlaß* remained fruitless. Joseph Kohnen, however, has done much to bring to light writings by Hippel believed lost. See, for example, "Zu einem unbekannten Hippel-Brief", *Recherches Germaniques* 15 (1985), 195–206.

[6] *Ueber das Autorschiksal*, p. 53.

⁷ The review appeared in the *Reichs-Postreuter*, where Albrecht Wittenberg had identified Leisewitz as the author of the *Lebensläufe*. Leisewitz subsequently denied having written the work in a letter to Wittenberg. Leisewitz does seem to have thought highly of the work, however, for as he wrote to Sophie Seyler-Braunschweig on 10 August 1779: "Unterdessen könte ich mein eigen Kind kaum so sehr lieben als diesen Fündling den man mir vor die Thür gelegt hat . . . . Es ist eines der witzigsten Dinge die ich kenne . . . Lessing und ich sind darüber eins daß es von dem Verfasser der Ehe ist." Johann Anton Leisewitz, *Briefe an seine Braut*, ed. Heinrich Mack (Weimar, 1906) p. 60; quoted in *Lessing im Gespräch*, ed. Richard Daunicht (Munich: Fink, 1971), p. 480.

⁸ For a presentation of all the pertinent material, including the draft versions Kant made of his "Erklärung," see Arthur Warda, "Kants 'Erklärung wegen der v. Hippelschen Autorschaft,' " *Altpreußische Monatsschrift*, 41 (1904), 61–93. See also Hamann's letter to Herder from 21 February 1779: "Kant, den ich wider zu besuchen anfange, findt in den Lebensläufen hundert Winke aus seinen Vorlesungen," *Hamanns Briefe*, (Frankfurt: Insel, 1959), IV, 55.

⁹ Vol. 44, p. 302. The correct date is 1780, not 1788, as given by Borowski, p. 56.

¹⁰ Hamann, in a letter to the publisher Hartknoch, erroneously attributed this article to Kant. "Daß Kant den unbekannten Verfasser als einen plagiarum seiner Vorlesungen in der Allg. Bibliothek in Anspruch genommen, ist bekannt." The reviewer was in fact on Chr. Fr. Glave. See Warda, pp. 64–5.

¹¹ Hippel is referring to the assertion made in the review that the author of the *Lebensläufe* had used "manche von *Kant* auf besondre Ausdrücke mit Absicht gestellte Definitionen, die nirgend anders her seyn können."

¹² *Hamburgische unparteyische Correspondenten*, Beylage zu Nr. 120, 27 July 1796, in Warda, p. 67.

¹³ See *Immanuel Kant's Anweisung zur Menschen- und Weltkenntniß*, (Quedlinburg und Leipzig: Ernst, 1830). "Vieles aus Kants Vorlesungen über Anthropologie, Moral u. s. w. hat der berühmte Hippel in seinen Schriften benutzt [. . .]" (p. viii). Also: *Immanuel Kant's Menschenkunde oder philosophische Anthropologie*. "Nach handschriftlichen Vorlesungen herausgegeben von Fr. Ch. Starke. [Motto:] Wer Menschen kennen lernen will, der muß sie nach ihren Wünschen beurtheilen. Hippel." (Leipzig, Expedition des europäischen Aufsehers, 1831).

¹⁴ It did, however, arouse the ire of Scheffner, who wrote an anonymous letter in Hippel's biography (signed: "v. K."). Referring to Kant's letter, Scheffner writes, "Mit ihren ersten Zeilen bin ich ganz zufrieden, aber alles nachfolgende dünkt mich eine Art von geistiger Guillotinirung [. . . .] An K. Stelle hätt *ich* blos die ersten Reihen dieser Erklärung mit dem Zusatz geschrieben: 'H. war einst mein Schüler, mein vieljähriger Tischgenosse, mein vertrauter Freund, mit dem ich bis an seinen Tod in engem Umgange lebte.' Wer sich aus solcher Anzeige nicht erklären könnte, wie Kantische Bächlein in Hippelsche Fruchtfelder geflossen, den lasse man bey seinem Glauben, und spare den weitern Trepan, aus Beysorge, Uebel ärger zu machen," (Schlichtegroll, pp. 460–63; that Scheffner was author of this letter has been shown by Arthur Plehwe, "Johann Georg Scheffner," Diss. Königsberg 1934, p. 82). And Abegg recorded in his diary a conversation he had with Scheffner: "Daß Kant in dem Intelligencblatt sich erklärt hat, als habe Hippel von seinem Heften eins u. das andere genommen, nimmt Scheffner ihm sehr übel. Kant soll einmal seine Philosophie so ins Leben und für's Leben verarbeiten, als es Hippel gethan hat," *Reisetagebuch von 1798*, p. 234.

¹⁵ In a draft version of the "Erklärung" Kant speaks of "mein Freund der sich nie für

einen der Philosphie beflissenen und selbst nicht in dergleichen Schriften Belesenen ausgab," (Warda, p. 87). This is a somewhat more precise formulation than the one Kant finally settled on, "mein Freund, der sich nie mit der Philosophie sonderlich befaßt hat."
[16] Schlichtegroll, p. 154.
[17] Kant, *Sämtliche Werke*, Akademie Ausgabe, XI, 472–73.
[18] Schlichtegroll, pp. 294, 299.
[19] Borowski, pp. 30–1.
[20] Here he was in agreement with Kant himself. See *Religion innerhalb der Grenzen der bloßen Vernunft*, AA VI, 118.
[21] See on the coexistence of pietistic and enlightened elements in Hippel's works esp. Dieter Kimpel, "Theodor Gottlieb von Hippel," in *Deutsche Dichter des achtzehnten Jahrhunderts*, ed. Benno von Wiese, (Berlin: Schmidt, 1977) pp. 462–81.
[22] Gerhard Lehmann's date for the lectures (Wintersemester 1781/2), given in his edition of the work (Berlin: Akademie, 1961), must be in error. This follows from Lehmann's own reference to Hippel in the *Akademie Ausgabe*, where he says that Hippel "fügte [. . .] eine Menge Kantischer Aussprüche—aus den Vorlesungen über Logik, Enzyklopädie, Anthropologie etc.—hinzu, so im 2. Teil der *Lebensläufe* (1779) ganze Passagen aus der Enzyklopädie [. . .]" (I. Kant, *Gesammelte Schriften*, AA XVIV, 2 = Vorlesungen I, 2, p. 958). This error has been pointed out by Giorgio Tonelli, Norbert Hinske and Michael Albrecht as well. See Tonelli's review of Lehmann's edition of the *Vorlesungen*, in *Filosofia* 13 (Turin, 1962), 511–14. Tonelli, without referring to Hippel, concludes that the lectures must have been delivered between 1775–1780. Hinske in his review (Deutsche Literaturzeitung 85, 6, June 1964, 486–90), does refer to Hippel, but incorrectly gives the date for the second volume of the *Lebensläufe* as 1778. The correct date, 1779, is given by Albrecht (*Kants Antinomie der praktischen Vernunft* [Hildesheim: Olms, 1978] p. 22, note 25), who limits the possible dates to the summer semester 1775 or winter semester 1777–78. Perhaps it is not possible to establish the date any more precisely than this. But to anyone familiar with Hippel's method of taking notes from daily life and including them in his novel, it would seem likely that Hippel came across the lectures at the same time that he was working on the second volume of the *Lebensläufe*. If one assumes that the lecture notes were newly written when they came into Hippel's hands, and that he was working on volume II in 1778, this would argue for preferring the winter semester 1777–78 dating to the earlier possibility. For the latest word on this subject see Manfred Kuehn, *Dating Kant's Vorlesungen über philosophische Enzyklopädie*, Kant-Studien, 74, 3 (1983), 302–13. Both Peterken (pp. 55–59) and Campe (pp. 133–35) make the error of comparing the examination scene in the novel with passages from the *Kritik der reinen Vernunft*, published two years after this volume of the *Lebensläufe*.
[23] For a comparison of the scene in Hippel with Kant's lecture, see *Appendix*. It should be added that the remote possibility exists that Hippel, if he was not using this precise book of lecture notes, was using one very similar to it. Joseph Kohnen and I, operating independently, discovered the relationship between the examination scene and Kant's lecture at the same time. Joseph Kohnen, *Theodor Gottlieb von Hippel, 1741–1796, L'homme et l'oeuvre*, p. 1031.
[24] To be sure, Kant also alludes to this passage from I Corinthians 8: 1, in his lecture, but in a different context.
[25] That Hippel did not want his audience to speculate on who the author of the *Lebensläufe* was is shown by his reply to Scheffner, who had asked why Hippel did not

reveal that he had written the work. "Ich habe einen Mann, der sehr unter Ihnen steht, als er den letzten Theil gelesen, so urtheilen gehört: 'Nachdem ich den 4. Th. gelesen, verflucht will ich seyn, wenn ich nach dem Verfasser ausgehe; wehe dem, der ihn sucht!' und das ließ mich, *wie Gott* weiß, vermuthen, der Mann hab es beim Zipfel gefaßt, er sey über das Buch *erleuchtet*," letter of 27 Jan. 1783 (XIV, 264–5).

[26] Thus at one point in the first volume Alexander introduces a long conversational passage with the remark, "Die Gespräche sind originalisirt" (I, 245).

[27] Kant, *Gesammelte Schriften*, AA, IV, 4, 239, (A 381).

[28] For another passage see Starke's edition of *Immanuel Kant's Anweisung zur Menschen- und Weltkenntniß*, "Mit Recht sagt Kant in einer ungedruckten Schrift: 'die Kenntniß des Menschen überhaupt ist schwer; die besondere Kenntniß eines anderen Menschen ist schon leichter und am leichtesten ist die Selbstkenntniß; denn mich selbst kann ich mir nicht verbergen und folglich fallen hier alle Decken weg, welche uns andere Menschen verhängen,' " pp. vi–vii. See also Starke, *Kant's Menschenkunde*, p. 8.

[29] Johannes 18: 38, "Spricht Pilatus zu ihm: Was ist Wahrheit?"

[30] *Vorlesungen über philosophische Enzyklopädie*, p. 54.

[31] In *Tristram Shandy*: "It is not actions, but opinions concerning actions, which disturb men," trans. J. A. Work.

[32] Kant's *Werke*, AA, IV, 4, 231, (A 382).

[33] Hippel's skepticism was, however, never entirely quieted. In *Über die bürgerliche Verbesserung der Weiber* (1792) he writes, "Jede Geschichte, jedes Faktum muß sich bequemen, sich nach uns zu richten, und der wahrhafteste Mann trägt zuvor etwas von seinem Selbst in jene Geschichte und jenes Faktum so, daß alles, was der Mensch berührt, etwas von seinem Ich, von seinem Selbst erhält." Here he takes the position that it is still undetermined, "ob die Seele mit sich selbst Erfahrung anzustellen vermag." More experience is needed before the question can be answered. (VI, 33.)

[34] Quoted in Williams, *Novel and Romance*, p. 238. At least one modern reader, however, seems to hold a view similar to that of *The Critical Review*. Henri Fluchère says that Tristram's "curious omnipresence" is responsible for a "permanent sense of authenticity," *Laurence Sterne: From Tristram to Yorick*, p. 337. For another view of Ernulphus's curse, see Herman Meyer, *Das Zitat in der Erzählkunst*, 2nd ed. (Stuttgart: Metzler, 1968) pp. 81–4. For more on documents in Sterne, see Michael Rosenblum, "The Sermon, the King of Prussia, and the Art of Interpretation in *Tristram Shandy*," *Studies in Philology* 75 (1978), 475–76.

[35] Only at the end of the sermon is the true history of the work's publication hinted at by Tristram in his assertion that "a certain prebendary" of York (a reference to Sterne himself, who held this post) had printed Yorick's sermon after his death in order to give rest to Yorick's ghost and to acquaint the public with the work (pp. 142–3). See also Rosenblum, p. 482.

[36] See Lansing Hammond, *Laurence Sterne's Sermons of Mr. Yorick*, Yale Studies in English, 108 (1948). See also Melvyn New, Richard A. Davies, and W. G. Day, *Laurence Sterne, The Life and Opinions of Tristram Shandy, Gentleman*, Vol. III: The Notes (Gainesville: Univ. Presses of Florida, 1984), p. 170 ff.

[37] See Arthur H. Cash, "The Sermon in *Tristram Shandy*," *ELH* XXI (1961), 395–417.

[38] Lansing Hammond, p. 105.

[39] In a comic continuation of this discussion the staunch Catholic Slop expands Walter's meaning of "description" by saying, " 'Tis only a description, honest man, quoth Slop, there's not a word of truth in it." To which Walter replies: "That's another

story" (p. 139). I cannot agree with James E. Swearingen's view that it is Walter, not Trim, who misunderstands the sermon. See his *Reflexivity in* Tristram Shandy, (New Haven and London: Yale Univ. Press, 1977), pp. 174–75. J. Paul Hunter points out that none of the characters responds appropriately to the sermon. See "Response as Reformation: *Tristram Shandy* and the Art of Interruption," *Novel*, IV (1970), 132–46.

[40] "Trim's extravagant over-reaction to the mention of the Inquisition raises the question of illusion and reality in a direct, Cervantic way." Max Byrd, *Tristram Shandy*, (London: Allen & Unwin, 1985), p. 101.

Conclusion

The narrative structure of Hippel's novel can be understood as a reply to that in *Tristram Shandy*, a reply for which Hippel found support in contemporary theories of the novel and in Kant's philosophy. It should be noted, however, that Hippel's very first work already reveals some of the idiosyncrasies that appear again in the *Lebensläufe*. Chief among them is a striving for totality.

Hippel's first work was a *Gelegenheitsgedicht* published anonymously in 1760 on the occasion of the marriage of his cousin.[1] "Das christliche Ehepaar" anticipates the *Lebensläufe* not just in the interest it shows in death, nor just in the highly self-conscious treatment of the (in this case: lyrical) *Ich*, which in stanza one is blasphemous and then pious, in stanza two humble and then proud, in stanza three a critic of its own past and a prophet looking to the future, and which then withdraws from the poem until stanza seven, where its farewell gesture is a confession of its own insufficiency, a confession that is followed in the final stanza by the bold attempt to portray the heavenly bliss of the faithful on earth. Even more than this, what is characteristic of Hippel is the impression of chaos given by the work, a chaos that is a reflection of the author's striving for totality; the apparent disorganization in the treatment of the poem's theme is on closer examination not so much a lack of unity as it is an explosion of themes that all reflect on the poem's central topic. The result of this endeavor to say in a short space virtually everything on its theme is that the poem presents an extremely condensed, convoluted surface, one that invites or even forces the reader to interpret, to think along with the persona, to re-conceive the poet's original conception and thus to become the poet's *Mitarbeiter.*

"Das christliche Ehepaar" is an early sign of what was to come in Hippel's mature production. Here he has not yet found the proper vehicle for expressing himself and is sometimes awkward, though his concerns and his approaches to themes are revealed to a degree that Hippel was first to show again in a work of fiction only in the *Lebensläufe.* Thus the basic characteristics of that work can be seen *in nuce* in this first poem, written long before Hippel came to know Sterne, theories of the novel, or Kant's *Enzyklopädie* lectures. Hippel's characteristic attempt to encompass everything, to create a work of art that can embrace themes in all their manifold and contradictory aspects, is an essential part of his creative process from the very beginning.

This striving to unite contradictory elements is not merely an idiosyncratic character trait, however, for it is anchored in the structure of contemporary Prussian society. Hippel's sometimes bitter social criticism (expressed in his anonymously published works) and the conformism of his public career (tempered, to be sure, by proposals for reform) ultimately reflect his position in a society which was in some ways enlightened and in others still very much a feudal society.

The impossibility of reconciling such contradictions perhaps can be said to account for the deformations in Hippel's character. There is an almost schizophrenic quality about this personality: on the one hand Hippel presents himself as the efficient mayor who could lay down his pen every evening in the certainty that all business had been taken care of; on the other hand he plays the eccentric hermit in his country house filled with symbols of death, complete with an imitation cemetery in the garden.

Hippel's striving for totality, for the reconciliation of contrary elements, the inclusion of diverse themes, is, among other things, a reflection of his social situation. His writings are deeply indebted to the Enlightenment, but the deformed elements peculiar to him separate his writings from the Enlightenment, and in this context his obsession with death and his passion for anonymity are often cited. An even more important deformation, however, one that gives Hippel's works (not just the novels) their idiosyncratic form, is that in them the striving for totality takes on a life of its own. In the *Lebensläufe* Hippel wants to include certain central aspects of life, "das gemeine Leben, so wie es da gemein ist," (III, pt. 2, 356), in their entire fullness, especially the process of maturation, the experience of love, of death, and man's reaction to the death of a beloved one. This desire for totality threatens to explode any literary form—except that of the Sternean novel. Thus Hippel takes up and transforms Sterne's techniques according to his own ends.

NOTES

[1] The text of the poem is given in the appendix to F. J. Schneider's biography, *Theodor Gottlieb von Hippel*, p. 139 ff.

Appendix

The left-hand column follows the text of the *Lebensläufe* as printed in Hippel's *Werke*, II, 148–167. The right-hand column contains excerpts from Lehmann's Berlin edition of Kant's *Vorlesungen über philosophische Enzyklopädie*. Only passages relevant to Hippel's text are quoted, and the numbers in the right-hand column indicate the page and line number of Lehmann's edition. All Biblical references are my addition and are in parentheses. Orthography and punctuation have been carefully modernized.

Hippel	*Kant*
Es gibt Natur-Philosophie und Kunst-Philosophie. Leben! Leben! Leben! und Schulweisheit. Philosophie, die bloß weiß, und Philosophie, die weiß und tut, gelehrten Wust und Weisheit. Aristoteles war ein Künstler, Epikur, Diogenes (mit Fleiß zusammen) waren Naturalisten und Sokrates desgleichen.—	Der Philosoph sieht die Regeln der Weisheit ein, der Weise handelt aber danach [34,8]. [. . .] Künstler der Vernunft, wie Plato und Aristoteles [35,26]. Diogenes, der Zyniker, und Epikur waren gleichfalls Lehrer der Zwecke [35,16]. Sokrates war der erste, der zwischen der Philosophie als Spekulation und als Weisheit einen Unterschied machte [35,6].
Die künstliche wird ganz und gar gelehrt, bei der natürlichen ist nur eine gewisse Methode, die gezeigt wird.	Der Philosoph ist als Führer der Vernunft ein Lehrer der Weisheit und als Vernunftkünstler ein Lehrer der Wissenschaft [34,17].
Das Faß des Diogenes, der Brei des Epikur, wie verehrungswert!	Er [Diogenes] wählte sich zur Wohnung ein kleines von Steinen aufgerichtetes Gebäude, dessen Gestalt wie ein Faß war, und entsagte aller Gemächlichkeit [35,34]. Polenta, eine Art von Gerstenbrei, war seine [Epikurs] Speise [35,22].
Die Fenster im Auditorio, wo natürliche Weisheit gelehrt wird, gehen alle ins gemeine Leben.—Die natürliche lehrt die Zeit gebrauchen, die künstliche sie vertreiben. Die Naturphilosophie ist fließend	

Wasser, Springwasser, die künstliche ist Wasser, welches steht. Die Kunstphilosophie treibt Kommissionshandel, die Naturphilosophie hat bloß eigenes Produkt. Das Leben der Naturphilosophie ist eine Copia vidimata ihrer Grundsätze, und zu ihren Angaben ein solch erklärender nachhelfender Beleg, daß ohne Beilage sub Vide ihre ganze Lehre, wie gar nichts ist. Wohl dem, der von diesem Wasser des Lebens getrunken hat! Die Idee der Weisheit liegt der Naturphilosophie zum Grunde, die nicht gleichgültig, sondern gleichmütig macht.—

Ist wohl ein passenderes Motto zur künstlichen Philosophie, als "die Herren werden doch wohl Spaß verstehen?" Will man ein Emblem, so ist's ein optischer Kasten.—
Vom natürlichen Philosophen sagt man, er *philosophiert*. Ein künstlicher Philosoph *hat Philosophie*. Er hat sie für Geld und gute Worte zum Verkauf und zur Pacht.— Man muß es bei der Philosophie nicht anlegen, ein Buch, den beliebten Autor, sondern die Sache zu verstehen. Man will sich vorzüglich selbst verstehen und das Buch Gottes, die Welt.—Diese Philosophie kann nicht auswendig gelernt werden; es ist was Inwendiges ein Philosoph zu sein. Denken und leben heißt: philosophieren. Wenn man die Wissenschaften in die der Gelahrtheit und die der Einsicht einteilt, so würde ich die künstliche Philosophie zur Gelahrtheit rechnen, und so wie man zum Exempel von einem Historikus sagen kann: er sei ein Gelahrter, er habe viel gelernt, so auch

[. . .]—kurz, man sieht, daß die Alten Lehrer der Weisheit waren. Sie forderten von ihren Lehrern Beispiele, sie sollten leben, wie sie lehrten [35,30].

Die Idee der Weisheit muß der Philosophie zugrunde liegen [. . .] [34,23].

Wir sind mit dem Namen eines Philosophen freigiebiger und legen ihn oft einem Menschen bei, der bloß gelassen ist und die Vorfälle des Lebens mit Gleichmütigkeit erträgt. Diese Gleichgültigkeit geziemt zwar, wenn sie aus der Selbstbeherrschung als aus ihrer wahren Quelle entspringt. Sie sieht aber sehr oft der stupiden Gleichgültigkeit und Gefühllosigkeit ähnlich [35,39].

Was uns anbeiangt, wir verstehen Scherz und nehmen es dem Philosophen nicht übel, wenn er auch nicht so lebt wie er lehrt [35,37].

Kein Lehrer der Philosophie muß den Autor bloß explizieren, sondern zu gleicher Zeit eine Instruktion geben von der Methode, wie man philosophieren soll [33,15].

Jemandes Gedanken nachahmen, heißt nicht philosophieren, sondern man muß selbst denken, und zwar a priori [33,14].

Eigentlich kann keine Philosophie auswendig gelernt werden [. . .] [33,6].

Die Wissenschaften sind 1. Wissenschaften der Gelahrtheit, 2. Wissenschaften der Einsicht. Zu den Ersteren gehört die Historie [31,21].

Zur Historie gehört alles, was gegeben wird. Wenn die Gelahrtheit sehr aus-

von einem Kunstphilosophen. Die natürliche Philosophie besteht nicht in Nachricht, sondern in Einsicht. Man kann nicht vom natürlichen Philosophen sagen: er habe viel gelernt, allein er kann viel lehren.

Alle Vernunfterkenntnis aus Begriffen gehört zwar zur Philosophie, allein der Philosoph ist eigentlich ein Führer der Vernunft und bringet den Menschen an Ort und Stelle. Der Mensch ist nicht bei sich, heißt oder sollte heißen: er habe diesen eigentlichen philosophischen Weg verfehlt. Die Bestimmung des Menschen und die Mittel, dahin zu gelangen, das ist das Ziel, wo alle philosophische Erkenntnis zusammentrifft. Es ist die Probe der Philosophie.

Der gemeine Mann *meint* und *wünscht*, und selbst dazu ist er ex speciali gratia privilegiert; der Weise denkt und will. Verstand und Wille zusammen ist eine Seele. Wer kann die Seele halbieren? Der Mann hat Geist und Leben, das heißt: der Mann ist ein Philosoph natürlicher Art. Zwar sagt man auch, dies Buch hat Geist und Leben, allein alsdann denkt man, der Verfasser, ein Philosoph der besagten Art, hat es geschrieben und es sich so ähnlich gemacht, daß er ihm etwas Geist und Leben abgegeben. Er hat es angehauchet—wie Gott den bis auf die Seele fertigen Adam. Der Mann ist im Buche getroffen!———Oft hab' ich gehört, wenn man den Mann sieht und sein Buch, sollte man sie wohl für Vater und Sohn halten? Ja—und wenn Ihr sie nicht dafür haltet, liegt es an Euch. Wie der Autor, so das Buch, per omnia saecula saeculorum. Jeder Physionomist muß den Autor aus dem Buch *abziehen* und zum Reden treffen. Das Buch hat Hand und Fuß, der Mann hat Hand und Fuß, heißt ein Mann

gebreitet ist, so heißt sie Polyhistorie [31,13].

Die Wissenschaft des Gelehrten besteht in Einsicht und nicht in Nachricht [31,26].

Der mathematicus kann nur im bürgerlichen Verstande ein Gelehrter genannt werden, denn er hat eigentlich nur viel gelernt [31,24].

Alle Vernunfterkenntnis aus Begriffen gehört zur Philosophie [32,16]. Der Philosoph, als ein Führer der Vernunft, leitet den Menschen zu seiner Bestimmung [34,13].

Seine Erkenntnisse gehen also auf die Bestimmung des Menschen [34,14]. Wenn der Philosoph alle seine Spekulation, Wissenschaft etc. mit den Zwecken, mit der Bestimmung des Menschen verbindet, dann ist er ein Führer und Gesetzgeber der Vernunft [34,20].

Was die Kräfte und Vermögen des Menschen betrifft, so sind ihrer zwei, Verstand und der Wille [36,27].

mit Winkelmaß und Wage, der alles mißt und paßt, und ein Buch von der nämlichen richtigen, abgemessenen Weise, wo weder Mangel noch Überfluß ist, sondern just die erforderlichen Gelenke.—Die Naturphilosophie ist keine Feindin von reinen Vernunftsbegriffen, allein sie bestätiget sie, wenn ich so sagen soll, auf der Stelle.—Sie schafft sich gleich einen Abdruck—wie Gott die Welt.—Die Religion fängt heutzutage mit dem Katechismus und die Philosophie mit einem Kompendio an.—Allein in Wahrheit, man sollt auf ein lebendiges Erkenntnis dringen, dann würde man doch einmal einen Philosophen zu sehen bekommen.—Rousseau, damit ich eine Bemerkung mache, die in unsern Tagen zu Hause gehört, Rousseau (schade, daß er tot ist!) war wirklich eine Spektabilität unter den Philosophen.—Der bloße philosophische Künstler weiß nichts Rechtes, nicht daß ein Gott ist; der arme Schelm! Man könnte die natürliche: *Philosophie* χατ'εξοχην, die künstliche: *Vernünftelei* nennen. Die Vernünftelei und die Zweifelsucht sind Grenznachbaren. Ein Zweifler und ein Abergläubischer sind Schwester und Bruder.—

Einige Alte haben sich dem Urbilde eines wahren Philosophen genähert, Rousseau gleichfalls, allein sie haben es nicht erreicht [34,29].

Er [Wolff] war eigentlich gar kein Philosoph, sondern ein großer Künstler für die Wißbegierde der Menschen [. . .] [34,27].

Ein Mensch, der sich der Vernunft bedient und sich mit derselben abgibt, kann betrachtet werden:
1. als ein Vernunftkünstler
2. als ein Gesetzgeber der Vernunft [. . .] [33,27].

Ein Zweifler macht sich sein Leben nicht gemächlich.—Nein, er hat sich mehr aufgelegt. Er hat Ja und Nein zu tragen, wenn er denkt. Im Fall er aber bloß spaßt, ist er nur ein Scheinzweifler und ein Mann, der alles der Nachfrage wegen hat. Man glaubt gemeinhin, ein Zweifler sei kein Vielwisser, allein er ist es im eigentlichsten Verstande, und es kann gemeinhin von ihm heißen: *das Wissen bläset auf.* Wer Dinge, die gang und gäbe sind, beprüft und keinen Stein auf den andern läßt, ist kein Zweifler, sondern ein Prüfer, im Fall er nämlich aus pro und contra, aus links und rechts, sich etwas auspunktiert, was Stich

Das Vielwissen bläht auf, die Philosophie aber drückt den Stolz nieder [39,3].
(Das Wissen bläst auf. 1 Kor. 8:1)
(Es wird hier nicht ein Stein auf dem andern bleiben. Matt. 24:2)

hält. Solch ein Mann ist nicht aufgeblasen, sondern bescheiden. Seine Zweifel leiteten ihn auf rechten Weg zur Überzeugung, zur Wahrheit und zum Leben.—Ein Lehrer der Naturphilosophie kann von sich und seinen Jüngern sagen: *Ich leb und ihr sollt auch leben.*—Wer hat je mit den Pietisten über die Wahrheit der christlichen Religion gestritten? Wer so lebt, als er lehrt, darf nur bitten, ihm die Ehre zu tun, bei ihm einzusprechen. Man ist heutzutage von der Naturphilosophie so abgekommen, daß man den, der so lebt, als er lehrt oder glaubt, einen Schwärmer nennt.—Sehr unrichtig!—

(Ihr aber sollt mich sehen, denn ich lebe, und ihr sollt auch leben. Johannes 14:19)

Allein heutzutage hält man den für einen Schwärmer, der so lebt wie er lehrt [38,19].

Meine Leser werden, hoffe ich, nicht vergessen haben, daß sie zu einem Picnic geladen sind, wo nur Se. Spektabilität und ich (meinen Vater kann ich immer mit einrechnen) ihr Schüsselchen auftrugen. Wenn ein Koch diese Schmauserei angeordnet hätte, wär es freilich abgemessener gewesen—ob schmackhafter, weiß ich nicht.
Ich bemühe mich auch hier, Lebensläufer zu sein, und diese Abschrift ist dem Original ähnlich.—Wir fielen von einem aufs andere. Wir scheitelten die Haare nicht. Würde ich nicht einen Roman schreiben, wenn ich nicht auch von einem aufs andere fallen und die Haare scheiteln sollte? Ein Roman! fern sei er von mir!—
Die Einteilung der Philosophie in die natürliche und künstliche ist die Haupteinteilung, die philosophische Einteilung der Philosophie. Sonst gibt es Einteilungen, Gott weiß wie viele!—In Absicht der Kräfte des Menschen, in Absicht der Prinzipien, in Absicht der Objekte, der Erkenntnisse.—
Ein Philosoph muß das Allgemeine in concreto und das Einzelne in abstracto erwägen, und wenn man gleich gern zugibt, daß bei jeder Wissenschaft die Idee des Ganzen die Avantgarde macht und daß aus der Einteilung des Ganzen die Teile entstehen und daß, um die Teile zu wis-

Folgende Einteilung müssen wir uns merken. Wir können sehen 1. auf die Kräfte des Menschen, 2. auf die Prinzipien, 3. auf das Objekt der Erkenntnis [36,25].

[. . .] zum philosophischen Talent gehört Witz und das Vermögen, sowohl das allgemeine in concreto, als auch das einzelne in abstracto zu erwägen [38,32].

Bei jeder Wissenschaft muß die Idee des Ganzen vorausgehen. Aus der Einteilung

sen, man erst das Ganze von Person zu kennen die Ehre haben müsse, so ist doch nicht gut, wenn ein erschrecklicher Eingang präludiert und prologiert wird, ehe man zum Thema schreitet [. . . .] Wozu die Prolegomena und das erschreckliche Geschrei: *da werden Sie sehen! da werden Sie sehen!* Gleich das Lied ist am besten! Wenn ich heißhungrig bin und der Wirt, der mich geladen hat, zeigt mir erst seine drei Porcelaine-Service und sodann sein Silberzeug und endlich seine Fayence, bis ich mich überhungert und keine ordentliche Mahlzeit tun kann, wie wenig Ursache habe ich, den Wunsch einer gesegneten Mahlzeit anzunehmen und mich ergebenst zu bedanken; ich wollte anbeißen und nicht mit der Gabel anspießen. Warum nicht kurz präsentiert: *Herr Gott, dich loben wir. Befiehl du deine Wege.* Philosophie! Verstandes- und Willensphilosophie, theoretische und praktische, wenn es ja nach der alten Leier gehen soll.

Vernunfts- und Erfahrungsphilosophie. Empirische und rationale, und damit die Einteilung in Rücksicht des Objekts nicht vernachlässiget werde—Philosophie der engelreinen Vernunft und der menschlichen Sinne.

Die Philosophie der Sinne heißt die Naturlehre.
Die Sinne sind zwiefach, innerlich und äußerlich.

Was ich mit dem innerlichen Sinn gewahr werde, ist einzig und allein meine Seele.
Also gibt's Seelennaturlehre und Körpernaturlehre.—

des Ganzen entstehn die Teile. Um nun zu wissen, was für Teile zum Ganzen gehören, muß man zuerst das Ganze kennen [31,4].

(Befiehl dem Herrn deine Wege und hoffe auf ihn, er wird's wohl machen. Ps. 37:5) Die Philosophie wird also eingeteilt 1. in die theoretische, welche die Regeln des Verstandes enthält, 2. in die praktische. Diese enthält die Regeln des Willens [36,28].

Die Philosophie, die ihre principia aus der reinen Vernunft entlehnt, heißt pura, entlehnt sie dieselbe aber aus der Erfahrung, so heißt sie applicata. Sie wird aber besser eingeteilt in rationalem et empiricam.
In Ansehung des Objekts ist folgendes zu merken. Das Objekt der Philosophie ist entweder ein Gegenstand der reinen Vernunft oder der Sinne. Die Wissenschaft, [. . .] deren Objekt ein Gegenstand der Sinne ist, heißt Physiologie. Diese ist zweifach, denn wir haben zwei Arten Sinne, äußere und innern. Die Natur des innern Sinnes oder die Gegenstände, die wir durch den innern Sinn gewahr werden, sind denkende Wesen. Weil ich aber nur mit mir selbst Erfahrungen anstellen kann, so ist meine Seele der Gegenstand meines innern Sinnes [36,34].
Die erste Art der Physiologie heißt die Seelenlehre. Die zweite Art ist die Physik,

Empirisch und rational kann jene und diese sein, und was kann nicht alles so sein?——

Ich kann zwar nur mit mir selbst Seelenbetrachtungen anstellen, allein ich kann nach dem Kennzeichen der Übereinstimmung auf andere schließen. Welch ein großes Wort: *Lern dich selbst kennen!*— Mancher Philosoph, der sich auf die Seelennaturlehre legt und viel drin philosophiert, kommt endlich zu einer Art nota bene, zu einer Art von Geisterseherei, von Anschauung vom Platonismus und mystischem Wesen. Er wird entzückt, und wenn man gleich mit dem Verstande nicht sehen, sondern nur denken kann, so ist er doch in einer Verfassung, wo es heißen könnte: Es hat kein Auge gesehen, kein Ohr gehört, es ist in keines Menschen Herz kommen, was Gott bereitet hat, denen, die ihn lieben. Oft versehen sich diese guten Leute so, daß sie an ihren Ort gestellt werden, der nicht der angenehmste ist.—Biegen oder brechen ist die Losung dieser Seher. Jammer und Schade, daß es gemeinhin bricht!—

Ist denn in den äußeren Sinnen Wahrheit, ihr Sinnengläubige? Sehet die Sonne an, geht oder steht sie? Selbst wenn unser Urteil mit der Erscheinung übereinstimmt und wenn man sagen kann, die Sache ist wahrscheinlich, ist sie drum so und nicht anders?

Gott allein kann die Gegenstände mit dem Verstand anschauen, denn sie sind durch ihn und in ihm.—Er hat alles in originali, wir uns selbst nur so.—

Was heißt: *Gott schauen und in Gott alle Dinge?*——Durch eine einzelne Vorstellung erkennen, könnte man anschauen nennen, durch allgemeine Begriffe erkennen, würde denken heißen. Man kann welche von Gegenständen der äußeren Sinne handelt. Die Wissenschaft der denkenden Natur, das ist der Seele, heißt Psychologie. Sie ist wieder 1. entweder rational oder empirisch [37,7].

Ich kann zwar nur mit mir selbst Beobachtungen anstellen, aber nach der Analogie, den Kennzeichen der Übereinstimmung, kann ich auch auf andere schließen [68,15].

(Kein Ohr hat gehört, kein Auge hat gesehen einen Gott außer dir, der so wohl tut denen, die auf ihn harren. Jesaja 64:3)

Wenn ich sage, die Sonne bewegt sich, so ist in dem Urteil ein Schein [40,20] [...] Wenn unser Urteil mit der Erscheinung übereinstimmt, dann ist es wahrscheinlich [40,23].

Gott allein kann die Gegenstände intellectualiter anschauen, denn sie existieren durch ihn [40,35] [...] Ich kann nichts originaliter anschauen (als mich selbst), [...]

Die esoterische Lehre [...] lehrte [...], daß der Mensch sogar die Gottheit anschauen kann und in Gott alle Dinge [41,3]. Durch eine einzelne Vorstellung erkennen, heißt anschauen. Denken ist die

physisch und mystisch schauen, durch Körper- und Seelenaugen. Die Seele hat, nach der Mystiker mystischem Dafürhalten, wie die Zyklopen nur ein Auge.

Erkenntnis durch allgemeine Begriffe; die Anschauung heißt physisch, insofern etwas unseren Sinnen erscheinen kann und mystisch, wenn etwas durch die Sinne nicht erscheinen kann, sondern durch den Verstand angeschaut wird. Dies war des Plato Meinung [41,11].

Die Logik ist Verstandes-Grammatik. Die lehrt uns von keinem Gegenstande etwas—selbst vom Verstande nichts; allein sie lehret uns von Dingen, die wir gar nicht kennen, viel, und was noch mehr ist, gelehrt—*reden*. Von Dingen, die man weiß, von denen man überzeugt ist, spricht man nur wenig. Man handelt, wie oben gezeigt worden. Dingen aber, von denen man nicht überzeugt ist, legt man durch eine gewisse Hitze einen Grund bei. Man legt es recht dazu an, sich dadurch, daß man den andern überzeugt, auch selbst zu überzeugen, und oft ist man hierbei glücklich, so daß man in der Tat auch hier durchs Lehren lernt. Es kann eine allgemeine Grammatik aller Sprachen geben, so auch eine des Denkens, die nämlich allgemeine Regeln des Denkens enthalten müßte. Was tun Wörter zur Grammatik! Allgemeine Regeln der Sprachen würd' eine allgemeine Grammatik sein.

Vielleicht hätte die lateinische dazu alle Anlage. Die Dialektik ist die Logik des Scheins. Wahrheit ist der Inhalt der Erkenntnisse, mithin kann sie durch die Dialektik nicht erkannt werden. Die Dialektik trägt die Livree des Verstandes, sie ist die Kunst des Scheins, die Wissenschaft der Sachwalter und der Skeptiker.—

Was die Grammatik in Ansehung der Sprache ist, das ist sie [die Logik] in Ansehung des Gebrauchs des Verstandes [39,17]. Die Logik lehrt uns also von keinem Gegenstande etwas, auch nichts vom Verstande [39,14]. Der eine Teil der Logik heißt die Analytik, der andere die Dialektik, hier werden wir gelehrt, von Dingen zu reden, die wir gar nicht kennen. Überhaupt man kann davon ungemein viel reden, was und wovon man nicht überzeugt ist, das es da sei [39,23].

So wie man eine allgemeine Grammatik der Sprachen hat, sucht man auch eine des Denkens zu erfinden, welche gewisse allgemeine Regeln des Denkens erhalten sollte. Eine allgemeine Grammatik enthält allgemeine Regeln der Sprachen, ohne auf das Besondere derselben, z. E. die Wörter etc., zu sehen.

Die lateinische Grammatik schickt sich für alle Sprachen, weil sie am besten ausgearbeitet ist [55,23].
Die Dialektik ist die Form des Verstandes, überhaupt die Kunst beliebiger Behauptungen, die Logik des Scheines [56,3] [. . .]
Da die Wahrheit der Inhalt der Erkenntnisse ist, so kann die Wahrheit dadurch nicht erkannt werden.
Die Dialektik ist die Kunst des logischen Scheins [56,6].
Die Dialektik war für die Sachwalter und Anwälte in den alten Zeiten für notwendig gehalten. Die Skeptiker bedienten sich ihrer gleichfalls häufig, [. . .] [56,12]

Die Römer waren nicht spekulativisch in der Philosophie, sondern gesund. Sie waren nicht Aristoteliker, sondern Menschen. Den Cicero machten die Wissenschaften ruhig, denn er sprach wenigstens, wie Sokrates lebte, und schon diese von der Naturphilosophie entzündeten Worte weheten ihm Ruhe zu.— Durch die Scholastiker ist dem Summus Aristoteles ein Ehrengedächtnis gestiftet. Der Ausleger weiß immer ein Drittel mehr als sein Autor; so geht es immer, und so ging es auch hier.

Sokrates hat sich nicht der spekulativen Philosophie ergeben. Die Römer waren von mehr gesundem Verstande als die Griechen und fanden daher keinen Geschmack an den Subtilitäten. Allein es kam ein Zeitalter der Spekulation. Dies war die Zeit der Scholastiker im 14. saeculo [...] [56,22] Die Schriften des Aristoteles [56,26] wurden ihnen in die Hände gespielt, sie gaben vor, daß sie dieselben erklärten; so wie aber ein jeder Ausleger mehr zu wissen glaubt als sein Autor, so machten sie auch so viele Zusätze, daß die ganze Logik auf pure Schrauben gesetzt wurde. Sie dauerte nach der Reformation der Wissenschaften noch lange fort, [...] [56,26]

Man findet von diesem Greuel der Verwüstung noch Überbleibsel, und vorzüglich sind diese Antiquitäten noch in der Logik zu sehen.—Da gibt es Altertümer die Menge. (Einen *Winkelmann* bei den Antiquitäten der Logik wünsche ich bloß der Seltenheit wegen; dieses ist ein Wunsch, der ohne Fingerzeig weit jünger als mein Examen ist.)

Aber vieles, z. E. die Syllogistik, ist noch darinnen kindisch [56,33].—

Des Aristoteles, Gott verzeih mir meine Sünden! oder vielmehr seiner *Ausleger* wegen—denn wahrlich, er, für seine Person, war ein Mann, der sich gewaschen hatte—sollte man eine Feindschaft wider alle undeutschen Namen in der Philosophie haben.—Die *Ausleger!* was sind sie meistenteils und was sind sie in casu besonders? Kanäle in die Kreuz und Quer, die dem Lande die feuchte Kraft nehmen und den Reisenden hindern.——
Viele behaupten, daß wir mit Erkenntnissen auf die Welt kommen, die man allmählich herausspinnt, wie Garn aus Flachs. Diese halten die Seele für eine beschriebene, andere halten sie für eine unbeschriebene Tafel. Beide für Tafeln von Wachs und nicht von Stein, wie die Tafeln Mosis.

Von den angeborenen Begriffen. Der eine Teil der Philosophen behauptet, daß wir mit Erkenntnissen versehen auf die Welt kommen, daß sich der Vorrat nur allmählich entwickele, und daß die Seele des Menschen gleichsam wie eine beschriebene Tafel sei. [...] [39,35] Der andere Teil behauptete das Gegenteil, die Seele sei wie eine tabula rasa [40,1].

Alle Sünden aus der Erbsünde herleiten, heißt: eben dadurch eine wirkliche Sünde mehr begehen.

Es waren schon Weise des Altertums, die der Meinung waren, daß alles noch Überbleibsel von unserer vorigen Gemeinschaft mit Gott wäre, daß alles, damit ich mich deutlich und christlich ausdrücke, aus dem Paradiese herkäme. Was mein Vater von angeborenen Begriffen dachte, konnte ich nicht anbringen, Se. Spektabilität überkreischten mich, und was Se. Spektabilität davon dachten, ergibt sich ziemlich deutlich aus dem Vorigen. Sie glaubten, der Tisch sei nicht mit Essen und Trinken besetzt; allein auf dem Tisch ständ ein Beutel mit Dukaten und Talern, groß und klein Geld, je nachdem die Fähigkeiten sind, Essen und Trinken anzuschaffen. Die Erkenntnisse mögen nun aus den Sinnen geschöpft werden, oder die Sinne mögen bloß Gelegenheitsmacher sein; dies sei der Weg zur Erkenntnis.——
Es ist die Frage, ob wir alle gut, alle böse oder bald gut, bald bös auf die Welt kommen.
Wenn wir in die Höhe wollen, müssen wir steigen.—Wenn der Mensch alles aus dem lieben Gott beweiset, so will er ohne Leiter auf den Kirchturm; glückliche Reise! So philosophieren, nenne ich einen leichtsinnigen Eid schwören. Man muß sich nicht anders auf Gott berufen, als bis Not am Mann ist. Du sollst den Namen deines Gottes nicht unnützlich führen!

—Euere Rede sei ja, ja, nein, nein, was drüber ist, ist vom Übel. So wie sich Gott durch die Werke offenbaret hat und der Mensch von allen Geschöpfen, die wir die

—Etwas als angeboren anzunehmen, ist der Philosophie sehr zuwider. Es ist eben so, als wenn man alle Laster von der Erbsünde herleiten will, da doch ihrer viele erworben sind [41,28].

Plato sagte, der Sitz der menschlichen Seele ist ursprünglich in der der ewigen Gottheit gewesen [41,5].

Aristoteles glaubte, daß unsere Erkenntnisse aus den Sinnen geschöpft sind und entspringen. Das lehrte Locke nicht, sondern daß sie bei Gelegenheit der Sinne entspringen [41,25].

Man muß in der Natur so lange bleiben, als es möglich ist und sich nicht unmittelbar auf Gott berufen, denn das ist sehr vermessen. Eine Naturbegebenheit hat ihre Ursachen in der Natur, und diese Ursache wieder eine andere. Die Ursachen steigen so, bis man zuletzt auf Gott kommt. Maximen von etwas Angeborenem oder von unmittelbaren Verhängnissen Gottes sind das Polster der Faulen [41,34].
(Du sollst den Namen des Herrn, deines Gottes, nicht mißbrauchen. 2 Mose 20:7)

(Eure Rede aber sei: Ja, ja; nein, nein. Was darüber ist, das ist vom Übel. Matt. 5:37)

Ehre haben zu kennen, sein Meisterstück ist, so will er auch keinen Sprung zu ihm hinauf, sondern will, daß es fein in dem Geleise der Natur bleibe, die nicht springt. Die Instanzien, die Gott angeordnet hat, müssen nicht übergangen werden. Schein ist ein Urteil, das aus der falschen Anleitung des Verstandes entspringt, Wahrheit ist die Übereinstimmung der Erkenntnis mit dem Gegenstande. Wenn also gefragt wird, was ist Wahrheit? reine gediegene Wahrheit? so kann man nicht besser drauf antworten, als: Wahrheit ist Wahrheit. Wenn mir nicht ein Gegenstand gegeben wird, so kann ja auch keine Probe der Übereinstimmung gezogen werden. Eine Erklärung der Wahrheit in der Art zu geben, daß sie auf alle Objekte ohne Unterschied paßt, ist unmöglich. Jeder hat seine Uhr, jeder seine Brille, jeder sein Pferd (und jeder seinen Hund, seinen Argos, setzte Herr v. G. hinzu). Ein allgemeines Wahrheitsmerkzeichen, wo ist es? Eine Regel, die alle Objekte umfaßt und sie herzt und küßt, wo ist sie?

Ein Urteil, was aus der falschen Anleitung des Verstandes entspringt, heißt Schein. [...] [40,22] Die Wahrheit ist die Übereinstimmung der Erkenntnis mit dem Objekt. [...] [45,14] *Was ist Wahrheit?* Es gibt viele Fragen, welche deswegen nicht beantwortet werden können, weil sie ganz unbestimmt sind. [...] [45,9] Da hier keine Merkmale vom Gegenstand angegeben werden können, so weiß ich nicht, wie ich mit demselben übereinstimmen werden. [...] [45,12] Die Erklärung der Wahrheit soll so beschaffen sein, daß sie auf alle Objekte ohne Unterschied paßt [45,16] Es bleibt also die Antwort auf die Frage, was ist Wahrheit? ganz unbestimmt, und es kann kein allgemeingültiges Merkmal, keine allgemeine Regel von der Wahrheit gegeben werden [...] [45,20].

Ich muß vergleichen Erkenntnis und Gegenstand; wenn ich aber keinen Gegenstand habe, wie kann ich es?

Wodurch kann man erkennen, daß etwas mit dem Gegenstande übereinstimmt? Dadurch, daß ich eine Vergleichung anstelle. Dies kann ich aber nicht tun, wenn ich den Gegenstand selbst nicht kenne [45,25].

Vielleicht könnte sie die Übereinstimmung der Erkenntnis mit den Gesetzen des Verstandes und der Vernunft heißen, und der Irrtum der Widerstreit der Erkenntnis mit den Gesetzen des Verstandes und der Vernunft—vielleicht!——
Die Seel' in jeder Sache, oder dasjenige in der Erkenntnis von ihr, was in allen Vorstellungen, die wir von der Sache haben können gilt, ist das Wahre darin.

Alle Wahrheit wird bestehen in der Übereinstimmung der Erkenntnis mit den Gesetzen des Verstandes und der Vernunft [...] [46,10]. Der Irrtum ist der Widerstreit der Erkenntnis mit den Gesetzen des Verstandes und der Vernunft [46,14].
Dasjenige in einer Erkenntnis, was für alle Vorstellungen, die wir an der Sache haben können, gilt, das ist das Wahre darin [47,22].

Insoweit sich eine Sache nicht widerspricht, insoweit ist eine Seitenwand zum Wahrheitsgebäude fertig, insoweit ist eine Bedingung da, unter der etwas wahr ist. Wer kann und will aber sagen: alles, was sich nicht widerspricht, ist wahr. Es kann wahr werden. Es ist in Gott wahr, jeder Gedanke bei ihm steht da. Das Prinzipium des Widerspruchs ist immer ein negatives Wahrheitskennzeichen. Es ist nur eine Laterne in der Hand, allein es gehört mehr dazu als meiner Mutter Handlaternchen, wenn man hier sicher und ohnangefallen an Stell und Ort kommen soll.

Die Sinne lehren das Formale eines Dinges, der Verstand das Materiale. Das, wodurch das Mannigfaltige auf gleiche Art gedacht werden kann, heißt Regel. Der Verstand ist das Vermögen der Vorstellungen nach Regeln.

Das principium contradictionis ist die erste Bedingung, unter der etwas wahr ist. Aber deswegen ist doch die Erkenntnis noch nicht wahr, wenn sie sich nicht widerspricht. Es ist nur eine conditio sine qua non, aber kein bestimmtes Merkmal [45,35].

Der Satz des Widerspruchs ist nur ein negatives criterium [46,2].

Von den Begriffen. Durch die Sinnlichkeit werden wir nur die Form der Dinge gewahr 1. Raum und 2. Zeit. Der Verstand aber ist das Vermögen der Vorstellungen nach Regeln. [. . .] [42,8] Etwas ist eine Regel, wenn das Mannigfaltige auf gleiche Art gedacht werden soll [42,11].

Wir haben viele Vorstellungen, die wir nicht wahrnehmen, deren wir uns nicht bewußt sind. Man kann mit einem Menschen sprechen, ohne daß man weiß, was er für ein Kleid hat, und man kann denken, ohne daß man es wahrnimmt. Ein abstrakter Kopf ist, der so denkt, daß er nur immer auf das sieht, was den Begriffen gemein ist. Das Vermögen, sich Dinge durch Begriffe vorzustellen, heißt denken. Einen Begriff analysieren, ihn klarmachen, ist ein Hauptstück der Philosophie.

Wir haben viele Vorstellungen, deren wir uns nicht bewußt sind, [. . .] [42,36] Nicht alles, was man denkt, nimmt man wahr [42,39].
So hat man mit manchem Menschen gesprochen, ohne sich hernach besinnen zu können, wie er gekleidet war [42,39].
Ein abstrakter Kopf ist, der so denkt, daß er nur immer auf das sieht, was den Begriffen gemein ist [43,23].
Das Vermögen, sich die Dinge durch Begriffe vorzustellen, heißt denken. [. . .] [43,27] Die Analysis der Begriffe ist die Klarmachung derselben [43,30].
Der größte und wichtigste Teil der Philosophie besteht in der Analysis der Begriffe [. . .] [43,32].

Sie macht Gold; denn wenn es aus der Erde kommt, ist es Erde, durch Läuterungen wird es Gold.—Ein Moralphilosoph kann keinen Buchstaben mehr als

Klar wird eine Erkenntnis nicht bloß dadurch, daß man die Merkmale, die in dem Begriffe liegen, entwickelt und macht, daß man sich derselben bewußt

dies. Läge der Begriff der Tugend nicht in uns, wie könnten wir von ihm überzeugt werden? Wie?—

Begriff, Urteil, Schluß, major, minor, conclusio!

wird, sondern auch dadurch, daß man neue Merkmale hinzufügt, z. E. wenn man vom Golde sagt, daß es nicht rostet [43,34].
Die ganze Moral ist so beschaffen. Denn wie könnten wir z. E. von dem Begriff der Tugend überzeugt werden, wenn er nicht schon in uns läge [43,34].
Da die Logik vom Denken überhaupt handelt, so werden darin vorkommen:
1. Begriffe, d.i. eine Kenntnis von Dingen durch allgemeine Vorstellungen.
2. Urteile, wenn ich im Verhältnis etwas erkenne.
3. Schlüsse sind das Verhältnis der Urteile untereinander [42,2].

Ein Übergang von einem Urteil zum andern heißt Schluß.
Major enthält mehr in sich als das Subjekt quaestionis. Es ist der Vater vieler Kinder, Söhne und Töchter. Ehe man sein Zimmer bezieht, sieht man den ganzen Palast.—Das Prädikat ist größer als das Subjekt.—
Es behaupten einige: Empfindung wäre die größte Wahrheit; allein sie gibt nur Stoff zum Urteil. Die Sinne urteilen nicht, die Vernunft urteilt. Die Sinne sind Stahl, Feuerstein und Zunder. Zum Irrtum (Heil mir und meinem Buche!) gehört so gut als zur Wahrheit Verstand. Die Unwissenheit allein kann sich ohn ihn behelfen. Der Verstand wird beim Irrtum anders gewendet.

Beim Irrtum ist Illusion des Verstandes. Sinne und Verstand sind Wasser und Wein. Wer hat Wein ohne Wasser getrunken? Schon in der Traube ist Wasser.—
Jedes muß sein Maß und Gewicht haben.

Von den Schlüssen. Ein Schluß ist ein Übergang von einem Urteil zum anderen [44,30].
Das Prädikat ist größer als das Subjekt, es enthält noch mehr in sich als dies eine Subjekt. Deswegen heißt der erste Satz, der ein Prädikat vom zweiten ist, major und der zweite als das Subjekt minor [45,1].
Die Empfindungen, behaupten einige, enthielten die größte Wahrheit. Allein sie enthalten weder Wahrheit noch Falschheit. Die Sinne geben uns nur data zum Urteil, und es kommt darauf an, wie wir sie anwenden [46,5].
Zum Irren gehört ebensogut Verstand als zur Wahrheit. Zur Unwissenheit bedarf man keinen. Der Unterschied zwischen Irrtum und Wahrheit besteht nicht darin, daß in der Wahrheit Verstand, im Irrtum aber keine sei, sondern daß beim Irrtum der Verstand anders angewandt wird als bei der Wahrheit [46,32].
Bei jedem Irrtum ist eine Illusion des Verstandes [47,12].
Irrtum entsteht aus der Mischung der Sinnlichkeit und des Verstandes [47,5].
Die Schranken und die Enge des Verstandes bringen nicht Irrtümer hervor,

143

Die Schranken des Verstandes bringen nicht Irrtümer hervor, sondern nur weniger Erkenntnisse. Ein engbegrenzter Verstand irrt weniger als ein großer! Bei Gelehrten sind mehr Irrtümer, bei gemeinen Leuten aber mehr Vorurteile.— Wenn man den Menschen bindet, so läuft er nicht davon.—Man sagt von großen Genies, ihre Irrümer, ihre Fehler wären schön.—Schmeichelei!
Ein Kleid hebt das Gesicht. Ein kleines Männchen kann so richtig gebaut sein, als der größte; es kommt nur auf das Verhältnis unter den kleinen Teilchen an.
Irrtum, wenn ihn ein Kluger begeht, ist Taschenspielerei; es gehört ein Auge dazu, den Trug zu entdecken, und dies Auge hat nicht jeder.
Irrtum liegt oft in Sätzen, oft in der Anwendung dieser Sätze. Ein Fehler in Absicht der Sätze heißt *wirkliche,* in Absicht der Anwendung *Schwachheitssünde.*

Erst buchstabieren, dann lesen, sagten unsere lieben Alten.—Erst ein Urteil über Bausch und Bogen, dann ein richtiges. Erst der Läufer, dann der Herr. Wer in seinen vorläufigen Urteilen das Rechte trifft, heißt: ein Glückskind, oder sollte es eher heißen, als der, in dessen Familie viele alte Tanten sind. Es wäre wohl wert, ein Buchstabierbuch in diesem Verstande, in diesem Sinn, herauszugeben und über die vorläufigen Urteile eine Anleitung zu erteilen. Die Franzosen sind vorläufige Urteiler.—Der erste Gedanke ist oft der beste, und in Wahrheit, es gibt vorläufige Urteile, die wert sind, in Rahmen gefaßt zu werden.
Vorurteile sind Urteile aus der bloßen Sinnlichkeit, die man für Urteile aus dem Verstande hält. Die Sinnlichkeit läuft dem Verstande vor. Den Grund, den wir sondern nur weniger Erkenntnisse [47,27]. Gelehrte haben mehr Irrtümer als gemeine Leute, diese aber mehr Vorurteile als die ersteren [51,3].
Große Genies begehen oft mehr Fehler und Irrtümer als eingeschränkte Köpfe, wenn sie nur die Schranken ihres Verstandes immer nur vor Augen haben.—Was den richtigen Gebrauch unserer Kräfte betrifft, so kommt es da alles auf die Proportion an [47,30].
Wenn man einem die Möglichkeit des Irrtums entdeckt, so heilt man ihn auch davon. Wir gehen unzufrieden von einem Taschenspieler und zwar deswegen, weil wir wissen, daß wir hintergangen sind, nur nicht wissen wie [48,28].
Aller Irrtum liegt 1. entweder in Axiomen, Lehrsätzen, oder 2. in deren Anwendung [48,32].
Nach Verschiedenheit der Regeln sind die Irrtümer auch von verschiedenen Folgen. Ein Fehler in der logischen Regel ist größer als der in der ästhetischen. Ein Fehler in Ansehung eines moralischen Gesetzes ist noch größer als in einer logischen Regel. Ein Fehler in Anwendung der Regeln heißt nur ein Versehen [48,34].
Wenn wir lesen, so buchstabieren wir zuerst. Und so handeln wir überall [49,12]. Dann wird es uns begreiflich werden, wie es möglich gewesen ist, daß wir das vorläufige Urteil (die Anleitung zum Urteil, die Präsumtion) für was Wahres halten konnten [48,23]. [...] man könnte eine Logik von den vorläufigen Urteilen schreiben [49.29].

Wenn etwas nicht aus objektiven, sondern aus subjektiven Gründen, nicht aus Gründen des Verstandes und der Vernunft, sondern der Sinnlichkeit etc.

haben, von einer Sache zu urteilen, der aber nicht aus den Gesetzen des Verstandes genommen ist, heißt ein Vorurteil.

entsprungen ist und doch für etwas als aus Gesetzen des Verstandes Entsprungenes gehalten wird, dann ist es ein Vorurteil [50,3].
Der Grund, den wir haben, von einer Sache vorhero zu urteilen, der aber nicht aus Gesetzen des Verstandes entstanden ist, heißt ein Vorurteil [50,24].

Die Eltern haben Vorliebe zu ihren Kindern, hieraus entsteht eine Vorsprache, welches die Redekunst des Vorurteils ist.—
Ein Vorurteil ist eine Lüge, nur daß sie nicht immer vom Vater, dem Teufel, ist.

Die Sprachen, die man gelernt, lobt man vorzüglich. Die Eltern haben eine Vorliebe zu ihren Kindern, einen Fürsprecher in sich für sie [50,31].
Es ist an sich strafbar, wenn man Vorurteile in anderen pflanzt. Es ist eine Lüge, die man an anderen begeht [51,18].

Große Köpfe stiften viel Gutes, allein auch wahrlich viel Unheil, denn sie werden verehrt, und niemand untersteht sich, weiter zu gehen. Sie sind ein Wall, den kein Remus zu ersteigen sich unterfängt. Jeder Mensch hat einen Hang, seine Meinungen andern mitzuteilen, und der Gelehrteste ist nicht gleichgültig gegen das Urteil seiner Wäscherin und seines Ofenheizers.

Große Genies haben mehr Schaden angerichtet als kleinere. In der ersten Zeit haben ihre Schriften viel Nutzen geschafft, vieles dunkele erklärt, aber sie machen auch, daß man sehr lange Zeit nicht von der Stelle weitergehen kann [51,23].
Ein jeder Mensch hat einen Drang, sein Urteil und seine Meinungen andern bekanntzumachen, und das ist keinem zu verdenken. [. . .] [52,7] Es wird ihm gewiß auch das Urteil, was der Geringste über ihn fällt, nicht gleichgültig sein [52,4].

Die Methode ist dogmatisch über apodiktische Wahrheiten, und dies ist die Methode der Unterweisung und Behauptung. Die Methode ist aber skeptisch, polemisch, wo man erst untersucht, ob etwas apodiktisch heißen kann. Dies ist die Methode der Untersuchung, Beprüfung oder Kritik. Die polemische Methode ist die Läuterung, das Streben, die Verwesung in der Kenntnis, ehe wir zum Licht und Leben kommen. Die skeptische Philosophie ist hiervon verschieden, von welcher wir oben loco congruo schon ein Wörtchen gewechselt. Zweifeln und sein Urteil aufschieben, ist so unterschieden, als vorurteilen und nachurteilen.

Der dogmatischen Methode kann man sich in der Philosophie bedienen, wenn die Erkenntnisse apodiktisch gewiß sind [52,19].

Es gibt also 1. eine Methode der Behauptung und 2. eine der Untersuchung. Dies ist die skeptische Methode, wo man erst untersucht, ob etwas apodiktisch gewiß sei. Die skeptische Methode ist die Methode des Widerstreits, wodurch wir die Wahrheit zu finden suchen. [. . .] [52,22] Zweifeln und sein Urteil aufschieben, ist sehr verschieden [55,13].

Hier eine schöne Predigt über die Worte: Der Glaube kommt durch die Predigt, viva vox docet.—
Ein mündlicher Vortrag verrät die Art zu denken. Sie zeigt den Lehrer unangekleidet. Beim Hören denkt man immer mehr als beim Lesen.

Hören ist auch natürlicher als Lesen. Zwar können auch Bücher erbauen, allein es ist hier das nämliche Verhältnis wie zwischen Kirchen- und Hausandacht.—

Man muß beim Lesen die Seele des Buches suchen und der Idee nachspüren, welche der Autor gehabt hat, alsdann hat man das Buch ganz. Zuweilen ist freilich die Seele schwer zu finden, wie bei manchem Menschen sie wahrlich auch schwer zu finden ist. Der Verfasser selbst würde Mühe haben, die Seele aus seinem Buche herauszurechnen—indessen hat jedes Buch eine Seele, etwas Hervorstehendes wenigstens, und gemeinhin pflegt sich hiernach das übrige zu bequemen.—
Es scheint in der Welt bei allen Sachen eine Fibel nötig zu sein, überall ein gewisser Mechanismus, überall eine Schule, eine Akademie.—Wer nur ein Buch lieset, vergißt, daß das Jahr vier Jahreszeiten und daß jeder Tag vier Tageszeiten habe. Man lese *vier* Bücher auf einmal, und man wird finden, daß dies dem Gemüte Erholung sei. Ein einziges Buch lesen, heißt im Seelenverstande: den Pflug führen oder dreschen.—Neue Beschäftigung ist wahrlich Erholung. Warum ist die Gesellschaft Erholung? Weil ein kluger Mann hier mehr als ein Buch lieset. Der hat es weit gebracht, der Menschen lesen kann!—
(Gott weiß, dies ist ein großes Studium! Die schönste Gegend, was ist sie gegen einen Menschen. Und wer die Gesellschaft aus diesem Gesichtspunkt nimmt,

(So kommt der Glaube aus der Predigt, das Predigen aber durch das Wort Christi. *Römer*, 10,17)
Ein mündlicher Vortrag, wenn er auch nicht ganz ausgearbeitet ist, hat sehr viel Instruierendes. Beim Hören denkt man auch immer mehr als beim Lesen [54,38].

Das Lesen ist auch nicht so natürlich wie das Hören. Durch Schriften muß freilich eine Wissenschaft vollendet werden, allein die Autodidachie, das Selbstlernen aus einem Instrument (welches nicht selbst erfinden heißt), ist nur eine Nothilfe [55,3].
Man muß das Charakteristische eines Buches kennen lernen, d. h. nicht den bloßen Inhalt, sondern das Eigentümliche, was es vor anderen Büchern besonders hat [54,20].
Man muß bei jedem Buch die Idee des Autors zu entdecken suchen. Das ist etwas Wichtiges und Schweres. Oft hat der Autor seine eigene Idee selbst nicht gewußt, und sie alsdann zu finden, ist um desto schwerer [53,18].

Ohne Mechanismus scheint in der Welt nichts recht fortkommen zu wollen [53,30].
Man kann nie ein Buch allein mit Aufmerksamkeit lesen, sondern man muß ein ganz anderes von verschiedenem Inhalt bei der Hand haben. Die Gesellschaft ist auch eine Erholung fürs Gemüt, denn sie ist gleichfalls eine Beschäftigung [54,1].

kann gelehrt werden, ohne ein gedrucktes Buch, das ohnehin selten Leben hat.)

Es gibt einen gewissen Lesegeiz, alles, was man lieset, in seinen Nutzen zu verwenden.—Einen Lesevielfraß, alles zu verschlingen—und da ereignen sich oft Kopfdrücken und Verschleimungen. Sich in einem Buche betrinken, heißt: darüber Sehen und Hören vergessen und es so vorzüglich finden, daß nichts drüber ist.— Wenig und gut lesen ist großen Köpfen eigen. Es ist schwerer, so schreiben, als so reden, daß es einen interessiert. Das Beste ist, sich selbst herausdenken, nicht bei Hand- und Lehrbüchern, sondern bei seinem Genie in die Schule gehen und ihm Folge leisten und die Logik dem natürlichen Gange seines selbst eigenen Geistes, so wie die Moral seinem Gewissen, zu verdanken zu haben. Wohl dem, der sich von allem entkleiden kann, was nicht er selbst (das letzte Hemde nicht ausgenommen) ist! Wohl dem, der seine Willkür dem Gesetz der Wahrheit und der Tugend unterwirft; wohl dem, der Wesen vom Schein, Schatten vom Licht absondert; Menschenfurcht, Menschenehre und den ganzen unwürdigen Troß von Vorurteilen, sie mögen gleich die höchste Stufe des menschlichen Lebens und ihre Achtzig erreicht haben und mit dem regierenden Hause in Einverständnis leben, vom Hauptpastor kanonisiert und vom Professore Philosophiae ordinario als ein Anhang dem Katechismus der Vernunft beigebunden sein, für das hält, was sie sind—Menschensatzungen und Tand!——Wohl—
Alles Rationale zusammengenommen, heißt Metaphysik. Sie ist die Seele der Philosophie.

Man muß bei jedem Lesen geizen und soviel wie möglich zu behalten suchen, wenn es auch nur ein lästiger Einfall etc. wäre, das kann uns auch nutzen und eine Gesellschaft aufgeräumt machen [54,12].
Wenn die Literatur oder viel Bücher zu kennen, unsere Absicht ist, so muß man viel lesen. Allein um vielen Nutzen vom Lesen zu haben, muß man wenig und gut lesen. Wer viel liest, behält wenig [54,29].
Es ist ein großes Verdienst, mit jedermann so sprechen zu können, daß es ihn interessiert [55,20].
Das Genie kann sich nicht den Regeln unterwerfen, denn sie sind nicht aus dem Genie geschöpft, sondern sie dienen ihm nur zur Anleitung [54,24].

(Ps. 90:10)

Wenn man alles rationale aus der Philosophie zusammen nimmt, alles was entweder durch die bloße reine Vernunft gegeben ist oder obgleich durch die Sinne gegeben, aber doch rationaliter oder durch die Vernunft betrachtet wird, so entsteht daraus die Metaphysik [37,17].

Die Metaphysik enthält Urteil des Verstandes, abgesondert von aller Er-

Die Metaphysik enthält Urteile des Verstandes, die abgesondert sind von aller

fahrung und von allen Verhältnissen der Sinne, wenn zum Exempel von der Möglichkeit, Zufälligkeit usw. gehandelt wird. Hier reden wir nicht vom Schein, sondern vom Sein, um dem Drosselpastor nachzuahmen. Die Metaphysik hat kein Verhältnis zu den Sinnen. Es will hier alles geistisch gerichtet sein. Sie ist ein Lexikon der reinen Vernunft, ein Versuch, die Sätze des reinen Denkens in eine Tabelle zu bringen.

Erfahrung und auch von allen Verhältnissen der Sinne, z. E. wenn die Rede ist von der Notwendigkeit, Möglichkeit, Zufälligkeit der Dinge [59,40].
Es muß einen doch aber wundern, daß ein Gebrauch der Vernunft ganz abgezogen von der Erfahrung möglich ist [60,3].
Die Kritik wird aus zwei Stücken bestehen, nämlich 1. aus der Analytik, 2. aus der Dialektik der Vernunft. Die erstere könnte man ein Wörterbuch der reinen Vernunft nennen; [. . .] [60,20] Wir wollen versuchen, die Sätze des reinen Denkens in eine Tabelle zu bringen [60,35].

Was in der Logik Urteile sind, sind in der Ontologie Begriffe, unter die wir die Dinge setzen, *Titel* des Verstandes, *Inhalt* der Vernunft. Die Metaphysik muß kritisieren. Ihr Gebrauch ist negativ, wenn—
Wir waren im Begriff, uns recht viel Metaphysik ins Auge zu streuen, allein siehe da! die Hausmütze Sr. Spektabilität, die Großmutter, würgte die Tür auf und blinkte durch ein Ritzchen. Man sahe, daß die alte Frau noch einen Brand im Auge hatte. Sie schlug einen Strahl ins Zimmer. Dieser Wink sollt ihren lieben Ehegatten zum Schluß bringen, weil sie ohnfehlbar beim Großsohn den Abend versprochen waren. Man sah es Sr. Spektabilität an, daß Sie wußten, was man einem Blick durchs Ritzchen schuldig wäre. Es ging über und über.—
Ich weiß nicht, ob ich dies über und über schriftlich werde nachmachen können.

Was in der Logik Urteile sind, sind in der Ontologie Begriffe, unter welche wir die Dinge bringen [61,27].
Die Metaphysik enthält also die Titel des Denkens und lehrt den Gebrauch des Verstandes in Ansehung aller angeblichen Dinge [58,36].
Die Metaphysik muß kritisieren, ihr Gebrauch ist negativ, sie lehrt uns ganz und gar nichts [68,7].

(Kant's servant was named Lampe.)

Die moralischen Maximen, fingen Se. Spektabilität, nach disem Blick durchs Ritzchen (ich weiß nicht, warum?) an, zeigen, wie ich der Glückseligkeit würdig werden könne, die pragmatischen zeigen, ihrer teilhaftig zu werden. Die Moral lehrt, der Glückseligkeit würdig zu sein; ihrer

Die moralischen Maximen zeigen, wie ich der Glückseligkeit würdig werden kann, und die pragmatischen, wie ich ihrer teilhaftig werden soll [67,13].
Die Moral ist, die uns lehrt, der Glückseligkeit würdig zu sein, ihrer teilhaftig zu werden, ist eine Lehre der

teilhaftig zu werden, ist eine Lehre der Geschicklichkeit. Es ist nicht möglich, die Regeln der Klugheit und der Sittlichkeit zu trennen. Es ist kein natürlicher Zusammenhang zwischen dem Wohlverhalten und der Glückseligkeit; um es zu verbinden, muß man ein göttliches Wesen annehmen. Ohne dies kann ich keine Zwecke in der Welt finden, keine Einheit.—Ich spiele in der Welt blinde Kuh.—Ohne Gott hab ich keinen Punkt, wo ich anfangen soll, nichts, was mich leitet. Gott ist *groß* und unaussprechlich!——	Geschicklichkeit. Die Metaphysik verbindet sie beide. Es ist nicht möglich, die Regeln der Klugheit und der Sittlichkeit zu trennen. Es ist kein natürlicher Zusammenhang zwischen dem Wohlverhalten und der Glückseligkeit [. . .] [67,21]. Um das Wohlverhalten mit der Glückseligkeit zu verbinden, muß man solches dadurch tun, daß man ein höchstes Wesen annimmt. Wenn wir ein solches Wesen nicht annehmen, so handelt man entweder als ein Tor oder als ein Bösewicht [67,27].—(Denn der Herr ist groß und hoch zu loben, mehr zu fürchten als alle Götter. Ps 96,4) Ohne dieses kann ich keine Zwecke in der Welt finden, keine Einheit des Weltganzen. Die Annehmung des höchsten Wesens ist eine notwendige theoretische Hypothesis, ohne die ich keinen Punkt habe, wo ich anfangen soll, nichts, was mich leitet, wenn ich außerhalb der Grenzen dieser Welt gehe.—Die Menschen bedienen sich ihrer Vernunft a priori, zum Nachteil des praktischen Gebrauchs, wenn sie nicht durch künstliche Schranken zurückgehalten werden. Die Metaphysik muß solchen Frevel steuern [67,38].
Die Menschen bedienen sich ihrer Vernunft a priori, zum Nachteil des praktischen Gebrauches, wenn sie nicht durch künstliche Schranken zurückgehalten werden. Dieses ist auch die Pflicht der Metaphysik.——(Zehnmal fingen Se. Spektabilität: quid est? an, und zehnmal macht ich eine Verbeugung, um ihn vom Fragen abzubringen.—)	
Das Erste, was ich bei mir gewahr werde, ist das Bewußtsein, dies ist kein besonderes Denken, sondern die Bedingung und die Form, unter der wir denkende Wesen sind. Wie schön bauen und wirken nicht manche Tiere, wie nah kommen sie uns nicht auf die Seele; allein eins, was nicht ersetzt werden kann, das Bewußtsein, fehlt, und wahrlich, es fehlt wenig, und es fehlt viel! Mein Reisegefährte wollte wegen der Hunde einwenden, indessen konnt'er nichts mehr als husten.—	Das erste, was ich bei mir gewahr wurde, ist das Bewußtsein. Dies ist kein besonderes Denken, sondern dasjenige, worunter ich die übrigen Vorstellungen etc. bringen kann, es ist die Bedingung und die Form, unter der wir denkende Wesen oder Intelligenzen sind [68,21]. Der Haupt- und beinahe der einzige Unterschied zwischen Tieren und Menschen ist das Bewußtsein, aber der ist auch so groß, daß er durch nichts ersetzt werden kann [68,26].
Alles, was da ist, ist im Raum und der Zeit. Raum und Zeit sind Formen der	Aber alles, was da ist, ist im Raum und der Zeit [. . .] [63,25]. Raum und Zeit sind Anschauungen, sie

149

Anschauungen, sie gehen den Erscheinungen vor, wie das Formale dem Wesentlichen. Ich muß Zeit und Raum haben, damit wenn Erscheinungen vorfallen, ich sie hinstellen und beherbergen könne. Die Objekte der äußeren Sinne werden im Raum, die der innern Sinne in der Zeit angeschaut. Hier ein ganz kleiner Kommentarius über den theologischen terminum technicum Zeit und Raum zur Buße, der, wie Se. Spektabilität sich ausdrückten, nicht außerm Wurf läge. Wie vielen Dingen mußten wir auf der Stelle, des Blickes durch die Ritze wegen, einen Scheidebrief geben. Wir nannten bloß ihre Namen und behalfen uns damit, daß wir diese Namen nannten und uns einander zulächelten.—Ein wahres Examen!—
Bei reinen Verstandesbegriffen haben wir keine Begriffe von Sachen, sondern nur Titel, worunter wir uns eine Sache denken können. Durch diese Titel können wir nichts ausrichten, außer, wenn wir sie auf Gegenstände der Erfahrung und Anschauung anwenden.

Wer kann aber, ohne die Titel des Verstandes vorauszusetzen, wer kann Erfahrungen anstellen? wer Fische ohne Netz oder Hamen fangen? Die Metaphysik enthält alles und enthält nichts. Sie macht nichts von den Gegenständen aus, allein ohne sie kann man nichts von Gegenständen ausmachen. Sie ist das Zollhaus, die öffentlichen Wage der philosophischen Erkenntnis. Sie enthält Titel des Denkens, allein keine Prädikata der Dinge. Nur die Erscheinungen verleihen Begriffe von den Dingen.—
Vernünftelei (Se. Spektabilität wurden von einer Mücke verfolgt, die um Sie herumsauste und sich nicht haschen ließ) ist das, was kein Objekt hat. Was eine Bedingung der Vorstellung und des Begriffs vom Gegenstande ist, machen wir oft zur Bedingung des Gegenstandes selbst, die subjektive Bedingung zur

sind keine Begriffe, sondern sie werden angeschaut. Sie sind Formen der Anschauungen und gehen den Erscheinungen vor.
Ich muß notwendig zuerst reinen Raum und Zeit haben, damit, wenn ich Erscheinungen habe, ich weiß, wohin ich sie stelle.
Alle Objekte der äußeren Sinne werden im Raum, und Objekte des inneren Sinnes werden in der Zeit angeschaut [62,3].

Bei allen reinen Verstandesbegriffen haben wir noch keine Begriffe von den Sachen, sondern nur Titel, worunter wir uns eine Sache denken können. Durch sie können wir nichts ausmachen, außer wenn wir sie auf Gegenstände der Erfahrung und Anschauung anwenden [62,35].

Die Metaphysik betrachtet die Titel des Denkens, unter welche ich die Objekte bringen kann [58,32].
Ohne Anschauung können wir nicht denken, ohne Titel des Denkens haben wir keine Anschauung [58,27].
Da die angeführten Verstandesbegriffe nicht von den Gegenständen entlehnt sind, denn kein Gegenstand erscheint mir mit der Notwendigkeit etc., so machen sie auch nichts von den Gegenständen aus, sie sind nur Titel des Denkens und keine Prädikate der Dinge. Nur die Erscheinungen geben uns Begriffe von den Dingen [63,1].
Vernünftelei ist das, was kein Objekt hat.—Was eine Bedingung der Vorstellung und des Begriffs vom Gegenstande ist, machen wir oft zur Bedingung des Gegenstandes selbst, d.i. die subjektive Bedingung zur objektiven [64,2].

objektiven.—Die Mücke verhinderte Se. Spektabilität, dieses Thema weiter auszuführen. Im Ernst, die Mücke hätte nicht besser ihre Sachen machen können, wenn sie von der Frau Gemahlin Sr. Spektabilität wär auf den Hals geschickt worden.

Der analytische Teil der Metaphysik enthält Definitionen meiner Begriffe, der synthetische Bereicherung von Erkenntnissen. Der Begriff von den Monaden muß billig nur auf denkende Wesen gedeutet werden, fingen Se. Spektabilität mit einem frischen Atemzuge nach einer geendigten Kadenz an und schienen noch sehr viel Metaphysik auf Ihrem Gewissen zu haben, allein die Türe ging auf.——

Der analytische Teil würde Definitionen meiner Begriffe enthalten, aber der synthetische ist eine neue Akquisition von Erkenntnissen [65,22].

Der Begriff der Monaden muß billig nur auf denkende Wesen appliziert werden [66,25].

Bibliography

Hippel

Hippel, Theodor Gottlieb von. *Biographie des Königl. Preuß. Geheimenkriegsraths zu Königsberg. Zum Theil von ihm selbst verfaßt. Aus Schlichtegrolls Nekrolog besonders abgedruckt.* Gotha: Perthes, 1801; rpt. with an Afterword by Ralph-Reiner Wuthenow (Texte zum literarischen Leben um 1800, ed. Ernst Weber, 4), Hildesheim: Gerstenberg, 1977.

———. Th. G. v. Hippel's *Sämmtliche Werke.* 14 vols. Ed. Theodor Gottlieb von Hippel (author's nephew). Berlin: Reimer, 1828–39; rpt. Berlin: de Gruyter, 1978.

———. Rev. of *Lebensläufe. Allgemeine deutsche Bibliothek,* XLI (1780), 469–70.

———. Rev. of *Lebensläufe. Der Teutsche Merkur,* 1779, IV, 286–89.

Other Sources

Abbt, Thomas. Rev. of Justi's *Psammitichus. Briefe, die neueste Literatur betreffend,* 12 (1761), 255–84.

Abegg, Johann Friedrich. *Reisetagebuch von 1798.* Ed. Walter and Jolanda Abegg, Zwi Batscha. Stuttgart: Insel, 1976.

Albrecht, Michael. *Kants Antinomie der praktischen Vernunft.* Hildesheim: Olms, 1978.

Anderson, Howard. "Answers to the Author of *Clarissa:* Theme and Narrative Technique in *Tom Jones* and *Tristram Shandy.*" *Philological Quarterly,* 51 (1972), 859–73.

Bach, Theodor. *Theodor Gottlieb von Hippel, der Verfasser des Aufrufs:* 'An mein Volk.' *Ein Gedenkblatt zur fünfzigjährigen Feier der Erhebung Preußens.* Breslau: Trewendt, 1863. (Contains letters from Hippel to his nephew.)

Baird, Theodore. "The Time Scheme of *Tristram Shandy* and a Source." *PMLA,* 51 (1936), 803–20.

Batteux, Charles. *Einleitung in die schönen Wissenschaften.* Trans. and with supplements by K. W. Ramler. 4th ed. Leipzig: Weidmann, 1774. Vol. IV.

Beck, Hamilton. *Hippel and the Eighteenth-Century Novel.* Diss. Cornell 1980.

———. "Historiography and Parody in the Eighteenth-Century Novel." *Journal of the History of Ideas,* XLVI (1985), 405–16.

———. "Kant and the Novel." *Kant-Studien,* 74 (1983), 271–301.

———. "*Tristram Shandy* and Hippel's *Lebensläufe nach aufsteigender Linie.*" *Studies in Eighteenth-Century Culture*, 10 (1981), 261–78.
Becker, Eva D. *Der deutsche Roman um 1780*. Germanische Abhandlungen, 5. Stuttgart: Metzler, 1964.
Bergk, J. A. *Die Kunst, Bücher zu lesen*. Leipzig: Brockhaus, 1799.
Blanckenburg, Friedrich von. *Versuch über den Roman*. Sammlung Metzler, 39. Leipzig and Liegnitz: Siegert, 1774; rpt. Stuttgart: Metzler, 1965.
Booth, Wayne C. *The Rhetoric of Fiction*. Chicago and London: University of Chicago Press, 1961.
———. "The Self-Conscious Narrator in Comic Fiction Before *Tristram Shandy.*" *PMLA*, LXVII (1952), 163–85.
Borcherdt, H. H. *Der Roman der Goethezeit*. Urach and Stuttgart: Port, 1949.
Borinski, Ludwig. *Der englische Roman des achtzehnten Jahrhunderts*. Frankfurt and Bonn: Athenäum, 1965.
Borowski, Ludwig Ernst. *Ueber das Autorschiksal des Verfassers des Buchs: Ueber die Ehe—der Lebensläufe nach aufsteigender Linie u.a.m. Eine Beilage zu den benannten Schriften*. Königsberg: Hartung, 1797.
Braudy, Leo. *Narrative Form in History and Fiction*. Princeton: Princeton University Press, 1970.
Breitinger, J. J. *Critische Dichtkunst*. Zurich: Orell, 1740; rpt. Stuttgart: Metzler, 1966.
Brenning, Emil. "Hippel der Frauenanwalt." *Altpreußische Monatsschrift*, XVII (1880), 417–24.
———. "Hippel, Theodor Gottlieb von." *Allgemeine deutsche Biographie*, XII (1880), 463–66.
———. "Hippel und Rousseau." *Altpreußische Monatsschrift*, XVI (1879), 286–300.
———. "T. G. v. Hippel." *Monatshefte der Comeniusgesellschaft*, XI (1902), 257–73.
Brodsky, Joseph. "The Soviet Union" (part of a Symposium on Literature and War.) *Times Literary Supplement*, May 17, 1985, pp. 543–44.
Byrd, Max. *Tristram Shandy*. London: Allen & Unwin, 1985.
Campe, Joachim. *Der programmatische Roman. Von Wielands "Agathon" zu Jean Pauls "Hesperus"*. Abhandlungen zur Kunst-, Musik- und Literaturwissenschaft, vol. 292. Bonn: Bouvier, 1979.
Cash, Arthur H. "The Sermon in *Tristram Shandy.*" *ELH*, XXI (1961), 395–417.
Chatman, Seymour. *Story and Discourse*. Ithaca and London: Cornell Univ. Press, 1978.
Czerny, Johann. *Sterne, Hippel und Jean Paul*. Berlin: Duncker & Humblot, 1904; rpt. Hildesheim: Gerstenberg, 1978.
Deiter, Heinrich. "Hippel im Urteile seiner Zeitgenossen." *Euphorion* 17 (1910), 306–13.
Deppe, Wolfgang G. *History versus Romance. Ein Beitrag zur Entwicklungsgeschichte und zum Verständnis der Literaturtheorie Henry Fieldings*. Neue Beiträge zur englischen Philologie, 4. Münster: Aschendorff, 1965.
Diderot, Denis. *Jaques* [sic] *le fataliste et son maître*. Edition critique. Ed. Simon Lecointre, Jean le Galliot. Geneva: Droz, 1976.
———. *Oeuvres complètes*. Ed. Assezat et Tourneux. Paris: Garnier, 1875–77.
Dieckmann, Herbert. "Introduction de Préface de *La Religieuse.*" With notes by Georges May. In: Diderot, *La Religieuse*, Edition Critique et annotée. Ed. G. May, H. Dieckmann et al. (Paris: Hermann, 1976).
———. "The Préface annexe of *La Religieuse.*" *Diderot Studies*, II (1952), 21–147.

———. *Studien zur europäischen Aufklärung*. Munich: Fink, 1974.
Düntzer, Hermann. "Zur Würdigung Hippels." *Allgemeine Monatsschrift für Wissenschaft und Literatur*, II (1850), 190–92. (Contains essay by Borowski written shortly after Hippel's death.)
Eichendorff, Joseph Freiherr von. *Der deutsche Roman des 18. Jahrhunderts in seinem Verhältnis zum Christentum*. Neue Gesamtausgabe der Werke und Schriften in vier Bänden. Stuttgart: Cotta'sche Nachfolger, 1851, IV.
Engel, Johann Jakob. "Ueber Handlung, Gespräch und Erzählung." Facsimile of the first version of 1774 from the *Neue Bibliothek der schönen Wissenschaften und der freyen Künste*, 16 (1774), 177–256; ed. and with an afterword by Ernst Theodor Voss. Metzler Reihe Realienbücher für Germanistik, 37. Stuttgart: Metzler, 1964.
English Theories of the Novel. Ed. Theo Stemmler. Tübingen: Niemeyer, 1970. Vol. II.
Fielding, Henry. *The History of the Life of the Late Mr. Jonathan Wild the Great. And: Journal of a Voyage to Lisbon*. Everyman's Library ed. London: Dent; New York: Dutton, 1932.
———. *The History of Tom Jones, A Foundling*. Ed. M. Battestin, F. Bowers. Wesleyan University Press, 1975.
Fischer, Richard. *Geschichte der Johannis Loge Zu den drei Kronen*. Königsberg: Als Manuskript gedruckt, 1910.
Fluchère, Henri. *Laurence Sterne: From Tristram to Yorick. An Interpretation of Tristram Shandy*. Trans. and abridged by Barbara Bray. London: Oxford University Press, 1965.
Frankfurter gelehrte Anzeigen 1772. Ed. and selected Hans-Dietrich Dahnke, Peter Müller. Leipzig: Reclam, 1971.
Fredman, Alice Green. *Diderot and Sterne*. New York: Columbia University Press, 1955.
Fritsch, Theodor (ed.). *Handbuch der Judenfrage. Eine Zusammenstellung des wichtigsten Materials zur Beurteilung des jüdischen Volkes*. 23rd ed. Hamburg: Gleipner, 1919.
Geißler, Rolf. *Romantheorie in der Aufklärung. Thesen und Texte zum Roman des 18. Jahrhunderts in Frankreich*. Berlin: Akademie, 1984.
Genette, Gérard. *Narrative Discourse*. Trans. Jane E. Lewin. Ithaca: Cornell Univ. Press, 1980.
Gervinus, Georg. *Geschichte der poetischen National-Literatur der Deutschen*. 3rd ed. 5 vols. Leipzig: Engelmann, 1846.
Godenne, René. "Les Nouvellistes des années 1680–1750 et *La Religieuse*." *Diderot Studies*, XIV (1973), 55–68.
Greenburg, L. "Narrative Technique and Literary Intent in Diderot's *Les Bijoux indiscrets* and *Jacques le fataliste*." *Studies on Voltaire and the Eighteenth Century*, LXXIV (1971), 93–101.
Greiner, Martin. *Theodor Gottlieb von Hippel 1741–1796*. Schriften der Justus Liebig Universität Gießen, 3. Gießen: Schmitz, 1958.
Grund, Uwe. "Studien zur Sprachgestaltung in Theodor Gottlieb von Hippels Roman *Die Lebensläufe nach aufsteigender Linie*." Diss. Berlin 1970.
Hahl, Werner. *Reflexion und Erzählung. Ein Problem der Romantheorie von der Spätaufklärung bis zum programmatischen Realismus*. Studien zur Poetik und Geschichte der Literatur, 18. Stuttgart: Kohlhammer, 1971.

Hamann, Johann Georg. *Briefwechsel.* 7 vols. Ed. Walther Ziesemer (vols. 1–3) and Arthur Henkel (vols. 4–7). Wiesbaden: Insel, 1955–1979.

Hammond, Lansing. *Laurence Sterne's "Sermons of Mr. Yorick".* Yale Studies in English, CVIII (1948).

Hays, Michael. "Dramatic Literature as History: Some Suggestions about Theory and Method." Literature and History, ed. Harry R. Garvin, *Bucknell Review* 23, Nr. 2 (1977).

Hegel, Georg Wilhelm Friedrich. *Aesthetik.* 2nd ed. 2 vols. Ed. Friedrich Bassenge. Berlin and Weimar: Aufbau, 1976.

———. "Ueber: Hamann's Schriften." *Sämtliche Werke.* Jubiläumsausgabe. 3rd ed. Ed. H. Glockner. Stuttgart: Frommann-Holzboog, 1958. XX, 203–75.

Heidegger, Gotthard. *Mythoscopia Romantica oder Discours von den so benanten Romans.* Facsimile of the first edition of 1698; ed. Walter Ernst Schäfer. Ars Poetica, 3. Bad Homburg v. d. H., Berlin, Zurich: Gehlen, 1969.

Heitmann, Klaus. "Das Verhältnis von Dichtung und Geschichtschreibung in älterer Theorie." *Archiv für Kulturgeschichte.* Cologne: Böhlau, 52 (1970), 244–79.

Herder, Johann Georg. *Briefe zu [sic] Beförderung der Humanität.* 2 vols. Berlin and Weimar: Aufbau, 1976.

Hettner, Hermann. *Geschichte der deutschen Literatur im achtzehnten Jahrhundert.* 2nd ed. 2 vols. Berlin and Weimar: Aufbau, 1979.

Hinske, Norbert. Rev. of Kant's *Vorlesungen über philosophische Enzyklopädie,* ed. G. Lehmann. *Deutsche Literaturzeitung,* 85, 6 (1964), 486–90.

Hönes, Theodor. *Theodor Gottlieb von Hippel. Die Persönlichkeit und die Werke in ihrem Zusammenhang.* Diss. Bonn 1909.

Home, Henry Lord Kames. *Elements of Criticism, with analyses, and translations of ancient and foreign illustrations.* London: Millar; Edinburgh: Kincaid & Bell, 1762.

Huet, Daniel Pierre. *Traité de l'origine des romans.* Sammlung Metzler, 54. Paris: Barbin, 1670; rpt. Stuttgart: Metzler, 1966.

Hunter, J. Paul. "Response as Reformation: *Tristram Shandy* and the Art of Interruption." *Novel, A Forum on Fiction,* 4 (1970), 132–46.

Jacobs, Jürgen. *Prosa der Aufklärung.* Munich: Winkler, 1976.

Kant, Immanuel. *Anweisung zur Menschen- und Weltkenntnis.* Ed. Fr. Chr. Starke (J. A. Bergk). Quedlinburg and Leipzig: Ernst, 1830.

———. *Gesammelte Schriften.* Vols. 1–22 ed. Preußische Akademie der Wissenschaften; Vol. 23 ed. Akademie der Wissenschaften zu Berlin; Vols. 24– ed. Akademie der Wissenschaften zu Göttingen. 1910–

———. *Menschenkunde oder philosophische Anthropologie.* Ed. Fr. Chr. Starke (J. A. Bergk). Leipzig: Expedition des europäischen Aufsehers, 1831.

———. *Vorlesungen über philosophische Enzyklopädie.* Ed. Gerhard Lehmann. Berlin: Akademie, 1961.

Keber, W. G. *Nachrichten und Bemerkungen den Geheimen Kriegsrath von Hippel betreffend. Ein Nachtrag zu seiner Biographie im Nekrolog.* Königsberg: Goebbels and Unzer, 1802.

Kermode, Frank. "Richardson and Fielding." *Cambridge Journal,* 4 (1950), 106–14.

Kimpel, Dieter. *Der Roman der Aufklärung.* Sammlung Metzler, 68. Stuttgart: Metzler, 1967.

———. "Theodor Gottlieb von Hippel." In *Deutsche Dichter des 18. Jahrhunderts.* Ed. Benno von Wiese. Berlin: Schmidt, 1977, pp. 462–81.

Kleinschmidt, Erich. "Fiktion und Identifikation. Zur Ästhetik der Leserrolle im deutschen Roman zwischen 1750 und 1780." *Deutsche Vierteljahrsschrift für Literaturwissenschaft und Geistesgeschichte* 53 (1979), 49–73.
Kohnen, Joseph. "Hippel und Hamann." In *Johann Georg Hamann*. Acta des internationalen Hamann-Colloquiums in Lüneburg, 1976. Ed. Bernhard Gajek with a Foreword by Arthur Henkel. Frankfurt a. M.: Klostermann, 1979, pp. 22–39.
―――. *Theodor Gottlieb von Hippel, 1741–1796, L'homme et l'oeuvre*. European University Studies, Series 1, German Language and Literature, Vol. 727. Bern, Frankfurt, New York: Lang, 1983.
―――. "Ottomar und der 'Sterbegraf'." *Germanisch-romanische Monatsschrift*, 29 (1979), 185–99.
―――. "Zu einem unbekannten Hippel-Brief." *Recherches Germaniques* 15 (1985), 196–206.
Krauss, Werner. *Essays zur französischen Aufklärung*. Berlin and Weimar: Aufbau, 1968.
Kundera, Milan. *Jacques and his Master*. Trans. Michael Henry Hein. New York: Harper & Row, 1985.
Kurth, Lieselotte E. "Historiographie und historischer Roman: Kritik und Theorie im achtzehnten Jahrhundert." *Modern Languages Notes*, 79 (1964), 337–62.
―――. *Die zweite Wirklichkeit. Studien zum Roman des achtzehnten Jahrhunderts*. University of North Carolina Studies in Germanic Languages and Literatures, 62. Chapel Hill: University of North Carolina Press, 1969.
Lämmert, Eberhard. "Zum Wandel der Geschichtserfahrung im Reflex der Romantheorie." In *Geschichte-Ereignis und Erzählung*. Ed. Reinhard Koselleck, Wolf-Dieter Stempel. Poetik und Hermeneutik, V. Munich: Fink, 1973, pp. 503–15.
Lange, Victor. "Erzählformen im Roman des achtzehnten Jahrhunderts." *Anglia*, 76 (1958), 129–44.
Laurence Sterne. Ed. Gerd Rohmann. Wege der Forschung, 467. Darmstadt: Wissenschaftliche Buchgesellschaft, 1980.
Lehmann, B. H. "Of Time, Personality and the Author. A Study of *Tristram Shandy:* Comedy." In *Studies in the Comic*. University of California Publications in English, VIII, 2 (1941), 233–50; rpt. in *Essays on the Eighteenth Century Novel*. Ed. Robert Donald Spector. Bloomington: Indiana University Press, 1965, pp. 165–84.
Lessing, Gotthold Ephraim. *Briefe, die neueste Literatur betreffend*. Stuttgart: Reclam, 1972.
Lessing im Gespräch. Ed. Richard Daunicht. Munich: Fink, 1971.
Lockemann, Wolfgang. *Die Entstehung des Erzählproblems. Untersuchungen zur deutschen Dichtungstheorie im 17. und 18. Jahrhundert*. Deutsche Studien, 3. Meisenheim am Glan: Hain, 1963.
Losno, Robert. "Optimisme et pessimisme dans l'oeuvre de Theodor Gottlieb von Hippel." In *Hommage à Maurice Marache 1916–1970*. Publications de la faculté des lettres et des sciences humaines de Nice, 11. Paris: Les belles Lettres, 1972, pp. 22–39.
―――. "Satire et Humeur dans l'oeuvre de Theodor Gottlieb von Hippel." In *Hommage à Georges Fourrier*. Paris: Les belles Lettres, 1973, pp. 243–61.
Lowenkron, David. "The Metanovel." *College English*, 38, 4 (1976), 343–55.
Mauzi, Robert. "La Parodie romanesque dans *Jacques le fataliste*." *Diderot Studies*, VI (1964), 89–133.

May, Georges. *Diderot et* La Religieuse. *Etude historique et littéraire.* New Haven: Yale University Press; Paris: Presses universitaires de France, 1963.

———. *Le Dilemme du roman au XVIIIe siècle. Etude sur les rapports du roman et de la critique (1715-1761).* New Haven: Yale University Press; Paris: Presses universitaires de France, 1963.

Mendilow, A. A. *Time and the Novel.* New York: Humanities, 1972.

Menzel, Wolfgang. *Geschichte der deutschen Dichtung von der ältesten bis auf die neueste Zeit.* Leipzig: Zander, 1875. Vol. III.

Meyer, Herman. *Der Sonderling in der deutschen Dichtung.* Munich: Hanser, 1963.

———. *Das Zitat in der Erzählkunst. Zur Geschichte und Poetik des europäischen Romans.* 2nd ed. Stuttgart: Metzler, 1967.

Michelsen, Peter. *Laurence Sterne und der deutsche Roman des achtzehnten Jahrhunderts.* Palaestra. Untersuchungen aus der deutschen und englischen Philologie und Literaturgeschichte, 232. 2nd ed. Göttingen: Vandenhoeck and Ruprecht, 1972.

Miller, Norbert. *Der empfindsame Erzähler. Untersuchungen an Romananfängen des achtzehnten Jahrhunderts.* Munich: Hanser, 1968.

Mundt, Theodor. *Kritische Wälder. Blätter zur Beurtheilung der Literatur, Kunst und Wissenschaft unserer Zeit.* Leipzig: Melzer, 1833.

Mylne, Vivienne. *The Eighteenth-Century French Novel. Techniques of Illusion.* 2nd ed. Cambridge: Cambridge Univ. Press, 1981.

———. "Truth and Illusion in the 'Préface annexe' to Diderot's *La Religieuse*." *Modern Language Review*, LVII (1962), 350-56.

Nadler, Josef. *Literaturgeschichte der deutschen Stämme und Landschaften.* 2nd ed. Regensburg: Habbel, 1923. Vol. II.

New, Melvyn, with Richard A. Davies and W. G. Day. *Laurence Sterne,* "The Life and Opinions of Tristram Shandy, Gentleman." Vol. III: The Notes. Gainesville: Univ. Presses of Florida, 1984.

Oetingen, Alexander von. Introduction to Hippel's *Lebensläufe. Eine baltische Geschichte aus dem vorigen Jahrhundert für die Gegenwart bearbeitet.* Leipzig: Duncker & Humblot, 1878. Vol. I.

O'Gorman, Donal. "Hypotheses for a New Reading of *Jacques le fataliste*." *Diderot Studies*, XIX (1978), 129-44.

Peterken, Paul. *Gesellschaftliche und fiktionale Identität. Eine Studie zu Theodor Gottlieb von Hippels Roman* "Lebensläufe nach aufsteigender Linie nebst Beilagen A, B, C". Stuttgart: Hans-Dieter Heinz, 1981.

Plehwe, Arthur. "Johann Georg Scheffner." Diss. Königsberg 1934.

Poser, Michael von. *Der abschweifende Erzähler. Rhetorische Tradition und deutscher Roman im achtzehnten Jahrhundert.* Respublica Literaria, V. Bad Homburg v. d. H., Berlin, Zurich: Gehlen, 1969.

Price, Lawrence Marsden. *Die Aufnahme englischer Literatur in Deutschland 1500-1960.* Bern and Munich: Francke, 1961.

Proust, Jacques. "Recherches nouvelles sur *La Religieuse*." *Diderot Studies*, VI (1964), 197-214.

Reichls philosophischer Almanach auf das Jahr 1924. Immanuel Kant zum Gedächtnis 22. April 1924. Ed. Paul Feldkeller. Darmstadt: Reichl, 1924.

Reill, Hans Peter. *The German Enlightenment and the Rise of Historicism.* Berkeley: Univ. of California Press, 1975.

Reminiszenzen. Goethe's Mutter; nebst Briefen und Aufzeichnungen zur Charakteristik

anderer merkwürdiger Männer und Frauen. Ed. Dr. Wilhelm Dorow. Leipzig: Hinrich, 1842.
Richardson, Samuel. *The History of Clarissa Harlowe.* New York, 1902; rpt. New York: AMS Press, 1970.
Rocholl, R. " 'Johann Georg Hamann.' Ein Vortrag." Hannover: Mayer, 1869; rpt. *Johann Georg Hamann,* Wege der Forschung, ed. R. Wild. Darmstadt: Wissenschaftliche Buchgesellschaft, 1978, pp. 91–118.
Rolle, Dietrich. *Fielding und Sterne. Untersuchungen über die Funktion des Erzählers.* Münster: Aschendorff, 1963.
Le Roman jusqu'à la revolution. 2nd ed. Ed. Henri Coulet. Paris: Armand Colin, 1968, Vol. II.
Romantheorie. Dokumentation ihrer Geschichte in Deutschland 1620–1880. Ed. Eberhard Lämmert et al. Neue wissenschaftliche Bibliothek, 41. Cologne: Kiepenheuer & Witsch, 1971.
Romberg, Bertil. *Studies in the Narrative Technique of the First-Person Novel.* Stockholm: Almqvist & Wiksell, 1962.
Rosenblum, Michael. "The Sermon, the King of Bohemia, and the Art of Interpretation in *Tristram Shandy.*" *Studies in Philology* 75 (1978), 472–91.
Scheffner, J. G. *Briefe an und von Johann Georg Scheffner.* Veröffentlichung des Vereins für die Geschichte von Ost- und Westpreußen. Ed. Arthur Warda. Munich: Duncker & Humblot. Vol. I (1916–18), Vol. II, 1 (1920), Vol. II, 2 (1926), Vol. III (1927–28), Vol. IV, 1 (1929), Vol. IV, 2 (1931).
———. *Mein Leben, wie ich Johann Georg Scheffner es selbst beschrieben.* Leipzig: Brockhaus, 1821.
Scherer, Wilhelm. *Geschichte der Deutschen Literatur.* Berlin: Knaur, n.d.
Schmalz, Guenter G. "Jean Paul Friedrich Richters Urteile ueber Theodor Gottlieb von Hippel." *Proceedings of the Pacific Northwest Conference on Foreign Languages.* 30, i–ii (1979), 71–74.
Schmidt, Julian. *Geschichte des geistigen Lebens in Deutschland von Leibnitz bis auf Lessings Tod 1681–1781.* Vol. II. Leipzig: Grunow, 1863.
Schneider, Ferdinand Josef. "Hippel und seine Freunde." *Euphorion,* XIX (1912), 110–22.
———. "Studien zu Theodor Gottlieb von Hippels *Lebensläufe.* 1. Die *Lebensläufe* und *Sophiens Reise von Memel nach Sachsen.*" *Euphorion,* XXII (1915), 471–82.
———. "Studien zu Theodor Gottlieb von Hippels *Lebensläufe.* 2. Über den Humor Laurence Sternes und Theodor Gottlieb von Hippels." *Euphorion,* XXII(1915), 678–702.
———. "Studien zu Theodor Gottlieb von Hippels *Lebensläufe.* 3. Hippel als Schüler Montaignes, Hamanns und Herders." *Euphorion,* XXIII (1921), 23–33, 180–90.
———. "Theodor Gottlieb von Hippel als dirigierender Bürgermeister von Königsberg." *Altpreußische Monatsschrift,* XLVII (1909), 534–69.
———. *Theodor Gottlieb von Hippel in den Jahren von 1741 bis 1781 und die erste Epoche seiner literarischen Tätigkeit.* Prague: Taussig & Taussig, 1911.
———. "Theodor Gottlieb von Hippel und Carl Georg Gottfried Glawe." *Euphorion,* XIX (1912), 735–46.
———. "Theodor Gottlieb von Hippels Schriftstellergeheimnis." *Altpreußische Monatsschrift,* LI (1915), 1–35.

Schröder, Ursula. *Theodor Gottlieb von Hippel's* Kreuz- und Querzüge des Ritters A. bis Z. Diss. Hamburg 1972.

Sembritzki, Johs. "Hippels Briefe an Scheffner." *Euphorion*, XVIII (1911), 406–11.

Shaftesbury, Anthony Earl of. *Characteristicks of Men, Manners, Opinions, Times*. 3rd ed. London, 1723.

Schklovskij, Viktor. *Theorie der Prosa*. Trans. Gisela Drohla. Frankfurt: Fischer, 1966.

Simon, Ernest. "Fatalism, the Hobby-Horse and the Esthetics of the Novel." *Diderot Studies*, XVI (1973), 253–74.

Sola, Emma. *Un Contemporaneo di Kant*. Bologna: Zanicelli, 1918.

Stanzel, Franz. "*Tom Jones* and *Tristram Shandy*." *English Miscellany*, V (1954), 107–48.

———. *Die typischen Erzählsituationen im Roman*. Wiener Beiträge zur englischen Philologie, LXIII (1955).

Sterne, Laurence. *The Life and Opinions of Tristram Shandy, Gentleman*. Ed. James A. Work. Indianapolis: Odyssey, 1940.

Stewart, Philip. *Imitation and Illusion in the French Memoir-Novel, 1700–1750. The Art of Make-Believe*. New Haven: Yale University Press, 1969.

Stockum, Th. C. von. *Theodor Gottlieb von Hippel und sein Roman* Lebensläufe nach aufsteigender Linie. Amsterdam: Mededelgn d. Kgl. Nederl. Akad. von Wetensch. Afd Letterk. N. R. 22, 7, pp. 251–65.

Swearingen, James E. *Reflexivity in Tristram Shandy. An Essay in Phenomenological Criticism*. New Haven and London: Yale Univ. Press, 1977.

Switten, Marlou. "*L'histoire* and *la poésie* in Diderot's Writings on the Novel." *Romanic Review*, 67 (1956), 259–69.

Theorie und Technik des Romans im 17. und 18. Jahrhundert. 2 vols. Ed. Dieter Kimpel, Conrad Wiedemann. Deutsche Texte 16, 17. Tübingen: Niemeyer, 1970.

Tiege, A. J. "A Peculiar Phase of the Theory of Realism in Pre-Richardsonian Prose-Fiction." *PMLA*, 27 (1913), 213–52.

Toliver, Harold. *Animate Illusions. Explorations of Narrative Structure*. Lincoln: University of Nebraska Press, 1974.

Tonelli, G. Rev. of Kant's *Vorlesungen über philosophische Enzyklopädie*, ed. G. Lehmann. Filosophia, 13 (1962), 511–14.

Traugott, John. *Tristram Shandy's World. Sterne's Philosophical Rhetoric*. Berkeley and Los Angeles: University of California Press, 1954.

Tschackert, Paul. "Th. G. Hippel, der christliche Humanist, als Student der Theologie 1756–1759". *Altpreußische Monatsschrift* XXVIII (1892), 355–356.

Vaihinger, Hans. "Als Ob-Stellen bei Theodor Gottlieb von Hippel." *Annalen der Philosophie und philosophischen Kritik*, IV (1924–25), 269–71.

Vor hundert Jahren. Elise von der Reckes Reisen durch Deutschland 1784–1786 nach dem Tagebuch ihrer Begleiterin Sophie Becker. Ed. G. Karo, M. Geyer. Stuttgart: Spemann, 1884.

Vormus, Helga. "Theodor Gottlieb von Hippel: *Lebensläufe nach aufsteigender Linie nebst Beilagen A, B, C*. Eine Interpretation." *Etudes Germaniques*, 21 (1966), 1–17.

Voßkamp, Wilhelm. *Romantheorie in Deutschland. Von Martin Opitz bis Friedrich von Blanckenburg*. Germanistische Abhandlungen, 40. Stuttgart: Metzler, 1973.

Wahrenburg, Fritz. *Funktionswandel des Romans und ästhetische Norm. Die Entwicklung seiner Theorie in Deutschland bis zur Mitte des achtzehnten Jahrhunderts*.

Studien zur Allgemeinen und Vergleichenden Literaturwissenschaft, 11. Stuttgart: Metzler, 1976.

Warda, Arthur. "Der Anlaß zum Bruch der Freundschaft zwischen Hippel und Scheffner." *Altpreußische Monatsschrift*, LII (1916).

———. "Friedrich Heinrich Jacobi und der Verfasser der *Lebensläufe*." *Euphorion*, XV (1908), 34–41.

———. "Kants 'Erklärung wegen der v. Hippelschen Autorschaft'." *Altpreußische Monatsschrift*, 41 (1904), 61–93.

Warning, Rainer, "Fiktion und Wirklichkeit in Sternes *Tristram Shandy* und Diderots *Jacques le fataliste*." In *Nachahmung und Illusion*. Ed. H. R. Jauß. Poetik und Hermeneutik, I. Munich: Eidos, 1964, pp. 96–112.

———. *Illusion und Wirklichkeit in* Tristram Shandy *und* Jacques le fataliste. Theorie und Geschichte der Literatur und der schönen Künste, Texte und Abhandlungen, 4. Munich: Fink, 1965.

———. "Jacques le fataliste." In *Der französische Roman*. Ed. Klaus Heitmann. Düsseldorf: Bagel, 1975, 210–33.

Watt, Ian. *The Rise of the Novel. Studies in Defoe, Richardson, and Fielding*. Berkeley and Los Angeles: University of California Press, 1957.

Weber, Ernst. *Selbstreflexion im deutschen Roman des achtzehnten Jahrhunderts. Zu Theorie und Praxis von "Roman", "Historie" und pragmatischen Roman*. Studien zur Poetik und Geschichte der Literatur, 34. Stuttgart: Kohlhammer, 1974.

Wellek, René. *Immanuel Kant in England 1793–1838*. Princeton: Princeton University Press, 1931.

Werner, Fritz. *Das Todesproblem in den Werken Theodor Gottlieb von Hippels*. Hermaea. Ed. Georg Baesecke and Ferdinand Joseph Schneider, XXXIII. Halle: Niemeyer, 1938.

Werner, Stephen. *Diderot's Great Scroll: Narrative Art in* Jacques le fataliste. *Studies on Voltaire and The Eighteenth Century*, CXXVIII (1975).

Wieland, C. M. *Geschichte des Agathon*. Frankfurt and Leipzig, 1776; rpt. Berlin: Akademie, 1961.

———. *Romane*. Ed. Friedrich Beißner. Munich: Winkler, 1964.

White, Hayden. "The Fictions of Factual Representation." *The Literature of Fact*, ed. Angus Fletcher. New York: Columbia Univ. Press, 1976.

Williams, Ioan. *Novel and Romance 1700–1800. A Documentary Record*. New York: Barnes & Noble, 1970.

The Winged Skull. Ed. Arthur H. Cash, John M. Stedmond. Kent, Ohio: Kent State Univ. Press, 1971.

Wölfel, Kurt. "Friedrich von Blanckenburgs *Versuch über den Roman*." In *Deutsche Romantheorien*. Ed. Reinhold Grimm. Frankfurt: Athenäum, 1974, I, 29–60.

Robert Godwin-Jones

TALES OF COURTSHIP BY JEREMIAS GOTTHELF

American University Studies: Series I, Germanic Languages and Literature. Vol. 35
ISBN 0-8204-0177-3   241 pp.   hardcover/lam. US $ 28.00

recommended prices - alterations reserved

Among the best short works of Jeremias Gotthelf (1797-1854) are six stories of courtship, appearing here together for the first time in English translation. Gotthelf varies masterfully the age-old motif of the scheming suitor in *How Joggeli Seeks a Wife, How Christen Wins a Bride* and *Michel's Courtship Adventures*. Rich in earthy humor, these stories portray well-to-do, traditional farm families who represent the patriarchal ideal Gotthelf proposed as a model for Swiss society at large. The well-known historical tale. *Elsi the Unusual Farm Maid,* offers a tragic example of how the break-down of a family exerts a pernicious influence on individual lives. *The Notary Gets Caught* provides a different kind of warning: it satirizes the actions of a suitor who marries only for money. In contrast, *The Broommaker of Rychiswyl* portrays a suitor unconcerned with money who, in a typically Gotthelfian twist, becomes rich in the end. The tales of courtship show Gotthelf at his best as a creator of vibrant and believable characters. They are preceded by a critical introduction.

Contents: Jeremias Gotthelf (1797-1854) was one of the greatest writers of peasant literature. Among the Swiss writer's best short works are six tales of courtship, appearing here for the first time in English translation. They are preceded by a critical introduction.

PETER LANG PUBLISHING, INC.
62 West 45th Street
USA - New York, NY 10036